EVALUATING SOCIAL WORK EFFECTIVENESS

WITHDRAWN

Juliet Cheetham
Roger Fuller
Gill McIvor
Alison Petch

Open University Press
Buckingham • Philadelphia

Open University Press
Celtic Court
22 Ballmoor
Buckingham
MK18 1XW

and
1900 Frost Road, Suite 101
Bristol, PA 19007, USA

First Published 1992
Reprinted 1994, 1996, 1997

A catalogue record of this book is available
from the British Library

Library of Congress Cataloging-in-Publication Data

Evaluating social work effectiveness/Juliet Cheetham . . . [et al.].
    p. cm.
  Includes bibliographical references and index.
  ISBN 0-335-19006-5   ISBN 0-335-19005-7 (pbk.)
  1. Social service – Evaluation.   2. Evaluation research (Social
action programs)   3. Social service – Scotland – Case studies.
I. Cheetham, Juliet.
HV40.E87   1992
361'.0068 – dc20   92-8572
                                                               CIP

Typeset in Hong Kong by Graphicraft Typesetters Ltd
Printed and bound in Great Britain by
Biddles Ltd, Guildford and King's Lynn

CONTENTS

ACKNOWLEDGEMENTS

This book has grown from the experience of the Social Work Research Centre, which was established at Stirling University in 1986 to study the effectiveness of social work services. The Centre, which is jointly funded by the Economic and Social Research Council (ESRC) and the Scottish Office, is intended to undertake interdisciplinary research of practical and theoretical importance to the development of social work services and to develop research methodologies appropriate to this complex area of enquiry. In tune with these objectives, this text has been written to be of interest and practical use to those who read and carry out research relevant to social work: practitioners, policy makers, students and academics.

The four authors of this volume have been with the Centre from its earliest days and we are thus able to draw on the Centre's large and varied research programme in developing and illustrating our argument. In so doing, we accumulate many debts to our colleagues in the Centre and elsewhere. The Centre has been fortunate in being able to attract researchers, too numerous to mention by name, from many disciplines: social work, social policy, sociology, psychology, psychiatry, economics and accountancy. Their labours, criticism and debate provide a solid foundation for this book. We are grateful for their stimulation and for their contributions to the development of the Centre. They must take much credit for whatever merits this book is found to have; its faults remain our responsibility.

We are grateful, too, to the many people who have given great practical support to the Centre, by no means an easy task in times which have been hard for social work, social services, universities and research councils. The Centre was the brainchild of Professor Raymond Illsley when chairman of the Human Behaviour and Development Committee of the ESRC. His enthusiasm for a research centre sponsored equally by a research council and government was matched by the practical support of David Colvin, the Chief Social Work Advisor at the Scottish Office, who continued to give much help to the Centre until his retirement in 1990.

The Centre has also been fortunate in the financial and other help it has received from the University of Stirling at a time when universities have not found it easy to give such support. We have particularly valued the advice and help of the University's Principals, Sir Kenneth Alexander and Professor John Forty.

Several colleagues in other universities were kind enough to undertake the time-consuming task of commenting on draft chapters. We thank David Challis, Martin Knapp, Robin Lovelock, Owen O'Donnell, Brian Sheldon, David Smith and Ken Wright for their help in improving the manuscript, and we apologize for the remaining deficiencies.

The authors of books need, but do not always have, the practical help of excellent secretaries. We are grateful to Pam Lavery for her organization of Centre business, which allowed us more time for writing, and to June Watson for her skill and good humour in bringing about the improbable union of different word-processing systems and messy manuscripts and transforming them into an elegant typescript.

Finally, and particularly important, we want to thank the countless users, providers and managers of social work whose patient, expert responses to questionnaires, interviews and other encounters with researchers made the Centre studies possible. We took a great deal of their time for which any return can only be indirect: this is the hope that needs will be better understood and services become more effective through the illumination research can provide.

1

EVALUATION IN SOCIAL WORK

If to do were as easy as to know what were good to do, chapels had been churches, and poor men's cottages princes' palaces.
Shakespeare, *Merchant of Venice*

No people do so much harm as those who go about doing good.
Bishop Creighton (1904) *Life*, Vol. ii, p. 503

Social work is contentious. Over the years in various guises which include charity, philanthropy and welfare, its preoccupations and activities have been extolled as essential to social reform and to the protection of the vulnerable and derided as reactionary forces which keep the poor in their place. Social work has been said both to uphold and to undermine the moral fabric of society and its practitioners have been regarded as courageous benefactors and as incompetent meddlers in human misery. There is no shortage either of day-to-day opinion about the needs of people who receive the attention of social workers or about what that attention should be. Because social work involves moral and political questions about rights and duties, freedom and fairness, ideological debate about its proper place and purposes is both inevitable and desirable (Cheetham, 1989). Unfortunately, however, debate and opinion are usually aired without reference to systematic information about the effects of social work on individuals or its impact on groups or organizations. Bold claims and harsh accusations are thus not substantiated and policy may be more influenced by reaction and fashion than by knowledge of its impact. One purpose of this book is, therefore, to encourage more informed comment on social work. A brief example of a familiar human dilemma will illustrate the enormity and intriguing complexity of the task of identifying and then evaluating the effects of social work intervention.

The care of very dependent and frail elderly people is a major contemporary concern. Few individuals or families escape the practical, moral and emotional dilemmas raised by such dependency. One important objective of services for elderly people is to prevent their inappropriate admission to institutional or residential care. How might such services be evaluated? One outcome, or practical measurable effect, is simply the numbers or proportion of very frail people who remain in the community, but few observers would be so easily satisfied. They would want to know also about the physical and emotional condition of elderly people outside institutions, perhaps compared with their peers in care. Elderly people's preferences about their lifestyle and satisfaction with services received might also be on the agenda; and not just once because these might change over time as frailty increases. The relative costs of community and residential care can also influence continued enthusiasm for their original objectives.

This already large field of enquiry has so far focused mainly on elderly people themselves. What are the outcomes for their relatives who may be the linchpin of community care policy and practice? The care they provide may well have some unhappy consequences for their own health, wealth and independence. In a few cases, the accumulation of unrelieved hardships may lead to the abuse or desertion of an elderly person. An unintended or unforeseen outcome is no less an outcome. At the very least, relatives' enthusiasm for community care objectives may differ from that of elderly people themselves, whose greatest dread may be institutional care. A cheerful initial evaluation of the success of the services in preventing institutional care must surely be tempered by some assessment of these other outcomes and perspectives. It might further be influenced by conflicting ideologies about the rights and responsibilities of individuals and families.

The supervision of offenders provides a further example of the challenges of evaluating the outcomes of intervention and how these may be influenced by public policy and legislation and by knowledge or assumptions about the effects of different styles of supervision. Although it is commonly assumed that the prevention of further offending is the main reason offenders are placed under supervision, as an alternative to other sentences such as fines or custody, there may be several other objectives which should be taken into account in evaluating the effectiveness of social work intervention with offenders. One important purpose of supervision can be to provide an alternative to a custodial sentence when this is regarded as counterproductive in terms of costs or influence on delinquent behaviour. A second objective can be the provision of help, both for humane and pragmatic reasons, for those offenders with a multiplicity of personal and social problems, some of which may be associated with their delinquency. Even when all this is disregarded and prevention of offending is held to be the *raison d'être* of social work supervision, several questions remain. Is the intention to prevent further offending forever, an extremely bold aspiration, or for a specified period after supervision has finished, or for a period equivalent to the custodial sentence the offender might otherwise have received and during which he could not have committed further offences? Sentencers, politicians, the public, probation officers and social workers, and no doubt offenders themselves, may all differ in their views about the priorities of supervision and the value which should be attached to particular outcomes. There are changing views, too, about what can be realistically achieved through social work intervention and these can also influence the selection of priority objectives.

It would be possible to design studies of services for elderly people and for offenders and the courts which took account of all these differing objectives and perspectives, but few evaluations of the effectiveness of social work services range so wide; time and resources simply do not permit this. These examples are given to illustrate the potential hazards of drawing large conclusions from limited information and the importance of recognizing conflicting interests. Most studies of social work outcomes are more narrowly focused on different aspects of a service. These might seek, for example, to examine the relationship between assessment of need and services provided or the sentence passed; to identify such possible consequences of service delivery as greater mobility, improved diet, higher morale; to examine offenders' response to supervision; to explore opinions and preferences about services provided. Such studies, which may involve a handful of service users or several hundred, could take only a few months or several years. They are the building blocks of evaluative research. A second purpose of this book is therefore to describe and discuss, in the context of recent research, different ways in which such studies can be pursued. Why is such a book needed?

External pressures for evaluative research

The demand for social workers and their managers to identify the effectiveness of their work is now very great. The pressures for this come from both within and outside their ranks. From outside social work, there are the contemporary pressures to pursue value for money and to scrutinize particularly carefully the ends, means and costs of services in the public sector. There is continuing demand for resources to be better targeted. The reports of the Audit Commission (1985, 1986) on community care and its devastating criticisms of poor planning and confused objectives, and the Audit Commission's (1989b) and Home Office's (1990) reviews of the probation service have pushed economy and efficiency into the vocabulary of social work. Both demand information about the effectiveness of services, and in a world where individual choice is extolled (probably more often than it is achieved) good sense demands that the context and implications of different choices should be as clear as possible. The frequent attacks on social work, often uninformed but still influential, also demand exploration of alleged shortcomings and failures. Equally important, the accumulating evidence of social work's success, as yet not properly recognized, must be further established and properly disseminated.

This last point may sound surprising to those more attuned to hear the failures than the successes of social work. It has been widely believed that social work emerges badly when subjected to research. It has until recently been far more common, for example, for social work's lack of impact on delinquent activity (Martinson, 1974; Folkard *et al.*, 1976) to be quoted than its achievements (Gendreau and Ross, 1979, 1987; Blagg and Smith, 1989; McIvor, 1990c). Many more people have heard about the famous clients of the Family Welfare Association who were bemused by the clash between their own and their social workers' agenda than about the third who said they had been helped (Mayer and Timms, 1970). The drifting, unplanned years of residential care that awaited children who were not rehabilitated within a few months of their admission, identified by Rowe and Lambert (1974), have left another apparently indelible impression of the shortcomings of social work. Simple and often single conclusions have had a more powerful influence than the well-argued critiques of the research and, indeed, the reservations and cautions of the researchers themselves.

More positive accounts of social work have also been ignored. For example, probably only the readers of academic texts know that Reid and Hanrahan's (1981) review of research involving experimental and control groups showed positive effects in nearly all studies of social work that had been carefully planned and executed; and not all practitioners are familiar with Sheldon's (1986) useful summary for the general social work reader of the accumulating evidence of the effectiveness of social work when it clearly identifies target problems, works extensively with them, applies task-centred or behavioural approaches, co-ordinates with other services with an agreed and definite policy, adopts a contractual style with clients and tries out rather than simply discusses possible solutions to problems. There are too, several studies which demonstrate the high regard clients can have for their social workers; and while it is often said this may simply represent low expectations, these clients' reactions should not be dismissed as irrelevant (Sainsbury, 1975, 1987; Rees and Wallace, 1982; Glendinning, 1986).

This brief glimpse of some of the more cheering examinations of social work must not be understood as implying that studies should only be pursued if they are likely to yield positive results or, indeed, that unequivocal conclusions are likely to emerge. The integrity of research demands that studies are neither designed nor interpreted to fit predetermined expectations. The point being made is that there are sufficient indications of the effectiveness of certain social work practices and approaches to demand further exploration of their impact in a variety of contexts and with increasingly difficult problems. A special impetus comes from the conclusions of recent substantial evaluative studies in the field of community care. Researchers at the Personal Social Services Research Unit at Kent University have demonstrated the effectiveness of case management by social workers in assessing and meeting, in the community, the needs of elderly people who might otherwise have lived in some form of institutional care (Challis and Davies, 1986; Davies and Knapp, 1988; Challis et al., 1989, 1990). By orchestrating and providing a variety of resources, social workers showed they could enhance individuals' quality of life and respond positively to their preferred options for care in the community, and that this could be done at the equivalent cost of residential care. The scope and impact of social work in promoting community care was further demonstrated by the Personal Social Services Research Unit's evaluation of the Department of Health's Care in the Community Projects (Knapp et al., 1990b), which were planned to enable the discharge of people from long-term institutions. To use the language of our times, social work can now claim to be cost-effective.

The White Paper *Caring for People* (HMSO, 1989), which outlined the major components of community care services, at least for the next decade, describes such research as 'impressive work in terms of quality and relevance for both policy makers and service delivery agencies' (para. 5.28, pp. 45–46). Further-more, it states that 'the government believes that research will continue to have an important contribution to make to the design and delivery of com-munity care services' (para. 5.31, p. 46). This is not, of course, to say that policies will in future always be congruent with the conclusions of research. The relationship between research and policy is notoriously elusive (Booth, 1988; Smith and Smith, 1992) and Sinclair (1990) has highlighted the many policy objectives of the *Caring for People* White Paper (HMSO, 1989) which are not grounded in any relationship to relevant research. Nevertheless, the language of effectiveness and evaluation is part of the rhetoric of govern-ments and, although this rhetoric is not matched by the appropriate resources, it cannot be ignored.

Internal pressures for evaluative research

The external pressures for evaluative research discussed so far can be viewed as a means of managerial control or even as a defensive response to ensure social work's continued existence. Equally important are the internal pres-sures for evaluation which arise from the general ethical and professional obligation upon social workers not simply to do their best for the people who need their help but to offer the help most likely to be effective. The Statement of Principles in the British Association of Social Workers' Code of Ethics outlines social workers' professional obligation to 'increase personal knowledge and skill . . . and to contribute to the total body of professional knowledge. This involves the constant evaluation of methods and policies in the light of changing needs' (n.d., para. 8). To put it more simply, social workers know that they must ask and answer the question 'what is the use of what I am doing?'

The ethical and practical importance of evaluative research as a component of social work practice and management are recognized, too, in the Central Council for Education and Training in Social Work's recently established Advanced Award in Social Work (Research). The Central Council also requires qualifying social workers to be able to use research findings and to evaluate the aims and outcomes of social work (CCETSW, 1989).

In some work with individuals, the identification of effectiveness has gained momentum through the approaches used. For example, this is greatly helped in task-centred work with its clarity about goals that can and cannot be achieved and, in some cases, about the different objectives of workers and clients. When task-centred work is properly recorded, clients, social workers and their managers can review what has been achieved and, from time to time, the relevance of the first objectives can be reassessed. Behavioural social work, again in its careful specification of the nature and incidence of problem behaviours and the strategies to tackle them, both allows and demands regular review of the impact of the work on the occurrence and severity of the problems (Hudson and Macdonald, 1986). Attention to the setting and achievement of objectives is also encouraged by reviews of children in care or on 'at risk' registers and of elderly people and others in residential care. Such approaches to the practice and the management of social work intervention discourage grandiose, unachievable aspirations and the tendency to blame, without further analysis, either clients or social workers for unsuccessful intervention.

This combination of external and internal pressures produces a positive climate for research which identifies and evaluates the effectiveness of social work, but if this research is to be of real value and to be taken seriously, it must recognize, and as far as possible take account of, social work's complexities. There are understandable suspicions of research which appears to deal in simple inputs and outputs and to inhabit a world devoid of conflicting objectives, unintended outcomes, huge and complex suffering, grand goals but limited means of relief. Social workers' daily experience teaches them, for example, that it is perfectly possible and indeed usual for the different interest groups involved in social work – clients, relatives, workers, managers and policy makers – to intend different outcomes and to differ in their views about the sensible means of achieving them. They know, too, that it is often possible only to deal with relatively minor components of an individual's troubles. Conclusions about the effectiveness of social work intervention must, if they are to have integrity, take account of these different perspectives and the resources available to social work. For example, the parents of a delinquent adolescent may desire above all their son's conformity with the law but disagree about how this should be approached: one may believe that greater enforcement of discipline in the home, curfews and contributions to the domestic economy are the best means of curtailing offences; the other that this will be better achieved by greater parental flexibility and understanding. The young man's main goal may be to leave home, to pursue his vision of freedom, whatever financial impoverishment this may mean for him. In such circumstances, there can be no one definition of effectiveness. Most poignant of all are the rare but well-publicized cases where parents wish, above everything, to retain care of a child but the social worker does not think this is in the child's best interest and there are no means to resolve satisfactorily the family's material, social and emotional problems. Here again there can be no simple criteria for effectiveness and if evaluative research does not have regard for this, it will not be surprising if social workers' commitment to identifying effective practice is tempered by the sober realization that this can be a hostage to fortune.

An approach to evaluative research

A major purpose of this book is, therefore, to encourage an approach to evaluative research which takes account of the complexities of the context, tasks and methods of social work and which produces studies that are seen as comprehensible and relevant to the different parties involved with it. These standards must be met by research which seeks to be useful for policy makers, for practitioners and for users. Ideally, therefore, it must be a collaborative enterprise in the identification of important research questions and the analysis and presentation of data and conclusions. In almost every study, difficult choices must be made about what can be examined and few single studies can do justice to all the questions of conflicting perspectives, multiple objectives and disparity between problems to be tackled and resources available. The price and the promise of such research is that it can raise as many questions as it answers, and it is unlikely to produce definitive conclusions about 'best practice' or about the success of whole enterprises. In the world of social work, there are few simple certainties.

The argument in this book and the approach described are derived from the experience of the Social Work Research Centre, which was established at Stirling University in 1986 by the Economic and Social Research Council and the Scottish Office to develop research which could evaluate the effects of social work intervention. In its first years, the Centre has undertaken over 20 studies of residential and fieldwork services for most major groups of clients. The programme has included research on services to promote the rehabilitation and community care of people with mental health problems, of alternatives to custody for offenders, and of fieldwork services and residential care for elderly people. Social work has, therefore, been interpreted broadly to include a range of activities from counselling to social care and its planning, undertaken by people, with a variety of qualifications, in social work, social services, probation and health care agencies. Such an interpretation is consistent with the Central Council of Education and Training in Social Work's definition of social work as:

> . . . an activity which enables individuals, families and groups to identify personal, social and environmental difficulties adversely affecting them. Social work enables them to manage these difficulties through supportive, rehabilitative, protective or corrective action. Social work promotes social welfare and responds to wider social needs . . . (thus) . . . social workers are part of a network of welfare, health, criminal justice and penal provision (CCETSW, 1989, p. 8).

The Centre studies, which have lasted from three months to three years, have focused on samples as small as 12 users and as large as several hundred and mostly on examples of social work services as they are found in agencies rather than on experimental projects planned specifically with evaluation in mind. While much can be learnt from studying such projects, especially those testing approaches which are, for whatever reasons, assuming some prominence, they are comparatively rare, particularly when the pressures on social work resources are very great. Contemporary developments in community care and in services for offenders are likely to present more opportunities for comparative studies of the effectiveness of innovative methods of intervention.

The studies have employed a wide range of methods and designs, most of which have been used elsewhere, although in quite different contexts. In the chapters which follow, the methods discussed will be illustrated by reference both to research conducted in the Centre and to other recently published studies of the effectiveness of social work.

It is the Centre's view that the demand for evaluative research and its scarcity, relative to other fields, together with the diversity of problems confronting social work, of the methods by which they are tackled and of its small and large settings, encourage a pragmatic approach; that is, one not wedded to the assumption that there is one research method to be preferred for its potential to illuminate and demonstrate social work effectiveness. Such pragmatism demands imagination, inventiveness and discipline; it is not a synonym for sloppiness. It assumes that progress in this much needed and little explored area of research will come, in the main, from rigorous applications, combinations and adaptations of available methods. It demands, above all, attention to what can and cannot be achieved in any one study. This requires clarity about the questions the research can address and their salience to the different audiences interested in social work. It thus involves alerting these audiences to the wider social and policy context of the problems and the services to be studied, so that neither too little nor too much is made of the research findings. Pragmatism also means deftness in matching, as far as possible, the research problems with the resources available. These include the access which will be allowed to sources of information and the time of those who will provide data for researchers. Evaluating the effectiveness of social work has therefore to be pursued and developed as the art of the possible, with full recognition that what is possible is also limited.

2

SOCIAL WORK EFFECTIVENESS: CONCEPTS AND PRIORITIES

The subjects that are most interesting in themselves do not lend
themselves best to accurate observation and systematic study.
                                              Michael Polanyi (1958)

Where is the wisdom we have lost in knowledge?
Where is the knowledge we have lost in information?
                                              T.S. Eliot (1919) *The Rock*

This chapter explores more deeply important concepts in the study of social
work which have so far been taken at face value, and in doing so examines
some features of social work which present special challenges to the researcher. The major purpose is to alert would-be researchers to the difficulty
of the terrain, while at the same time to encourage journeys through it. It
is the Centre's experience that wariness and boldness can go hand in hand.
Appreciation of the complexities of social work should not be a deterrent to
research, but a spur to the selection of priority questions and feasible methods; it also adds depth to the analysis and evaluation of research findings.

Despite much apparently straightforward use of the word, 'effectiveness'
is not something which has an object-like reality 'out there' waiting to be
observed and measured. Like any other data, empirical evidence about the
effectiveness of social policies and programmes is a product of data collection procedures and the assumptions on which they are based. The concept
of effectiveness derives from particular ways of thinking and makes sense
only in relation to its context. One such way of thinking is that of politicians preoccupied with the congruence between the aims of a service and the
social policies of their parties ('Will these criteria for eligibility ensure that
more families care for their dependent relatives?'). Managers or finance
officers may urgently question the cost-effectiveness of services ('If we spend
money on this, will it save money on that?'). Another way of thinking is
that of practitioners anxious to know whether their activities are making a
worthwhile impact on the lives of clients ('Is what we are doing having the
effect we are hoping for?'). The term would probably come less easily to the

lips of users themselves, who may not naturally use the language of objectives and effectiveness; perhaps the equivalent questions for them might be 'What am I getting out of this service; is it any practical help or comfort to me?'

This is to say something more than that different people have different expectations. It also implies that effectiveness derives from a variety of perspectives and assumptions, and itself forms part of one or more of a range of different rhetorics – the language of value for money, say, or that of professional accountability, meeting customer demand, or maximizing satisfaction. Often, and not always comfortably, students of social policy find themselves shuttling between such languages, and are forced to ponder the gap between any given rhetoric and the reality of the intervention in question. To change the metaphor, they sometimes feel, particularly over the last decade, that the goal posts are constantly moving, occasionally on to terrain where the markings of the pitch are scarcely recognizable.

These considerations are central to the understanding of how concepts of effectiveness are currently used and what and whose purposes they may serve. They should be taken into account in choices about the focus of research, and thus the data to be collected and the methods used, but they are generally bracketed off once the effectiveness researcher gets down to the task. Finding a way into a particular topic is often dependent upon temporarily putting aside these underlying issues, and the ensuing discussion will do so, without distracting the reader by the insertion of inverted commas whenever effectiveness is mentioned. The challenge is to arrive at working definitions of effectiveness in specific situations, and hence of methods of studying it, which do not permanently lose sight of its conceptual context. One useful working definition, often adopted by researchers, managers and practitioners, is that social work is effective in so far as it achieves intended aims.

Viewed in this way, effectiveness is separate from, but linked to, the practice of evaluation. The effectiveness of an activity may be studied without proceeding to a statement about what value might be given to it by various parties; but an activity cannot be evaluated without some knowledge of its outcomes and effectiveness. Evaluation therefore goes beyond the identification of effectiveness in its commentary, for example, on the worth of alternative objectives or perspectives, or its comparison between innovative and other services. It may conclude that intervention has been successful in terms of objectives achieved, but argue that these objectives are either trivial, inappropriate or misconceived. To evaluate social work, therefore, involves assessing it within the broader context of social policy.

Is evaluation essentially subjective, as Goldberg and Connelly (1982, p. 9) contend: 'Evaluation is in some sense assessing the value or worth of an activity, but if this is accepted it inevitably follows that there is no objectivity in evaluation: "value" and "worth" are essentially subjective judgements . . .'? This seems too polarized a view, and one which elides two rather different questions. First, it surely adopts too subjectivist a stance: 'value' and 'worth' may begin as subjective judgements, but there is widespread consensus that among the problems social workers address, certain things are undesirable and certain outcomes preferable. It is possible to study the effects of intervention designed, for example, to keep children out of residential care in such a way that informs a debate on how far (and with what kind of exceptions) this is a worthwhile aim, i.e. one which serves some higher and agreed value of serving the needs of children for whom residential care might be considered a possible option.

Second, the process by which such worth is assessed may be more or less 'objective'. It is, of course, true that much of what is described as evaluation does not follow the systematic procedures and safeguards of social research, or is not (as some would prefer) 'scientific'. Although in some quarters informal or ill-grounded procedures have given evaluation a bad name – a piece of jargon whereby policies are justified and promoted, or sabotaged and sidelined, according to managerial whim – there are many situations in social agencies where practice can be usefully reviewed without invoking the whole panoply of research methodology. Nevertheless, this book is about those instances where systematic empirical enquiries are pursued. To adopt Suchman's (1967) useful distinction, the subject matter is evaluative research rather than the more all-embracing abstract, evaluation.

Social work: diversity, elusiveness and specificity

The broad interpretation of social work adopted in this book has already been outlined. Its scope and content entail certain characteristic features which, as well as creating hazards for those who would define social work effectiveness, make the research task especially challenging. The language of effectiveness implies that the problems social work is expected to take up, its objectives, its methods and its outcomes are capable of being expressed in language which has some degree of precision. It is an understatement to say that this is not always easy. Social workers who apply to their activities the simple working definition outlined earlier, which relates effectiveness to the achievement of intended aims, are likely to experience unease. This will not be relieved by the rather more elaborate accounts of effectiveness given by other authorities.

- a method of determining the degree to which a planned programme achieves the desired objectives (Suchman, 1967, cited approvingly by Goldberg and Connelly, 1982 and Thomas, 1984);
- the success of a social care service is measured in terms of the extent to which its objectives are achieved, that is, the extent to which the needs of clients are met (Knapp, 1984, p. 22).

Are programmes always 'planned' with specified goals? Whose definition of needs is to count? And who is to judge whether they have been met? Something of the unease is expressed by the Barclay Report (1982, 11.43 *et seq.*), where queries are raised about the universal applicability to social work of a concept of effectiveness, borrowed from medical research, which seems to assume a model of the curing of social ills. Although the analogy may be fair in some instances, other types of social work intervention (for example, assessment and referring on, the prevention of deterioration) appear to resist the 'treatment and cure' approach and to require more subtle consideration of what an outcome is. A distinction hinted at by Sainsbury (1987) is relevant here. Some social work is about *helping*, while some may emphasize *caring*. Helping clients seems to imply some observable difference made to their lives; and there are indeed some quite clear-cut, tangible social work tasks, for example providing information or arranging a specific service, the presence of which can be noted as one outcome of intervention. Caring, on the other hand, may involve the intangibles of a personal relationship without necessarily making an outwardly observable difference. Furthermore, if social work is to take account of the distinction Ignatieff (1984) draws between what is needed in order to flourish (love, respect, honour, dignity, solidarity with others) rather than simply to survive, the nature of the relationship within which any help is given will influence its effectiveness:

> Giving the aged poor their pension and providing them with medical care may be a necessary condition for their self-respect and dignity, but it is not a sufficient condition. It is the manner of the giving that counts and the moral basis on which it is given: whether strangers at my door get their stories listened to by the social worker, whether the ambulance man takes care not to jostle them when they are taken down the steep stairs of their apartment building, whether a nurse sits with them in the hospital when they are frightened and alone. Respect and dignity are conferred by gestures such as these. They are gestures too much a matter of human art to be made a consistent matter of administrative routine (Ignatieff, 1984, p. 16).

Equally ambitiously, England (1986) raises particularly difficult issues for those in search of a definition of effectiveness that is easily operationalized. Significantly, like Barclay, he is responding to hostile accounts of the profession when he complains that 'the terms employed by the critics of social work demand a materialist reply, a reply about externally measurable procedures and effects' (p. 4). He goes on to develop a case for the 'artistic', essentially personal and intuitive, nature of a social work whose skills are deployed through the formation of relationships and through purposeful talk, and whose consequent requirement is for a mode of evaluation more akin to the procedures of artistic or literary criticism than to a medical model of evaluative research.

This sense of unease will be viewed differently by different people. For some (e.g. Sheldon, 1986) it is evidence of the nervousness or squeamishness of social work in the face of justified challenges to its claims to effectiveness, challenges which deserve to be met by 'hard evidence' derived from rigorously controlled empirical research. Sheldon derides practitioners who evaluate their practice by asking themselves whether it 'feels right'. For others, it remains as a residue of dissatisfaction with the results of effectiveness research, on the grounds that they rarely tell the whole truth. England might well argue, in contrast to Sheldon, that 'right feeling' is precisely the kind of criterion which social work above all demands.

So what are the features of social work which might be cited as objections to neat or suspiciously simple definitions of effectiveness? The first is its acknowledged diversity. To deal only with social work with individual clients, the activities of social workers cover a wide spectrum: assessment; providing information, advice, and sometimes counselling designed to alter behaviour or attitudes or to increase understanding; arranging service provision or arguing for it with other agencies; providing personal care in residential and day care settings; offering general support to clients and their carers; mobilizing community resources. Their goals can range from attempting to help vulnerable individuals to improve their quality of life or social functioning; to maintain these at an acceptable level or to arrest deterioration; to influencing systems within and outside social work, sometimes by playing a gatekeeping role; to performing some kind of controlling function, by rationing access to scarce resources, by trying to change deviant behaviour in the interests of 'society' or of deviant individuals themselves, or by using compulsory powers of removal from home.

Social workers will also argue, some more vigorously than others, that social work significantly involves a range of activities, perhaps preventive in spirit, which are not directly concerned with individual clients. These may be based in the broader communities that they serve or in the political world of argument for increased resources or changes in policy emphases.

To compound the diversity yet further, many of these activities and goals may coincide in the same case, sometimes even in the same client encounter. Social work is rarely a tidily delimited activity in which these multiple concerns may be disaggregated. Often, it is not obvious where, in an encounter with a client or in discussion about a client between professionals, 'social work' (of one kind or another) begins and ends. At the same time, the input of a social worker will be only one of many influences on a client's life. Although this is less true in those social work settings, such as residential care, which approximate to total institutions, it makes for difficulties in establishing relationships between receipt of social work help and the effects of that help. This extremely complex research problem is discussed further in Chapter 5.

A related feature is that social work may not consist of easily identifiable units whose content or meaning are generally accepted. This makes it unlike, say, the drugs or other treatments that may be prescribed by a doctor. Except on paper, there is little in social work equivalent to the drug cupboard with shelves of items labelled 'task-centred casework', 'counselling' and the like, which the worker may take down and dispense to the client. Admittedly, this is not equally true of all items in the social worker's repertoire. Group work is relatively distinct from individual casework; day care from the provision of home help. It is no doubt also possible to exaggerate the extent to which other helping professions such as medicine operate in a world of perfect consensus as to the meanings of treatment options. Nevertheless, it remains observably the case that many intervention methods will be used in different ways, with differing and often multiple purposes and for different categories of client, by different social workers, even those whose meaning seems the least problematic, such as the provision of home help. It is also the case, as we have seen, that in social work's more 'personal' manifestations, the way a technique is practised, and the degree of skill which the individual worker brings to bear, may be as important as the choice of technique itself.

It is important to dwell for a moment on possible reasons for this apparent confusion. There are elements of vagueness and loose formulation in much of the terminology of social work. Practitioners (and researchers) have been repeatedly urged to define more closely what is meant by such terms as 'inadequate' or 'support' which figure so largely in descriptions of social work and in its case records. Indeed, much of the progress identified by optimistic commentators on the development of social work lies in an increasingly precise matching of problems experienced by clients to responses developed by practitioners. It is likely, nevertheless, that however rigorous these attempts, a residue of difficulty will remain which cannot be put down to sloppy thinking or the persistence of grey areas. This is partly because many of the problems taken up by social workers, and many of their goals, are contested concepts. Ideological or other value preferences will enter into the ways in which key items are conceptualized, whether in the origins of problems, in responses or in desired end-states (deprivation, family therapy, adequate parenting).

Objectives and outcomes

The comparatively simple language of 'objectives' and 'outcomes' also presents difficulties when these are considered in the context of social work. First, what *is* an objective? The word has become increasingly prominent with the development of managerialist approaches to social work as to other areas. Objectives, preferably clear, are generally recognized as good things to have, whether at the level of an agency as a whole, a subdivision of an agency or individual client, and at the agency level working parties spend many hours trying to determine an appropriate form of words in which to express them. This induces a certain amount of cynicism, and although actors may be asked what their objectives are, there is no empirical way of establishing that *stated* objectives are those which have *actually* been applied in any given example of social work. The status of social workers' objectives is in fact empirically variable. They may be agreed, clear and unambiguous, or vague and conflicting. They will almost certainly belong to different dimensions and time-scales, and may sometimes be determined by public relations rather than realistic assessment of what is feasible.

For researchers seeking precision, these are problems which might, in a perhaps rather odd ideal world where there is infinite time for discussion, be capable of resolution. More interesting difficulties arise from the frequency with which intervention involves several parties with different perspectives – and therefore objectives. These problems can be compounded by the largely individualized nature of social work services, which might have a general service objective, such as maintaining clients in the community, only for it to be qualified by some such phrase as 'according to need' or 'appropriately'.

These barriers to identifying objectives with certainty are mirrored in the identification of outcomes for clients. A basic point is that social work may often be about creating potentialities rather than final states. Social workers may direct their efforts towards increasing clients' understanding of themselves and their circumstances *vis-à-vis* family, peers, or systems or agencies with whom they are involved; towards increasing their use of available services; towards their protection from inappropriate intervention, or other short-term evils; towards longer-term improvements in personal or family functioning. This may or may not result in a better quality of life for clients, and whether or not it does depends commonly on factors beyond the reach of the social work intervention. They are, nevertheless, goals which cannot be ignored by researchers. It may be contentious to suggest that social work differs from other forms of intervention in this respect, but it does appear a particularly significant feature of social work. And by their very nature, the extent of the achievement of these perfectly legitimate but intangible states is extremely difficult to determine. Viewed in this light, to conclude that, for example, 'clients received the service, and fell into the appropriately specified category of need, but there is no evidence that they are better off as a result', is to subject the service to an unfair test.

To summarize, researchers may be able to identify a set of outcomes which may be measured relatively easily, for example those defined in services terms like avoiding entry to care, domiciliary services arranged, foster parents selected and child placed or, in more individual, client-based terms, such as an improvement in the relationship between parent and child, or diminished depression. There is, however, a further set which are more intangible, for example, the potentialities referred to earlier. The restrictive position here would be that researchers should limit themselves to outcomes that are carefully specified either in operational or individual terms and easily measurable, and in some circumstances this may be perfectly acceptable. The difficulty arises when the social workers' agenda, or a significant proportion of their efforts, are based on the second and less tangible set of 'outcomes'; and hence to treat the first type of outcome as paramount amounts to a misrepresentation of the intervention.

Over the years, studies of the effectiveness of social work have reflected its changing goals. When aspirations were high, in the preventive arena for example, or in times when delinquents were thought capable of being reformed by 'casework', criteria for effectiveness were set up that social work was almost bound to fail. At the other extreme, an unduly relentless drive for clarity and specificity on the part of the social worker and researcher can produce objectives which are so modest, relating to minor changes in behaviour in limited or artificial situations, that 'success' becomes scarcely worth achieving (Reid and Hanrahan, 1981; Sheldon, 1986). As Mattinson and Sinclair (1979, p. 24) remark, 'often in social research apparent certainty is bought at the price of relevance'.

Tackling the problems

It is not, then, difficult to construct a picture of social work which would take account of all these complexities and would seem to make it highly resistant to effectiveness research. The goals, processes and effects of social work are both diverse and difficult to capture in the terminology of standardized 'variables' that researchers commonly and necessarily employ. As the scientist and philosopher Michael Polanyi (1958, p. 139) observed:

> If the scientific virtues of exact observation and strict correlation of data are given absolute preference for the treatment of a subject matter which disintegrates when represented in such terms, the result will be irrelevant to the subject matter and probably of no interest at all.

Any worthwhile research approach to effectiveness of social work is likely to have to live with various kinds of imprecision or elusiveness in some of its key terms.

The danger of stressing these features as 'difficulties' is that the effect may be to present research into social work effectiveness as so problematic that it may as well not be attempted. The would-be evaluative researcher needs to balance the problems which need to be solved against the possibility that failing to tackle them will result in research becoming even more marginal to the business of evaluation than many claim that it is already. Attempting to produce a perfect research design may well induce research paralysis! So how is a researcher, alive to the reasons outlined earlier why social work deserves to be held accountable to systematic research scrutiny, to proceed?

The first point to make is the simple one that despite all the complexities of definition and interpretation discussed earlier, effectiveness must derive from the objectives of social work services, in so far as these are articulated. No doubt the overall objective of social work is invariably to make some positive impact on the well-being of clients or communities, but while this may be salutary as an occasional reminder, such an abstraction, even platitude, is rarely helpful for theorists, for managers or for researchers of social work. Once contextual detail is supplied, the diversity outlined above has to be confronted, and since objectives are diverse, criteria for effectiveness will also be diverse. There is, therefore, no one model of social work effectiveness; it is, inevitably, context-specific. Services to children and families may involve different criteria for effectiveness than services to old people, and within the latter group the effectiveness of residential care will, despite some overlap, look different to that of meals on wheels.

Diversity may also be found within a comparatively restricted field. Suppose, for example, a social services agency wishes to know about the effectiveness of its child protection services. The objectives of the services may well include:

- the child protection procedures are followed;
- systematic and comprehensive recording takes place;
- liaison with other agencies takes place at relevant times;
- intrusive interviews and examinations of victims are kept to a minimum;
- criteria for placing on the child protection register are clearly understood and consistently applied;
- the safety of abused or at risk children is secured;

- offering appropriate counselling or other therapeutic services to families of abused children;
- when children are removed, plans are made for permanent placement or rehabilitation, according to need;
- preventive work takes place through public education, group work with vulnerable parents, and other means as appropriate.

This list could no doubt be extended, but it already illustrates the multi-dimensional nature of effectiveness even within a set of activities relating to a single client group. Effective service in this context inheres in a range of widely differing criteria and loci: from matters of procedure within and between agencies, to relatively objective, outwardly manifested aspects of clients' circumstances, to the more subjective areas of family and individual functioning, behaviour and understanding, and finally (in the last clause) to the prediction of likely future events.

Nor is it a matter of diversity alone. The various criteria of effectiveness implied by the objectives belong to different conceptual orders, some being procedural, some in observable events, some in the perceptions of a variety of professionals and a variety of service recipients. They also belong to different time-scales. Their investigation thus calls for different kinds of data and methods of collecting it.

The same example also illustrates the kind of work that needs to take place in order to turn the language of, say, social work management into that of effectiveness research. For as they stand, some of the objectives suggest measurable criteria to a greater degree than others. Here it is a question of finding the researchable equivalent to an objective that is stated in vague or inappropriate terms. 'Systematic recording' is clear enough, assuming some agreed format has been stipulated, and it would not be difficult to arrive at a criterion for establishing whether interviews with victims have been minimized. More difficult problems are set by talk of 'appropriate counsel-ling' and by 'placement according to need', and the preventive objective is likely to yield only crude and approximate evidence of effectiveness. In this instance, the researcher might begin by establishing what the child protec-tion procedures are, and what observable criteria would determine whether they had been followed. This would no doubt involve scrutiny of recording practices, liaison with other agencies, procedures for investigation, calling case conferences, and registration, and this initial work suggests a design based on the examination of agency records and procedures. Subsequent study would tackle the more challenging issues of securing the safety of children at risk and the effectiveness of counselling and longer-term plan-ning, for which the methodological repertoire would need to be extended, to include for example interviews with clients and professionals and some longitudinal follow-up.

It is one thing, therefore, to state what constitutes effectiveness in social work, but another to operationalize it. These are the kinds of conceptual operation with which researchers in many fields are familiar and, again, the problems are there to be solved. How this may be tackled is discussed further in the following chapters.

An incremental approach

In practice, although the skills of the researcher are likely to be put to stringent test because of the features of social work outlined above, two factors mitigate the problems. One is the opportunity for discussion with managers and practitioners which should precede any study of this kind, in which the aims of intervention can be clarified. If not invariably, and not without informed prompting from the researcher, this will often result in a re-ordering and recasting of objectives in more researchable form, and sometimes in a frank admission by managers or practitioners that the more ambitious (often the least tangible) service objectives are not seriously attempted.

The second factor is the likelihood that in the interests of feasibility, the focus may be narrowed, so that not all aspects of the effectiveness of intervention need be captured in a single study. There are some important distinctions to be made here, and researchers will often find themselves pulled in conflicting directions. There is a fundamental difference between a study which seeks a holistic approach to a given service, as in the child protection example, and one which focuses more narrowly on a given method of intervention such as behaviour modification, and seeks generalization across different contexts and client groups. The former approach will entail an obligation to be as comprehensive as possible in the coverage of different levels of objectives and outcomes, and will thus involve judgements about how objectives relate to each other in a hierarchy of importance, and how to give sufficient attention to the areas less amenable to research. Some evaluation is thus inescapable. The latter will encounter the difficulty of ensuring the true comparability across different contexts of the method studied, because without this it will be less immediately useful to agencies. Some implications of these two rather different kinds of undertaking will be briefly taken up again at the end of this chapter.

Decisions about the selection of a focus, and therefore about the exclusion of some objectives from investigation, will be made in a number of ways. Often, as the first step to a more comprehensive study, the concentration may be on the more immediate and more easily measurable short-term goals – what services have been delivered to whom, and with what lapse of time – rather than, say, the longer-term impact of these services. Two Centre studies which bear on large and complex questions of policy and practice have proceeded in this way.

The first seeks to explore a largely unresearched question of major importance to contemporary social work in which the reorganization of service delivery is endemic: how do differences in the organization of social work teams, such as specialist, generic and patch, affect the ways in which social services are delivered? This challenging question needs to be addressed in several linked studies. The work concentrated initially on trying to establish distinctive patterns of initial response to referrals of elderly people, in terms of how many were allocated, how they were assessed and who received what. This small study (Fuller and Petch, 1989, 1991) revealed some distinctive patterns of service delivery and indicated that the research strategy and methods would be feasible in larger-scale research. A substantial study was therefore designed which covered a larger number of organizational types and sought to expand the consideration of outcomes for clients and their carers. More studies relating to other client groups and exploring the new patterns of delivery of community care services will be needed to illuminate further the relationship – of which much is expected but little known – between organization and service delivery.

A second example to have adopted an incremental approach is concerned with the effectiveness of community service schemes for offenders. The first study (McIvor, 1989) sought to identify factors associated with the successful completion of orders rather than trying to investigate longer-term effects on criminal behaviour. A subsequent study identified reconviction during the three-year period after the completion of orders and examined the relationship between reconviction and offenders' experiences on community service (McIvor, 1992a,b).

Often, the priority is to fill important gaps in knowledge derived from previous research. The broad dimensions of the effectiveness of a given activity may be well enough known within its own terms, but the extent to which it fits the expectations or requirements of other agencies involved may be unclear. To take the last example above, once policies and practices associated with successful completion of community service orders had been identified, it became apparent that their effectiveness was also likely to be related to the kind of individuals who received a sentence of community service and to the types of work they were required to do. At the outset, it was also clear that the impact of the sentence as part of penal policy must be a crucial issue. How far do sentencers perceive and use community service as a real alternative to custody? To clarify this question, the Social Work Research Centre conducted a study of the perspectives of sentencers (Carnie, 1990). Finally, since one of the objectives of community service is to provide help for community groups and vulnerable individuals, a study of the experiences and views of beneficiaries illuminated how this is achieved (McIvor, 1992b, and forthcoming). Thus, with the ramified subject of community service, the strategy pursued by those who planned the research was to identify the important research issues which should be investigated in a series of linked studies, clarify the scope and limitations of each individual study, and embark first on the one which would yield crucial baseline data, in the hope that the others would be accomplished as time and resources permitted.

Decisions about individual studies turn on a mixture of factors, including the perceived priorities of agency managers and research sponsors, the context of previous work, the resources available to the researcher, his or her own interests and the unevenly developed technology of evaluative research. Vital tasks in initial discussion with agencies and sponsors are to reveal priorities among the various objectives that may be in question and to clarify what the available methods and resources can and cannot discover about effectiveness. The choice of objectives on which to focus is sometimes a difficult process involving delicate judgements between the desirable and the feasible.

Methodological pluralism

Finally, it should be noted that there are major methodological implications to the many-sidedness of social work activities stressed in this chapter. As suggested at the end of Chapter 1, the methodological approach of this book is an eclectic one, not wedded to a single allegiance. In part, this methodologically pluralist stance is indicated by a subject matter – social work services – characterized by diversity, occasional elusiveness and the generally shifting sands typical of social policy in action. To insist, as for example does Thyer (1989), that the first principles of practice research demand random sampling, assignment of subjects to experimental and control groups, validated assessment methods and extensive follow-up periods, would risk leaving much social work activity unresearchable, though opportunities for using such designs do exist. Readers of the *British Journal of Social Work* will be familiar with the debate joined in its pages (Raynor, 1984; Sheldon, 1984a; Smith, 1987) on the applicability of positivist approaches to social work research. Increasingly, and healthily, practitioners of evaluative research use a range of strategies in a single study.

A second consideration is also relevant. It has been noted that the demands of evaluative study differ markedly according to whether what is being studied is a single intervention method or technique, or whether it is an agency's performance in relation to a set of services or a client group. To re-employ earlier examples, the researcher wishing to establish whether the behaviour modification technique is effective, with whom and in what circumstances, will proceed rather differently, in terms of research design and methods, from one who is studying the child protection services of an individual agency. This may be seen as a particular version of the distinction between pure and applied research. The student of behaviour modification, interested in generalizable findings, will seek out examples of the technique in a 'pure' form, or may even set one up specifically for research purposes; in such a context, consideration of a classic experimental design may well come into play. This laboratory-like approach is unlikely to suit the study of child protection services, where such 'purity' is not appropriate, and where, indeed, the realities of shifting definitions and differing perspectives held by different parties are themselves of central concern. Here the researcher is more likely to be influenced by the seminal insight of 'pluralistic evaluation' (Smith and Cantley, 1985), discussed in Chapter 3, and by methods such as the semi-structured interview, often – if misleadingly – described as 'softer'.

These difficult choices are discussed more fully in the next chapter, which reviews the repertoire of methodological approaches available to the evaluative researcher.

3

REVIEW OF EVALUATIVE
STRATEGIES

On Monday, when the sun is hot
I wonder to myself a lot:
'Now is it true, or is it not,
That what is which and which is what?'

A.A. Milne (1926) *Winnie-the-Pooh*

The whole range of the methodological spectrum has been drawn on by different parties in seeking appropriate strategies for the evaluation of social work activity. The contention of this volume, however, is that the nature of social work will lead to certain evaluative methodologies being adopted with much greater frequency than others. In this chapter, the range of available methodologies is introduced with an indication of the potential and limitations which each can offer. The intention is not to give the definitive account of each strategy which can be found in the appropriate reference text, but to assist in the selection of the optimum choice for a given research problem. The options discussed range from experimental and cross-institutional designs to user and pluralistic evaluations. A distinction should be understood between this broader methodological strategy and the specific research technique (e.g. interview, time-monitoring, coded questionnaire), with similar techniques being acceptable across different strategies. The range of potential techniques with their particular strengths and weaknesses will be addressed in the following chapter.

It is important to clarify the various dimensions which are embedded in the different research strategies outlined below. To a certain extent, the classification is one of convenience, reflective of everyday practice, rather than of a coherent framework. Thus, for any one study there will be a time *dimension* – the observations will be over time (longitudinal) or they will be based on a single period in time. There will be a *comparison* of some form – between individuals or groups in receipt and non-receipt of a service, or between individuals or groups at different stages. And there will be representation from one or more *perspectives*, ranging from the user perspective to pluralistic evaluation, discussed later in this chapter. The priority given to each of these parameters will vary according to the focus of the study. In the exploration below, therefore, we have highlighted from across the dimensions the strategies which are most commonly debated in research in the social welfare arena.

Experimental and quasi-experimental designs

It is traditional to begin such reviews with the more positivist methodologies derived from the scientific tradition, in particular the experimental and quasi-experimental design. The attraction for some of the experimental design may lie in its apparent abstraction of the unit under study from the surrounding detail, its reduction of the elements of interaction to a simple relation of cause and effect. Central to the experimental design is the notion of control. In its pure form, the experimental unit would receive some input designed to stimulate some form of change. The outcomes for this group would be compared with those for a control group, identical to the experimental group on key dimensions but not in receipt of the specified input. The medical analogy is of the treatment group who receive a new drug and a control group who receive no drug or a placebo. Effects which are not present in a control group receiving only a placebo are deemed to be attributable to the drug itself.

A major problem in managing the experimental design in social welfare research is the control of the input under scrutiny. Much of social welfare delivery does not come in specifically identifiable components, the nature of which remains constant throughout intervention. Thus even if change is observed in the experimental group, it may be difficult to be exact as to what this change should be attributed to. Moreover, the alternative of a placebo outlined above in the drug analogy does not have an immediate social work equivalent.

Those who hold that social phenomena cannot readily be equated with those of the natural world will be sceptical of the application of the laws of the inanimate to circumstances moulded by the human spirit. Whatever view is taken on this, however, the creation for an experimental design of an experimental group and a control group can have both major practical and ethical problems. In ideal form, subjects should be allocated through a random mechanism to one of the two groups. In the drug analogy, this would mean receipt or non-receipt of some service. This is not, however, always a feasible option in the field of social welfare. Intervention may be a statutory requirement or the denial of a service may be considered ethically or politically unacceptable. Even without these considerations, allocation mechanisms or the timing of service delivery may militate against the accumulation of cases into two parallel groups.

Experimental designs are, none the less, accomplished. Good examples include those by Gibbons (1981) and Corney and Clare (1983), and it is perhaps not entirely without coincidence that these are both within the health sphere where there is a more ready tradition of comparison and specification in service delivery. An important consideration also may be that the experimental design is more readily accommodated in the evaluation that focuses on a specific, fairly self-contained intervention rather than on the totality of a multifaceted service. Gibbons was concerned to evaluate the provision of task-centred work to those seen at a casualty department who had deliberately poisoned themselves. In describing her study, she highlights the criteria that the experimental design must meet. In addition to the division into two groups, the intervention must be clearly defined, with evidence that it is delivered, and there must be baseline and outcome measures which can address for both groups the effects of receipt or non-receipt of the intervention. Expected differences are most often addressed in the form of hypotheses, in this case that the experimental cases who received the task-centred crisis service rather than the routine service would repeat self-poisoning and become psychiatric patients less often in the following year, would have less psychotropic drug treatment from general practitioners, would show greater improvement in depressed mood and social problems (as measured by standard schedules) and would express greater satisfaction with the service. On three of the outcome criteria (use of psychiatric services, improvement in social problems and satisfaction with service), significant differences between the two groups, attributable to the task-centred work, were demonstrated.

Corney and Clare (1983) applied an experimental design to the determination of the effectiveness of work by social workers attached to general practices with women presenting with depression. Randomly allocated to a control or experimental group, those in the control group were referred back to their doctor for routine treatment. No immediate differences on outcome measures between the two groups were evident after six months, although more detailed analysis did reveal differences for certain sub-groups. In particular, it appeared that a combination of a number of factors was important: the duration of the client's depression, the quality of her relationship with her partner and the support received from others, the motivation to be helped and the nature of her social problems. Thus, for those experiencing marital problems and having 'acute or chronic' depression, 80 per cent of the experimental group were judged to be clinically improved compared with only 31 per cent of the control group.

A detailed review of experimental studies in the field of social work can be found in Sheldon (1986), who maintains that 'experiments remain the strictest test of therapeutic good-intent' (p. 239). He identifies two waves of such studies: the first in the early 1970s of 20 or so studies of general focus; the second, more recent, addressing more specific questions in greater detail. With the move to this more focused assessment, outcomes for experimental groups began more often to emerge as favourable and increased methodological rigour ensured that the nature of the therapeutic intervention was defined more accurately. Most recently, Rushton (1990) has reviewed the evidence available from randomized control trials for the debate on community or hospital care for those with acute mental health problems. He finds methodological flaws in several of the studies, but highlights three where he considers the design to be sound, one a project at the Maudsley Hospital where those requiring immediate admission are randomly allocated to standard in-patient service or to the Daily Living Project, a 24-hour community support service. Initial results from 187 patients, 92 in receipt of the Daily Living Programme and 95 of standardized hospital care, show that home care reduced the length of hospital stay by 80 per cent. Clinical scale ratings were not significantly different between the two groups, although trends favoured the home care programme. Patient and relative satisfaction was significantly greater with the innovative programme. Again, however, it should be noted that these examples are very much rooted within the clinical tradition; their applicability to the sometimes very different interventions central to much of social work practice has to be explored with caution.

A further and oft-quoted example of an experimental study is that of Clarke and Cornish (1972), which is discussed in further detail in Chapter 5. In this case, two randomly selected groups were allocated to different treatment interventions. This may overcome to some extent the ethical objections to the withholding of intervention or some other form of service from one of the groups. In whatever form, however, experimental models can be exceedingly difficult to implement adequately in practice.

No doubt for practical reasons, experimental designs are often employed at the level of the individual case (Sheldon, 1983; Thyer, 1992). Often rooted in a behavioural modification model, the single-case (or single-system) design takes the argument for focusing-down from the global to its limit. Indicators, usually behavioural, relate to the presence or severity of problematic incidents and can be used to monitor change over time. A baseline measure is obtained for this indicator pre-intervention and subsequent measures obtained over the period of intervention. Recording techniques may vary from various forms of timed observation to self-report or mechanical recording, the time interval being determined appropriate to the subject under scrutiny. The selection of the dependent indicator (alias outcome measure) is the key to the single-case design: the measure must be reliable, valid and amenable to repeated measurement.

Various types of single-case experimental designs have been distinguished. The most straightforward is a before and after comparison (AB), e.g. ten days a month off school prior to the intervention being introduced and only two after. For full confirmation of the effect of intervention, advocates of this method argue that there should be a return to baseline (ABA) or, preferably, a return and then recommencement of the intervention (ABAB). Further refinements allow for situations where intervention begins before establishment of a baseline (BAB), the intervention being temporarily halted for a period, or where there are multiple baselines. Single-case designs can thus, in their different forms, address these two questions: did the client improve *during the course* of social work intervention and did the client improve *because of* social work intervention? They do not require an elaborate array of research techniques and may therefore be regarded as particularly suited for practitioners who wish to study their own cases. It is important to bear in mind, however, that these models are only possible where the effects of the intervention under scrutiny can readily be negated when the intervention is removed. Time spent in a certain activity or exhibiting certain behavioural characteristics can cease; the acquisition of, for example, greater confidence or assertiveness may disappear less immediately (if at all) on the removal of the stimulus.

The question of causality, to be addressed more generally in Chapter 5, is central to the experimental design. Perhaps more clearly than for any other research strategy, conclusions can be drawn as to the presence or absence of the intervention being the likely explanation for observed differences in outcome. For the more rigorous, Thyer (1992) regards the distinction drawn above between the AB single-system design and the more rigorous ABAB formulation as that between an evaluative and an experimental design, only the latter providing the certainty for attribution of causality.

In practice, the conceptual purity of the experimental design can often not be attained. Social work delivery is only but an element in the panoply of influences on daily life and the extent to which one can match for the huge range of community influences is questionable. A further stumbling block can be the ethical or political consideration of withholding a service from the control group or of stopping and starting a supposedly therapeutic intervention. Where the effectiveness of the intervention under scrutiny has not yet been demonstrated, this should be less of a concern, although it would appear to preoccupy the social work profession perhaps rather more than their medical colleagues. An alternative, however, is to look to the naturally occurring experiment, the intervention that appears in retrospect to have modelled the conditions of an experiment. This imposition of an experimental format on events which have already happened is termed a quasi-experimental design. Cases subject to the experiment are compared with controls outwith the experience. This design may also be created on a prospective basis where experimental subjects are contrasted with those in perhaps another geographical area where the system under scrutiny is not in operation.

The quasi-experimental design is exemplified in the study of parenting reported by Rutter *et al.* (1983). Primarily interested in potential links between childhood experiences and parenting behaviour, both retrospective and prospective samples were sought, with families where children had been taken into care contrasted with a general population sample where children had remained in the home. Relevant hypotheses could then be explored. Obviously, receipt into care could not form the subject of an experimental design; selection of appropriate elements, however, allows for reconstruction in quasi-experimental form.

A quasi-experimental design was also adopted in the examination of the effect of social worker attachment by Cooper *et al.* (1975). In this case, the focus was a single group practice and chronic neurotic illness. For both the experimental and the control groups, assessments of both psychiatric status and of social adjustment and functioning were made at the time of referral and after 12 months. In order to avoid contamination, controls were drawn from neighbouring practices without access to the attached worker, a modification on the random allocation principle. A matching of cases individually on key variables was not possible; instead, comparison of the two groups had to be made at the end-point to ensure that they were not significantly different in terms of these key variables.

It is perhaps necessary to stress that adequate experimental or quasi-experimental designs are comparatively rare. The formulation may exude an authority which perhaps exposes it to less critical scrutiny than apparently less vigorous strategies. It is the contention throughout this volume, however, that whatever the point on the research continuum, the rigour of the methodology must be maintained. To this end, the reappraisal by Logan (1972) cites the seven prerequisites for the experimental design which closely accord with the features cited by Gibbons (1981) above. His conclusion from examining a range of experimental studies in the criminological field was that not one of the 100 studies under review met all of the specified criteria. The question that must be asked is whether this was due to sloppy research or to the attempt to apply a less than appropriate strategy.

The Social Work Research Centre (SWRC) to date has made little use of experimental designs. A random allocation mechanism was possible in the Centre's evaluation of pre-prosecution reparation and mediation schemes (Warner, 1992). The limited capacity of the experimental project meant that the number of potentially suitable cases heavily outweighed the places available. Although the short period of random allocation to the project or to normal criminal justice processing was useful in identifying the likely alternative outcomes of project cases, further generalizability of the findings was unwarranted: there were reasons to believe that other temporary factors had contributed to the unexpectedly high non-prosecution rate of control group cases.

More often in social welfare, however, a comparison rather than a control group is introduced. This model was adopted for the study of rehabilitation of patients from the Royal Edinburgh Hospital by Simic *et al.* (1992) and for the evaluation of a domiciliary health and social work project for very dependent elderly people (EPIC) being carried out by Bland, Hudson and Dobson at Stirling. In the first study, those who were discharged from the hospital were matched on a number of key items (age, length of stay, diagnosis) with individuals remaining within the hospital. Comparisons of mental state, social functioning and quality of life at different points could then be made from a number of the research instruments which identified areas of divergence and similarity. The EPIC study has adopted the device of a comparison group from outside the study area who though similar on a number of characteristics do not have the particular facilities of the project on offer to them.

Cross-institutional design

An alternative to the rigorous experimental design is one which seeks to compare outcomes for varying forms of intervention across a number of different sites, i.e. the cross-institutional design. This requires detailed information about the characteristics of the individuals receiving the services. By controlling statistically for differences in intake at the different sites, the aim is to attribute different outcomes to the effects of different models of intervention (Fuller, 1987a). Originally developed for penal research, the cross-institutional design has been applied in contexts ranging from probation hostels and approved schools to residential nurseries and old people's homes (Sinclair, 1971; Dunlop, 1974; Tizard *et al.*, 1975; Booth, 1985). Sinclair and Clarke (1981) suggest that the minimum number of research sites should be eight and this obviously means that such studies require substantial resources. The recent work by Booth (1985), for example, which sought (without success) to relate certain features of institutional regime to increased dependency, embraced 175 residential homes for the elderly in four local authorities.

One of the key advantages of the cross-institutional design is its 'naturalistic' approach, that is its ability to capitalize on existing diversity of practice within a given area of service delivery or intervention. This, it is said, enhances the generalizability of results. Moreover, since there is no need for the researcher deliberately to manipulate or control the research environment, practice does not have to change to accommodate the research.

The approach does, of course, have its limitations and can present researchers with substantial measurement problems. The selection and measurement of outcomes is an obvious case in point, although the difficulties posed in this respect should be no greater than those encountered in any design where aggregate measures of the impact of intervention are required.

The identification of intake variables (or client characteristics) to be controlled statistically in the analysis also requires careful consideration. If important background factors are disregarded, erroneous conclusions may be reached about the effectiveness of specific components of the intervention. If, for example, no attempt was made to control for the age of clients across different sites, yet age was an important determinant of the success of intervention, then observed differences in outcome might be attributed to aspects of the intervention when they were, in fact, due to the uncontrolled variable of client age. Again, however, the problem is not confined to the cross-institutional design: experimental and quasi-experimental designs also require that all relevant intake variables are controlled for across the treatment groups.

A measurement problem that is more specific to the cross-institutional research design concerns the identification and measurement of potentially relevant features of the intervention (including, for example, the attitudes and orientations of staff as in Sinclair's study of probation hostels) in such a way that permits their ranking across the different research sites included in the study. In the community service study (McIvor, 1989, 1992b), the ranking of schemes according to their strictness in enforcing requirements was achieved through first ranking the schemes according to the average numbers of unacceptable absences which were tolerated prior to the issuing of a first warning and the average numbers of such absences that were tolerated prior to an offender being breached. An overall ranking of strictness was obtained through averaging the ranked positions on these two composite measures.

As with the identification of relevant intake variables, the selection of social work processes or features of the intervention or 'institution' to be examined may be guided by prior research or may be premised upon theoretical assumptions. Familiarity with the operation and objectives of the programme under scrutiny will also facilitate identification of each of the key components which might be expected to have a bearing upon outcome.

Sinclair (1971), for example, appears to have made choices about process variables to be examined in his study of probation hostels on the basis of hypotheses generated through prolonged involvement with the hostels.

The ranking of processes across research sites may be based upon quantitative data or upon qualitative data that has been quantified in some way. Dunlop (1974), for example, developed 'emphasis scores' for each approved school regime based on intensive interviews carried out with boys in each school. The interviews identified ten key topics which were both prominent in the minds of the boys and discriminating between schools; examples included trade training, adult relationships and punishment. The schools were then ranked according to the proportion of boys in each school who gave answers to a variety of questions indicating an emphasis on the relevant regime topic.

In application, the cross-institutional design has often yielded interesting and useful findings and has generated hypotheses which might form the basis of further research. A major drawback, however, in addition to its scale and complexity, is the amount of research energy that has to be expended before it is even apparent that the design can be applied in its strictest sense in analysing the relationship between process and outcome. The design is dependent upon there being differences in both process and outcome across the research sites. Apparent differences in outcome may, however, disappear when account is taken statistically of variations in intake to the sites. This occurred, for example, in the Centre's study of community service schemes (McIvor, 1989, 1992b). Although the 12 schemes differed according to the percentages of offenders who successfully completed their community service orders, they also contained differing proportions of offenders who, in terms of a number of background characteristics, were less likely to succeed. The relevant statistical controls revealed that the variations in success rates could be accounted for by the differential incidence of 'high-risk' offenders across schemes. Accounting for intake variables can therefore lead to a collapse of the cross-institutional rationale. Given the riskiness of the strategy, therefore, the intrepid researcher would be wise to ensure that at least some important components of the research (such as the exploration of the relative effectiveness of different types of work placements in the community service study) are not wholly dependent upon the successful application of a cross-institutional model and to have alternative strategies waiting in the wings.

The case study

The unique advantage of the individual case study is that it throws light on how policy decisions are actually made and on the role various participants play.

Saran (1973, p. 2)

Twill be recorded for a precedent
And many an error by the same example
Will rush into the state.

Shakespeare, *Merchant of Venice*

The case study, a term that is used somewhat imprecisely in social research, may serve a number of different functions and be useful in a range of contexts. Its distinguishing characteristic is that the uniqueness of the individual 'case' is retained, whether that case is an individual client, an area, an event, a team, or indeed any identifiable entity. Unlike the approaches previously detailed, the case study variables are not abstracted or tightly controlled; indeed, changes or developments in the course of a study are themselves valuable data rather than 'contaminating' factors, and numbers are not necessarily crucial. Although there is a certain emphasis on descriptive and qualitative methods, no particular system of data collection or analysis is entailed or excluded. Yin (1989) has reviewed a range of case study designs and methods.

The danger of the case study approach is that it may become merely an extended anecdote without evaluative relevance. This is the risk run if the case is selected for study on a wholly opportunistic basis. To avoid this, a conceptual framework of some kind is necessary to provide a rationale for choosing the individual case. As Heclo (1972, p. 107) remarks, in the absence of a general framework what is provided is 'at best an interesting contribution to historical scholarship and at worst an uninteresting episodic narrative'.

One such basis for selection is when a single example is chosen for individual in-depth study from a larger group of cases about which something is already known or reasonably hypothesized. Thus case study material may be used in the context of a larger study, or the case study may be separately undertaken. From a general survey or previous work, one or more cases may be selected on the grounds that they are in some way interesting, whether because they have been identified as typical, or conversely as deviant, as extreme or 'pure'. Here the point of interest is likely to lie in how observed outcomes came about. Why did the one case succeed while others failed, or vice versa? How did one project avoid financial difficulties? Why did one team have such an unusual referral rate? What in detail characterizes the typical example of a group of Intermediate Treatment (IT) projects?

A second context where the case study may be employed is that of the innovatory or unique instance, where precisely because of its uniqueness a design based on a comparison group is not readily available. One example of this is Ferri's (1981) evaluation of innovatory combined nursery centres. Although where appropriate a wide variety of research techniques may be employed in this design, Ferri demonstrates why certain contexts may demand more flexible and exploratory devices. Innovative projects will be particularly prone to shifting objectives and practices and evaluative methodologies must be able to adjust and respond to such variation. Strategies which require the rigid structure of, for example, the experimental design will not survive. On the other hand, the case study must not disperse into an amorphous collection of data which loses sight of the objective of the exercise. Ferri's study, for instance, sought objective measures of children's progress (outcomes), but placed this within the context of the process of establishment and development of the centres, thus addressing very much the substance as well as the product of the innovation.

One case study carried out at the Centre was the M.A.R.S. study described more fully in Chapter 6. In this instance, a project which worked intensively with adolescents on the brink of removal from home was chosen for detailed study because it offered a highly unusual example of an agency reputed to carry out intensive social work with a client group with whom such methods had not elsewhere been successful. The structure built into the design was to monitor rigorously the achievement of objectives with individual cases while attempting to describe systematically the social work processes involved. A second Centre example is the study of a pioneering joint initiative in a Scottish region between the social work department and the police for the investigation of child abuse (Brown and Fuller, 1991b). The rationale and main emphasis of this study was in the addition to a small body of similar case studies elsewhere, all of schemes differing slightly from each other; here, however, there was a quasi-experimental element with a limited comparison sought with another area without such a scheme.

Longitudinal studies

A dilemma for many attempts at evaluation is that adequate assessment of outcomes requires the passage of a reasonable period of time. Social work interventions are not usually of a form designed to produce instant results; only after 6, 12, or 24 months can tentative conclusions be drawn. For example, in the study of reprovision from the Friern and Claybury hospitals being undertaken by the Team for the Assessment of Psychiatric Services (1990), only after the third year is the first cohort beginning to suggest some tentative improvement in social functioning. It is not unusual, therefore, for studies to adopt some form of longitudinal perspective, returning to subjects at a series of time intervals. Some of the best known longitudinal studies, for example the National Child Development Study (Fogelman, 1983) and the Cambridge delinquency study (West and Farrington, 1973, 1977; Farrington and West, 1981), have tracked individuals over a considerable number of years. This is the intention also of the recently established Economic and Social Research Council (ESRC) Centre for the study of Micro-Social Change at Essex University. More frequently, the goal is more modest, two or three follow-ups over 6 or 12 months. The focus of the repeated observations will vary according to the aim of the study; it may be successive measurements of functioning or well-being, it may be determination of the number and nature of supports during a specific programme of intervention. As highlighted above, however, the time dimension is one of the key parameters in the research process.

Practical considerations can feature prominently in longitudinal studies. Although systematic evaluation might ideally follow a cohort for several years, few agencies are willing or able to wait this long for some notion of their effectiveness. Likewise, few recipients of social work services remain trackable for long periods of time and increasing numbers may be lost to a study over time. Questions may also arise as to the nature of the intervention being evaluated. In certain circumstances, 'survival' itself may be the focus of attention, e.g. the numbers that with an enhanced service are retained in the community. At other times, however, the interest may lie with the process that is taking place, and to assume consistency of this process over any extended length of time may be inappropriate.

As with the case study, the proviso introduced at the start of this chapter should be borne in mind. Adoption of the longitudinal design determines certain features of the study, but within these there is still wide scope to employ other research strategies and a range of research techniques. Within a longitudinal design, the focus might be upon the user perspective or upon a quasi-experimental component. A battery of quantified scaling devices may be scored or the interest may lie in the variation in subjective accounts over time.

By nature of being concerned with outcomes, virtually all of the studies undertaken by the Centre have an element of the longitudinal in them. Those according most closely to the traditional understanding of the longitudinal study, however, are probably the studies in the mental health field which have focused on time-sampling at specific intervals. Thus the study of supported accommodation projects sampled each project at three six-monthly intervals, the respondents being classified according to their length of stay in a project (Petch, 1990, 1992). The Royal Edinburgh Hospital study, likewise, sought interviews and psychiatric assessments within a month of leaving hospital, at three months and at nine months. For the study of homemakers, time-sampling was at intake, at three months and at closure, with further follow-up six months after closure.

User perspective

> We thought – them do-gooders, they must know what they're doing; we'll abide by their ways.
>
> A service user

It should be emphasized again that the research strategies being addressed are not all mutually exclusive. A case study could incorporate a longitudinal element; a longitudinal design could encompass a pluralistic perspective. User studies are none the less treated separately because of their current high profile within social work research. They continue very often to provide a rallying cry, a cry which must be analysed carefully in terms of methodology and interpretation.

The work by Mayer and Timms (1970) is very much seen as a historical landmark, the first attempt to explore how those on the receiving end might experience a service. Some would argue that attention to the user perspective was stimulated by the somewhat negative effects of the early global attempts to demonstrate social work effectiveness. Certainly, the impetus for a 'bottom-up' rather than 'top-down' approach steadily grew, nurtured by an increasingly participatory ethos and by an increasingly critical stance towards the status quo.

The reviews by both Rees and Wallace (1982) and by Fisher (1983) track the substantial development in studies focusing on the user perspective.

They also pinpoint a number of potentially problematic areas, a necessary antidote to the often seductive attraction of the perspective. 'Client evaluation is a complicated, confusing and often seemingly contradictory phenomenon which requires sensitive and detailed analysis' (Rees and Wallace, 1982, p. 86).

An important consideration in studies of this type is the concept of satisfaction. To ascertain levels of satisfaction is often the major motivation of a user study, but too general a notion of satisfaction can be problematic. It can be demonstrated across a wide range of phenomena that general satisfaction will be expressed by approaching 80 per cent of recipients (Gutek, 1978; Berger, 1983). Moreover, in relation to various forms of therapy (Ware, 1978), levels of satisfaction have been shown to vary with client characteristics. Thus older people, those at higher occupational levels and females express higher levels of satisfaction; those with lower educational attainment, lower income and from larger families are generally less satisfied. It can therefore be less than helpful merely to replicate such global ratings, particularly given the evidence in certain services that outcome appears unrelated to satisfaction ratings for the help received (Glendinning, 1986). At the very least, generalities must be disaggregated, and the context from which individuals are evaluating their experience must be explored.

There are implications within this discussion for the nature of the techniques through which the user perspective is sought. Many of the early studies argued that a concern with this perspective reflects a concern for the individual's subjective experience and as such arises from a very different theoretical base to the scientific rationality that lies behind the experimental and quasi-experimental design. User studies tend to be associated with the subjectivist or interpretative tradition of sociological thought, seeking to understand the nature of perceived reality rather than striving to explain a reality considered from the more positivist tradition to be objective. In seeking to explore these multiple interpretations of the user, it is argued that the most appropriate techniques are those at the softer end of the continuum, the exploratory interview, the semi-structured strategy that gives much of the initiative to the respondent. In this way, it is argued, there can be a closer approximation to the understandings and perceptions of those on the receiving end. The traditional 'measurement by fiat', forcing responses into arbitrary categories, is avoided.

Recently, there has been greater diversity in the techniques adopted for user studies. This has probably been prompted in part by practical considerations; the conduct and analysis of semi-structured interviews can be a lengthy and exhausting process. To stick rigidly to such a technique might reduce considerably the areas which could be exposed to user comment. Exploration of a wider range of techniques has recently been evident, including, for example, Fisher's (1983) combination of both more quantitative and more qualitative strategies.

One of the leading exponents of the user study has written recently of their potential contribution to the practice agency (Sainsbury, 1987). To achieve this potential, Sainsbury argues, a broader context must be adopted. Client studies must be extended into comparative areas and must be focused on specific issues. They may also, he suggests, provide a mechanism for the in-volvement of both service providers and users in the design and conduct of research. In terms of techniques, however, Sainsbury is less inclined to ex-ploration. He does not, for example, advocate the use of questionnaires: 'the relationship between person and paper is even more problematic than that between person and person' (p. 640).

The Centre has been committed to having the user perspective as a key component of many of its studies. The most extensive platform for the user has probably been extended in the study of supported accommodation pro-visions where 255 in-depth interviews were conducted with project users. Scales derived from Lehman (1983a) were used as summary adjuncts to per-sonal accounts in a range of areas and provided at analysis a useful framework for the more subjective accounts and acted more pragmatically during the interview as a staging device.

A number of studies have explored the extent to which less time-consuming techniques may none the less yield valuable material. In the series of studies on community service, both the initial study (McIvor, 1989) and the subse-quent study of beneficiaries (McIvor, 1990b) sought the views and experi-ences of the recipients through the completion of questionnaires. While there were the inevitable features of response rates (both studies had ap-proximately a third of the questionnaires returned) and of the need for a fair degree of structure, both these exercises were considered to have yielded worthwhile data. It is perhaps too early to judge to what extent such techniques can substitute for the more lengthy interview: more systematic exploration of the potential across a range of client groups and subject situations could be of value. For example, in the community service studies, the open-ended responses which were sought referred to situations the re-spondents had experienced rather than seeking more speculative comment. In a recent study by Smith (1991b) which sought, through a similar ques-tionnaire, comment and aspiration from those with mental health problems on service delivery, the responses to the limited number of open-ended questions were less illuminating.

Pluralistic evaluation

The approach which has been labelled pluralistic evaluation (Smith and Cantley, 1985) has been developed by those who argue that it is false to force the social work world into the traditional scientific model of evaluation which thrives on assumptions of objectivity, rationality and experimenta-tion. Individuals are not optimizers but satisficers; disjointed incremental-ism is a more appropriate model for the policy process than rationality. Ambiguity and diversity rather than clarity of goals is the norm for a social organization, with the distinction between means and ends an artificial and shifting one. Perhaps most importantly, traditional evaluation demands an assumption of consensus, of unity among all parties within an organization. Agreed criteria of success can then be defined and the extent to which these are attained can be measured. Pluralistic evaluation acknowledges that consensus is absent, and rather than struggling to force the illusion on unwilling subjects brings centre stage the multiple, possibly conflicting criteria of success of different parties to the process.

> Ambiguity and lack of agreement in perception between parties of the policy-shaping community would then be a central feature of the research, rather than an embarrassment as is the case when the presumption of consensus prevails (Smith and Cantley, 1985, p. 9).

It will be apparent that to engage in pluralistic evaluation is not merely to select a particular research strategy, as might be the case with a longitudinal design, but to accept, implicitly or explicitly, the validity of the arguments which invoke it. Indeed, it is probably more accurate to characterize pluralistic evaluation as a research orientation in order to distinguish it from the methodologies of the earlier parts of this chapter.

In practical terms, a commitment to pluralistic evaluation involves identifying the major parties involved in the initiative or process under scrutiny and comparing them with each other in terms of ideological and operational perspectives. Differing notions of success are identified and defined, and the strategies which the different parties adopt in striving for such success are recorded. Finally, an assessment is made of the extent to which success has been attained on each of the different criteria employed by the various parties.

Smith and Cantley illustrate their arguments with the evaluation they undertook of a psychogeriatric day hospital. The parties whose views were sought included medical practitioners, nurses, social workers, administrators and patients' relatives. Hospital meetings were attended over a two-year period, hospital records were scrutinized and referral data were analysed. Some field observation was also carried out on hospital routines and a relatives' support group. Such triangulation of techniques, whereby the strengths and weaknesses of different approaches are complemented by multiple usage (see Chapter 4), is frequently a feature of the pluralistic evaluation. Across the different parties, six varying meanings attributed to success were identified and the extent to which they were achieved was assessed. Very often evaluation of this nature will produce divergent answers – success on certain criteria for certain groups. Its advocates, however, would argue that this is the basis on which the most realistic intervention can then be planned.

A second example which has been worked in detail is the study of a travelling day hospital (TDH) for the elderly mentally ill by Evans *et al.* (1986). As the researchers explain, the day hospital exemplifies the type of intervention which is not amenable to the controlled causal explanation of the scientific model of evaluation:

> By its nature the service is relatively unspecific, and one where many other factors impinge on a patient during the six days and eighteen hours when he or she is not attending a centre. If dramatic and measurable changes occurred in his or her psychiatric condition, they could not be attributed with certainty to the work of the TDH (Evans *et al.*, 1986, p. 28).

Moreover, and of central concern to the pluralistic evaluation, is recognition of the fact that the different interests set very different agendas with regard to the goals of the day hospital. Three key groups are isolated: the patients themselves, their relatives and other informal carers, and the professionals involved either in direct care of patients or in the planning and management of services. Nine aims which were identified as the main focus for the study were linked to their primary reference group. Thus the aim of promoting the social well-being of users is linked to patients, while providing an alternative to residential care is seen as a concern of professionals.

Arguments consistent with the approach presented by pluralistic evaluation would appear implicit, at times explicit, in much of the debate that surrounds the Centre's work. Certainly, there would appear to be agreement with many of the basic tenets of the argument, an acknowledgement of the often very divergent interpretations that lie with different interest groups. In following through studies, however, it may often be that elements from the pluralistic argument are pursued rather than the total package. Two or three of the parties only may be addressed, the individual nature of their definitions of success will be accepted, but a global analysis of the total range of potential definitions will not be sought.

It would also appear that some of the detail of pluralistic evaluation is less clearly defined. Some important methodological debate, for example, has yet to be clarified. The underlying rationale would appear to dictate the use of certain methodologies rather than others; yet it may be appropriate in order to answer certain parties' notions of success to use, for example, traditional measurement devices. Moreover, some would argue that to specify the need for all perspectives to be gathered may be an advance but is not the final point. What, having specified the differing criteria of success and the extent to which they have been achieved, is to be done with that information? There still has to be – though not necessarily for the researcher – some process of moderation or judgement which determines priorities among the differing respondents. Evans and colleagues (1986, p. 239), for example, conclude: 'on the sometimes confusing continuum of aims from improved cooperation and liaison, through coordination, towards contributing to modest forms of integrated support, we have found the TDH achieving varying degrees of success'. It may have to be acknowledged that some of these aims are of greater import than others : whether it is the role of the researcher to moderate across these aims is one of the constant debates of the research arena. The answer, moreover, to this particular dilemma, may depend on whether the interest is in a particular party (applied research) or in a more detached and holistic account (pure research).

The aim of this chapter has been to provide a broad overview of the major research strategies which can be pursued in the evaluation of social work. Strategies cannot be divorced from the philosophical contexts in which they lie, and therefore the emphasis throughout the discussion has been on the interpretation of the particular advantages and constraints this relationship lends to each strategy for the purposes of the current evaluative task. While it would be true to say that many of the Centre's studies are heavily influenced in their formulation by the principles of pluralistic evaluation, the approach as a whole, as highlighted in Chapter 2, is more readily characterized as methodologically pluralist. Indeed there may be an argument that the concept of pluralistic evaluation was important for a time as an important critique of overly rationalistic planning, but that the debate has now become more specific. Thus in the Centre's work a range of strategies are drawn upon as appropriate for the particular research problem under consideration, but with clear recognition of the particular limitations or potentials that, given the nature of much of the social work task, are attached to each. Thus, for example, while the experimental design would not automatically be ruled out, the limits both of the conceptual philosophy in which it is rooted and of the practical requirements for its implementation would severely restrict the situations in which it might feature as a potential strategy. Different interest groups, varying scales of study, shorter and longer time periods may all have an influence on the particular strategy adopted for each research question. The prerequisite is that the limitations and potentials of each approach in terms of the underlying rationale are thoroughly understood. In the next chapter, the specific techniques which may be employed once the particular strategy has been selected will be discussed.

4

METHODS OF DATA COLLECTION

If no single measurement class is perfect, neither is any scientifically useless.

Webb *et al*. (1966, p. 174)

A number of different techniques or methods are available to document or measure the activities of social workers and their effects. Each of these techniques may be applicable across a range of research methodologies (see Chapter 3). This chapter describes the various means by which information about the process and outcomes of social work intervention might be gathered within a broader research framework concerned with assessing the effectiveness of services or practice. Although researchers' theoretical orientations, and sometimes those of their audience, may influence to a considerable degree the choice of methodology and data collection methods, such decisions will more usually reflect clearly pragmatic concerns, such as the purpose and objectives of the evaluation and the practical constraints imposed by the research environment.

In many, and perhaps most, evaluative studies, a range of data collection techniques will be appropriate within an overall research strategy and will be used in such a way as to maximize the value of the information obtained and strengthen the conclusions arising from the research. Some approaches (such as observational methods) are clearly more useful for describing and documenting the interpersonal components of intervention, whereas others (such as the use of documentary material, interviews or questionnaires) can more usefully provide information about the receipt of services and their impact on clients.

This chapter does not present a detailed methodological critique of the range of data collection methods available to the applied social researcher. A useful discussion of different techniques can be found in Bailey (1978) and in other texts listed in the annotated bibliography at the end of this volume. Here the main factors which will influence the choice of method will be highlighted. Examples of Centre and other studies will be drawn upon to illustrate the trade-offs between different techniques and how decisions concerning their use have been made.

Interviews and questionnaires

One of the most common means of obtaining information about the processes and outcomes of social work intervention is through the use of interviews and questionnaires, methods which are widely used in social science research more generally. Space does not permit a detailed exposition of the relative merits and shortcomings of these methods of data collection in their various forms, but the main factors that will be taken into account when deciding upon the choice of instrument will be discussed.

Breadth and depth of coverage

Questionnaires generally sacrifice detail for breadth of coverage and may be considered appropriate where larger sample sizes are required. They provide a means of gathering, in a structured and standardized format, the experiences and attitudes of a potentially large number of individuals which are usually collated to provide some aggregate picture of the issues under study.

Frequently, questionnaires require respondents to choose, from a limited range of responses, the one which best represents their experiences or views. Often, as in the Centre's studies of community service schemes (McIvor, 1989, 1992b), the recipients of community service work (McIvor, 1990b and forthcoming) and the quality of care in old people's homes (Bland *et al.*, forthcoming), fixed-choice questions are interspersed with open-ended questions to enable the meaning of responses to be further explored with a large sample of respondents, albeit in a necessarily limited way.

The use of fixed-choice responses in questionnaires may serve to reduce the amount of time required for completion and thus enhance the likelihood of participation. Open-ended questions, on the other hand, generally call for a more detailed and lengthy response and the inclusion of many such questions may discourage individuals from participating in the research. An appropriate balance is therefore needed if the quality of data available through questionnaires and the response rate are to be maximized, while keeping to a manageable level the amount of effort that will be required for subsequent analysis.

If depth of coverage of an issue is considered more important than the involvement of a large sample size, then the interviewing of respondents will usually be preferred. In their most structured form, interview schedules may be largely indistinguishable in content from questionnaires, but the face-to-face interaction between the researcher and respondent enables clarification of questions as necessary. By involving oral rather than written communication, interviews may also circumvent literacy difficulties which might otherwise prevent the completion of questionnaires.

Detailed explorations of an issue are obtainable through the use of either semi-structured or unstructured interviews which, because of their labour-intensiveness at both the data-collection and analysis stages, will often be deemed inappropriate with larger samples of respondents. A possible compromise, which was adopted in the assessment of offenders' experiences of community service (McIvor, 1989, 1991a), is to combine the use of questionaires with less structured interviews, the latter being employed to explore relevant issues in greater depth with a sub-sample of questionnaire respondents.

Clients' meanings

A major criticism of questionnaires, however structured, is that the predetermination of the questions constitutes the imposition by researchers of their interpretation of an issue or service which may or may not correspond to the perceptions or experiences of the respondent. Responses received may be misleading if questions cannot be understood by the respondents or have been misconstrued. The inclusion of open-ended questions may not prevent misunderstandings from occurring, but they do increase the likelihood of any such misconceptions or misunderstandings being identified.

Structured interview schedules are open to similar criticisms, but because of their greater flexibility and their potential to provide a richness of data usually not obtainable through questionnaires, semi-structured and unstructured interviews will often be preferred to other methods of eliciting social workers' and clients' experiences of and understanding of the social work process and its outcomes. In her study of supported accommodation for people with mental health problems, Petch (1990, 1992) conducted 255 loosely structured interviews involving 145 different individuals: 'The intention was to offer a relaxed opportunity to reflect on various aspects both of the projects and of their own lives' (Petch, 1990, p. 7).

Respondents may provide thoughtful and reflective responses to openended items in questionnaires. In the Centre's postal survey of the recipients of community service work, for example, most of the individual and agency respondents provided detailed responses to the open-ended questions and many took advantage of the opportunity to offer additional detailed comments on completing the questionnaire (McIvor, 1990b). The potential to elicit personal meanings and interpretations is, however, maximized through the use of relatively unstructured interviewing techniques, even if this in some instances necessitates the involvement of smaller samples of respondents.

Resources

The type of information desired by the researcher will usually have to be counterbalanced by a consideration of the resource implications of different methods of data collection. Ultimately, the decisions reached will reflect some form of trade-off between the information optimally desired and various practical constraints relating to its collection and analysis. Clearly, compromises will have to be made in ways which reflect the relative importance of issues such as sample size, depth of coverage and the need for the respondents' understanding and interpretation of issues to be explored. The time required to collect interview or questionnaire data will be an important determinant of the sample size and method of data collection. If time is limited, and it usually will be, the feasibility of conducting large numbers of interviews will be called into question. This problem is exacerbated when respondents are no longer in touch with the social work agency. As Cheetham (1991) found, some very disadvantaged and mobile people prove notoriously difficult to track down. If large samples and relatively undetailed responses are required, the prospect of a low return rate from postal questionnaires (and the associated interpretational problems) may be more acceptable than the prospect of spending days or weeks knocking (usually unsuccessfully) on doors with notebook and interview schedule in hand.

The use of postal questionnaires has been criticized on the grounds that the lack of information about non-respondents may introduce an unidentifiable bias in the results. In the postal survey of community service work beneficiaries, for instance, the anonymity of the responses meant that it was impossible to ascertain the precise extent to which the views expressed were representative of the total population to whom questionnaires were sent. In the study of offenders' attitudes towards community service, on the other hand, the questionnaire respondents and non-respondents were found to be indistinguishable in terms of each of the background characteristics on which they were compared. These included gender, age, marital status, employment status, previous convictions and sentences, current offence, length of community service order, and history of social work involvement. Offenders who had breached their community service orders were slightly under-represented among the questionnaire respondents, but some of this former group could not be contacted, either because they had changed their address and failed to notify the scheme (which in itself constituted the grounds for breach) or because the community service staff were reluctant to send questionnaires to offenders following an acrimonious breach procedure. Thus, there was no reason to believe that an unrepresentative sample of questionnaire respondents had been obtained.

The social work researcher will usually have given some thought to such resource issues when planning a study. Often, though, less detailed consideration will be given at the outset to the resource implications at the analysis stage of different techniques of data collection. Completely structured questionnaires or interview schedules will be relatively undemanding of time at the point of analysis, save that required to transfer the data to computer. Open-ended items in questionnaires present an additional stage of categorization and coding, since the range and type of responses received will usually not be wholly predictable in advance. The analysis of loosely structured or unstructured interviews, however, will be most demanding of resources, particularly if the interviews have been tape-recorded and literal transcription is required. The use of software packages, such as BRS Search, which facilitate the sorting and analysis of qualitative data, and which enable the cross-tabulation of interview material, may circumvent some of the stages required in the traditional 'cut and paste' method of qualitative data management, but considerable effort is still required to generate response categories and ensure that relevant responses are allocated to them.

Practical experience led the Centre to give some detailed consideration to the relative merits and disadvantages of taped interviews and their subsequent transcription. Full literal transcription of an interview may take several hours for even an experienced audio secretary to complete, while selective transcription will be highly demanding of researchers' time. The issue was highlighted in the study of supported accommodation (Petch, 1990, 1992), in which the impracticality of fully transcribing 255 often lengthy interviews was apparent. A strategy was adopted whereby the majority of first interviews were tape-recorded but, at subsequent interviews, unless an individual was known to be particularly voluble, the tape-recorder was replaced by a detailed written recording of the responses. Similar considerations led Warner (1992), in her study of two reparation and mediation schemes, to take written notes during her interviews with victims and accused, and transfer them to tape for ease of transcription by secretarial staff. Neither researcher considered that the taking of notes had seriously hampered the flow of the interviews or had unduly limited the scope of the information obtained.

As a result of these and other experiences, the Centre has agreed that in most circumstances it will be unnecessary to tape-record interviews. Exceptions to this general rule include those situations where it may be important to capture the subtle nuances of an argument or position and, if necessary, to provide material confirmation of statements which were made. Such situations include certain types of policy interviews, particularly with elite informants (see, e.g. Carnie, 1990); interviews where detailed contextual analysis will be required; and intensive analyses, such as those which are concerned with conceptual exploration (see, e.g. Petch, 1988). In such instances, full rather than partial transcription will be required. If other than full transcription is indicated, then careful note-taking should normally suffice.

Standardized schedules

A technique for data collection which is often used in conjunction with other methods is the standardized assessment schedule or rating scale. Designed with a very specific purpose in mind, for example assessing the self-care skills that can be performed by an elderly individual or the extent of negative symptoms exhibited by a person with schizophrenia, the use of such devices can produce some standardized score or measure which can be compared across a large number of subjects and for the same individuals over time. The number of such standardized measures is countless, and particularly in areas of social welfare bordering on the health sphere their use is fairly widespread. A number of detailed examples are cited in Chapter 7 on the discussion of measures of client state; the purpose here is to highlight more general principles.

A strong argument for the adoption of such a measure in a study is that it can yield summary and comparable data, often without the expenditure of too much effort. Certainly, it is the policy of the Centre, where such a measure is deemed appropriate, to cast about for one whose use has become established rather than to attempt the design of a scale *de novo*. Not least this arises from the lengthy process necessary to test for reliability and validity before any such measure can be accepted with confidence, a path which would only be embarked upon by the most persistent or by those determined to capture a new area.

The validity of a scale reflects its ability actually to measure what it claims to measure – is, for example, a scale concerned with dependency really addressing this area or has it become enmeshed with some other concept such as cognitive functioning? Three forms of validity are usually distinguished. Content or face validity ensures that the important relevant areas are included and that the range of items appropriate to the situation has been covered. Criterion validity tests the measures of the particular scale against those obtained from some alternative, either concurrently or through prediction of some future outcome. Finally, construct validity seeks to establish whether the results support the bases on which the measure was constructed in the first place.

The concern with the reliability of a measure addresses the need for the measure to achieve consistency over time or between different investigators. At the design phase, instruments will be subject to various test and retest mechanisms to ensure that the schedule can be confidently predicted to perform satisfactorily on these criteria. None the less, if contemplating the use of a particular scale in circumstances very different from those where reliability was originally established, it may be necessary to make additional checks to ensure continued reliability.

In selecting an appropriate scale for any particular study, the specific issues to be addressed will obviously provide a starting point: the potential device must be relevant to the issues under scrutiny. In addition, however, to ensure that reliability and validity are satisfied, as above, more pragmatic concerns should also be addressed. Does the chosen model make sense and does the researcher feel comfortable with the language and the concepts that are used? Is the time which it takes and the level of comprehension it demands appropriate for the target group? The use, for example, of the Schedule for Affective Disorders and Schizophrenia (SADS) (Endicott and Spitzer, 1978) in the Centre's Royal Edinburgh Hospital study was felt by the psychiatrist involved, despite its established reliability and validity, to be both too lengthy and too complex for the seriously disabled population for which it was purportedly designed.

Of importance also is the actual measurement device within the particular scale or schedule. Is there a form of ranking, of scaling, or of cumulative scoring? Whatever the device, does it make sense in the context of the area being addressed? What is the effect of missing values; does any weighting or sub-scale procedure provide information that will be useful to the purpose of the investigation? Has the schedule been widely used or is it the pet notion of a small clique?

The wealth of detail which can accompany the various rating scales and schedules can produce a situation of increasing confusion as a breadth of knowledge accumulates. The advice and practice of the Centre has been to make judicious use of such instruments as and when they contribute to some greater whole, with motives varying across studies from the desire to curry credibility with a particular professional group to an interest in extending, say, the use of the Malaise Inventory, to a new group of respondents. In the main, excessive complexity should be eschewed, and while researchers should be aware of the learned debates over the precise distinctions between different variants, their excessive proliferation in more arcane forms should be neatly sidestepped.

Documentary material

The use of documentary material to obtain information relevant to the process or outcomes of social work activities constitutes the employment of what Webb *et al.* (1966) have referred to as an 'unobtrusive measure'. By definition, unobtrusive data collection methods do not impinge directly upon the participants in the intervention process and as such avoid the criticisms often levelled at certain other data collection techniques (such as some types of observation) that they serve to distort the responses and patterns of interaction that otherwise would have occurred. Documentary sources, such as official statistics, referral data and case records appear, on the face of it, to provide a temptingly convenient source of information about the recipients of social work services, the social work process and its outcomes. They may, in particular circumstances, be indispensable (when, for instance, the use of retrospective samples is required), but their potential limitations need to be acknowledged and addressed.

When data are collected from a secondary source in a pre-coded format, the categories employed and the way in which individuals are allocated to them will be influenced by the frame of reference adopted by the coder. Furthermore, certain types of statistical information are not as comprehensive and unflawed as is commonly supposed. These points have been amply illustrated with reference to criminal justice statistics (e.g. Shipman, 1981; Bottomley and Pease, 1986). Researchers making use of national or local (including agency) statistical data should be aware of possible biases, gaps and flaws in these data and exercise caution accordingly.

Caution is similarly called for in the use by researchers of data derived from social workers' case records. Descriptions of intervention in case notes are, by their very nature, selective and subjective accounts by social workers of their work with clients. Potentially relevant information (for research purposes) may be omitted, the assumptions underlying descriptions of clients and their problems may be unclear and the meanings attached by clients to the intervention are likely to be unrepresented. On a more immediately practical level, the information contained in case records will often be incomplete, insufficient or inappropriate to the needs of the evaluative researcher. McIvor (1989), for example, found in her evaluation of practice across community service schemes, that while accurate and detailed information relating to absences from work placements was usually readily accessed from case records, instances of casework with, or practical intervention on behalf of, clients were less likely to have been recorded in what were primarily administrative tools.

Similar difficulties were encountered in the Centre's pilot study of different organizational arrangements for the delivery of social work services to the elderly (Fuller and Petch, 1989, 1991), where the recording of certain types of information in case notes varied from team to team and from case to case. For example:

An attempt was made to identify patterns of consultation during the assessment process, whether with other professionals or with people in the community. The data are unfortunately patchy, owing to apparent inconsistencies in recording, which made it difficult to decide with any confidence who had been consulted and, indeed, what 'consultation' meant (Fuller and Petch, 1989, p. 13).

The lack of directly accessible material in existing records may be at least partly remedied, as it was in the subsequent study of the impact of organizational arrangements on the provision of services for the elderly, by the development of instruments (such as case monitoring or review forms) designed specifically to provide the necessary information relevant to the research. Unless such instruments can replace existing recording systems, however, or unless their completion as a means of supplementing existing sources of information places little additional burden on social workers, their introduction may be (often justifiably) resisted by already overstretched staff. Examples of the use in Centre studies of practitioner-completed monitoring forms are presented in Chapter 8.

Existing documents and statistics can provide a useful source of data about the process and outcomes of social work and, as has already been suggested, may prove particularly alluring when retrospective samples are necessary. The preceding limitations should, however, be borne in mind. Documentary sources do not permit access to the meanings attached to intervention by social workers and (especially) their clients. This type of information is likely to be achieved only through direct questioning or through certain types of observation of the participants in the social work process.

Observation

The most direct method of determining the content and process of social work intervention is to observe what actually happens, particularly in the context of meetings and other contacts between social workers and their clients or service users. Observational methods will be of particular relevance when the interest lies in the nature of the interaction between individuals or in the styles of intervention adopted by social workers – how, for example, do they manage the necessary but often difficult balance between care and control? How do nurses or residential workers actually fulfil their objectives to treat those in their care with dignity and to maximize their choice? (McGlew *et al.*, 1991).

Observation may take a number of forms, it may require the involvement of the researcher in different roles and it may serve different purposes. In the early stages of a research project, for example, a period of more or less structured observation may help to familiarize the researcher with the practice or service to be evaluated, enable the identification of pertinent research questions and facilitate the development of appropriate research instruments and techniques.

As a method of direct data collection, a more systematic approach to the observation of practice will be required. Observational techniques can, in broad terms, be classified in two ways. The first is according to whether or not the researcher participates in the interaction or activity to be studied and the second is according to whether or not the subjects of observation are aware that they are being observed. For ethical and practical reasons, overt rather than covert observation is most usual in social work research. The substantive decision required by the researcher is more likely to be whether to assume the role of the participant or detached observer. The involvement of the researcher as an overt but detached observer may prove most feasible in the study of the social work process, but it is also open to the criticism that workers' and clients' awareness that they are being observed may result in a distorted picture being obtained of the interactions or activities that would otherwise have occurred.

Fuller's (1988) observation of work with clients in the M.A.R.S. project exemplifies this particular approach. Here, there was no attempt by the researcher to conceal his presence or purpose. Nor did the researcher take an active part in the interactions or activities being observed. Fuller acknowledged the potentially distorting impact of his presence as an observer, but concluded that this had not been a serious problem in the M.A.R.S. study:

> It may be unlikely that the adult client at least would have raised any very difficult personal issues in his [the researcher's] presence. On subsequent discussion with the workers this did not seem to be a major factor in the particular sessions chosen. The researcher had already met and interviewed two of the clients (Fuller, 1988, p. 38).

The taping or filming of interactions in the absence of the researcher but with the full knowledge of the participants would similarly fall into this category of observational approach.

In her evaluation of the 'open door' accommodation project, on the other hand, Lyon (1989) spent a considerable amount of time based in the project, engaged in informal observation and interaction with residents and staff. The role of the overt participant observer may be the most difficult to manage, since it requires a degree of integration into the activities and interactions which are being observed, while simultaneously guarding against over-involvement, over-identification with the project and stepping beyond predetermined responsibilities and roles.

The participative involvement of the researcher may, over time, lessen his or her potentially distorting impact on the focus of study and may provide greater insights into the meanings attached to his or her behaviour by workers and clients. The risk, of course, is of over-identification with the subjects of study which may lessen the researcher's critical faculties. While some would argue that a realistic and meaningful understanding can be achieved only through interaction with individuals and groups who are unaware that they are the subject of research interest, such an approach is rare in the evaluation of social work effectiveness. One exception is the study by Vass (1984), who posed as an offender on community service to gain an understanding of the enforcement process and its interpretation by, and impact upon, offenders on orders.

The choice of observational approach will be influenced both by the theoretical and methodological perspective adopted by the researcher, by the purposes of the research and by the nature of the intervention to be observed. The type of observation and the utility of the data derived will also be influenced by practical considerations such as the time available for the researcher to engage in direct observation of practice. Where the observation of the entire intervention process is impractical, as it often will be because of the labour-intensiveness of this approach, then the researcher may elect to observe a sample of client–worker interactions. Such an approach was adopted by Fuller (1988) in his evaluation of the M.A.R.S. project, but was acknowledged to have resulted in the under-representation of certain aspects of the project's work. While sampled observation of this nature may provide useful insights into the intervention process, it would not, on its own, provide a complete picture of the activities and interactions involved in the social work process and would need to be supplemented, as it was in the M.A.R.S. study, by other methods of data collection such as interviews or careful analysis of case records.

If observational methods are deemed feasible and appropriate decisions also have to be made about what types of information are to be gathered and how, is it necessary for the entire session to be recorded or will sufficient information be obtained through the use of time-sampling methods which capture the process of intervention at specified intervals? A variant of the latter approach was adopted in the M.A.R.S. evaluation which entailed the researcher, as an independent observer, recording, at ten-minute intervals, the activities which had occurred since the previous sampling point, including the patterns and types of interaction between the participants. The purpose was to document the styles of work engaged in by project staff.

If more detailed information about the intervention process is required and that process is sufficiently complex to limit the utility of note-taking, the direct recording by tape or film of the interaction(s), though not always feasible, may be of some value. This method permits the researcher retrospectively to identify and describe the most salient aspects of the intervention. The potential also exists for participants in the intervention (be it a group setting or one-to-one interaction) to comment retrospectively upon the meaning of their responses or behaviour and their understanding of the significance of the interaction and exchanges that occurred, thus circumventing one of the main criticisms of non-participative observational techniques.

Triangulation

It will be clear that any evaluation of the process or outcome of social work intervention is likely to draw upon a range of research techniques. The concept of triangulation (Denzin, 1970) is perhaps most often cited in relation to the systematic combination of different methods of data collection to study the same phenomenon (between-method triangulation). The term can also be applied to the triangulation of data sources and to within-method triangulation which involves the use of multiple strategies (such as the use of different scales) within a single method to examine data.

Triangulation of data, which involves the collection of similar information from different samples at different locations or points in time, can enhance the generalizability of findings and reduce the likelihood of erroneous conclusions arising from reliance on a single data set. Triangulation of method in which several different methods of data collection are employed in a single study provides a means of validating information derived from different sources and permits the weaknesses and strengths of different data collection methods to be balanced. A fuller discussion of triangulation, including examples of a range of potential mixes, is to be found in Patton (1980).

In the Centre's study of community service schemes (McIvor, 1989, 1992b), information about specific aspects of practice was obtained from case records, through interviews with staff and offenders and through the completion by community service officers and offenders of questionnaires. Information about the enforcement policies which operated in the 12 schemes, for example, was obtained through the questioning of staff; their implementation was assessed through examination of staff responses to absences as detailed in individual case records; and the offenders' understanding of the policies and the ways in which they operated in practice were gathered through interviews and questionnaires. In this way, the relationship between scheme policy and its implementation could be addressed and its impact upon the offenders ascertained through the triangulation of data obtained by the use of different research methods.

The use of different data collection methods and data sets may also enhance the theoretical relevance of research by enabling the researcher to address a wider range of issues and perspectives and thus obtain insights that would not have been possible through the use of one method of data collection or one source of data alone. For the above reasons, the Centre has, in most of its studies, drawn upon a range of techniques to study the process and outcomes of social work practice, as will be illustrated in the following chapters.

5

THE SOCIAL WORK PROCESS

> More attention should be paid to the processes actually involved
> in social work activities; it is no good saying that 'casework' does
> not work or that intermediate treatment does, unless we have
> some idea of what is meant by these notoriously ill-defined terms.
> Smith (1987, p. 413)

In the evaluation of social work effectiveness, the primary preoccupation is generally with the definition and measurement of the outcomes of intervention to determine whether or not a desired or intended effect has been produced or a particular outcome avoided. In other words, what are the objectives of intervention and have they been achieved?

Typically, less attention is paid to the actual process of social work intervention than is given to the identification and measurement of outcomes. This chapter argues that some detailed consideration of the social work process is often necessary if a clear understanding of the potential for social work to impact upon the lives of its clients is to be gained. The introductory quotation from Smith (1987) highlights the importance of specifying in some detail what social work intervention actually involves. Given the range of activities and approaches subsumed under such broad headings as 'casework' or 'intermediate treatment' or 'counselling', failure on the part of the evaluative researcher to specify the nature of the social work input leaves the reader of research reports unsure of exactly what was evaluated and severely limits the generalizability and utility of the results. There are, however, other important reasons why the study of the social work process should be accorded greater prominence. The present chapter will begin by outlining these reasons before turning to a discussion of the methodological challenges involved both in studying the social work process and in identifying the relationship between the process of social work intervention and its outcomes.

Programme integrity

First, it is important to determine the degree to which intervention or service provision corresponds to that which is actually proposed or planned. Programme integrity can only be assessed through detailed consideration of the social work process. The importance of establishing whether or not a given plan of intervention was fully implemented has been highlighted in particular by Quay (1977), who used a study by Kassebaum *et al.* (1976) to illustrate how poor programme implementation might have accounted for the failure of prison-based group counselling to have an effect upon subsequent reoffending. Quay argued that the group counselling was provided by minimally trained and inexpert staff; that there was little attempt to select, or even identify, inmates who were more likely to have benefited from the programme; and that there was no attempt to compose the counselling groups in any systematic way. He suggested that under the circumstances, any conclusions about the effectiveness of the group counselling programme should have been tempered by a consideration of the extent to which programme integrity was seriously lacking.

Even if the counselling had been implemented as intended, it is possible, of course, that the method was intrinsically ineffective and that no significant impact on recidivism would have been observed. The risk, however, is that failure to attend to the issues relating to programme integrity may result in the rejection of intervention as ineffective when, if properly implemented, positive outcomes could have been achieved. Before we can conclude that a specific method of social work intervention does not produce its intended outcomes, it is necessary to be sure that in its implementation the integrity of the planned intervention was maintained.

In the 1970s, for instance, rehabilitative efforts aimed at reducing recidivism among convicted offenders suffered a serious blow when Martinson (1974) concluded from his review of over 200 studies that none of the existing approaches could be guaranteed to reduce re-offending consistently among all types of offenders. When the Panel on Research on Rehabilitative Techniques in the United States (Sechrest *et al.*, 1979) re-examined the evidence upon which Martinson and his colleagues (Martinson, 1974; Lipton *et al.*, 1975) had based their pessimistic conclusions, they were led to conclude that:

> When it is asserted that 'nothing works', the Panel is uncertain as to just what has ever been given a fair trial. If we are to arrive at sound conclusions about the prospects for rehabilitation, *future research must pay far more attention to issues of strength and integrity of treatments along with the adequacy of experimental designs* (Sechrest *et al.*, 1979, p. 8; emphasis added).

Contact and relationship

Close attention to the social work process will also be demanded in research which takes as its primary focus of interest the nature of the interaction or relationship between client and social worker or between members of a family unit. Some studies (e.g. Rees, 1978) have been concerned directly with studying the process of change. Others have attempted to identify the characteristics of effective counsellors (e.g. Truax *et al.*, 1966) or to match social workers and clients on the basis of personality attributes and styles of working to maximize the potential impact of intervention. An early but much discussed example is California's Community Treatment Programme (see, e.g. Palmer, 1973), in which it was found that workers with certain combinations of personal and professional characteristics were better able to engage with particular types of young people and achieve more positive outcomes.

For some clients, the process of social work intervention is as significant as the outcome; the journey, in other words, is as important as the destination. The importance to clients of social workers' personal attributes and skills has been documented by Rees and Wallace (1982). They concluded from their review of client studies that a concerned and friendly approach is much valued by clients, though dissatisfaction may be expressed if initial promises of services or help are not fulfilled.

Sainsbury (1975), for example, in his study of a family service unit, showed how their relationships with their social workers were often more important to clients than were the longer-term objectives of intervention:

> When a client sees the worker–client relationship as having an intrinsic value (i.e. beyond the requirements of his problems and needs), his perceptions of purpose and success are related more to short-term achievements than to long-term goals of independent social functioning (Sainsbury, 1975, p. 122).

In their study of task-centred casework in a social services department, Sinclair and Walker (1985) similarly found that some clients valued the process of social work intervention as much as, or even more than, they did the achievement of specific goals: 'A small number looked to their social worker as a "mother" or general source of moral support. These clients placed less emphasis on the social workers' practical efficacy than they did on their availability and their care and concern' (p. 77). Likewise, Glendinning's (1986) study of an intensive support scheme for the parents of severely handicapped children vividly documents the importance parents attach to the regular visits of informed and sympathetic social workers, despite the fact that their best efforts produced minimal measurable change in the circumstances and morale of the families.

While debate will no doubt continue as to whether services can be justified when they appear to produce no measurable outcomes or change, failure to address users' views about the services they have received and the manner in which they have been delivered ignores both important components of social work practice and, even more serious, the voice of those for whom the services are intended.

Process and outcome

Frequently, studies in the field of social welfare seek to compare the relative effectiveness of different procedures or approaches within a given area of service delivery. In their evaluation of a joint police–social work child protection investigation team, for example, Brown and Fuller (1991a,b) aimed to establish, among other things, whether such an initiative engendered a more child-focused enquiry compared with the traditional procedures that had previously operated within the area. The ability to compare and contrast different procedures or methods of intervention requires some clear understanding of what these different approaches involve. So, too, does the identification of the components of effective practice. From their detailed studies of task-centred casework, for example, Goldberg *et al.* (1985) identified the social work skills which appeared most closely related to successful intervention. Briefly, these included: an ability to listen to the clients; a focus on the present rather than the past; an ability to negotiate with the client; an ability to enter into a partnership with the client; and an ability to close cases appropriately.

The desirability of relating the process of intervention to the effects that have been observed and thus enhancing explanatory power is the final, but by no means least important, reason for giving fuller attention to the social work process when attempting to evaluate the effectiveness of social workers' activities with or on behalf of their clients or service users. Neglect of what happened in the course of the intervention or service provision means that we can only say whether or not a particular effect has occurred or a given outcome has been achieved (and even then often only with various caveats or qualifications) and not how it was achieved or why. As Clarke and Cornish (1972, p. 19) have argued, 'knowing that something has made a difference is very little use unless it can be identified'.

The nature of the social work process

The social work process can be characterized as the activities that are undertaken by social workers with or on behalf of clients or the services that are provided with a view to achieving (or preventing) one or more specific outcomes. But this brief definition belies the complexity of much social work intervention. It implies, for instance, that both the objectives of intervention and the means by which they are pursued can be identified with some degree of specificity. Frequently, however, this will not be the case. The activities undertaken in the context of social work intervention and the objectives of the intervention can be more readily specified and described with certain social work approaches than with others. Behavioural or task-centred methods, for example, require that both the objectives to be pursued and the means of achieving them are specified with some precision at the outset. These particular methods have been more consistently associated with successful outcomes than other, less tangible, approaches (see, e.g. Reid and Hanrahan, 1981; Sheldon, 1983, 1984a,b; Goldberg *et al.*, 1985) in which the means and ends may be less clear. This does not necessarily indicate that behavioural and task-centred methods are always inherently superior to others. Because the objectives can be specified precisely and their achievement can be more readily measured, such approaches have been more closely scrutinized than others which are less amenable to evaluative research methods. The observation (Goldberg *et al.*, 1985; Sheldon, 1986) that task-centred or behavioural methods are successful only if properly applied underlines the need for close attention to be paid to the manner in which interventions have been implemented and the degree to which the implementation corresponds to what was actually planned.

Even if they can be specified with some clarity at the outset, the original objectives of intervention may undergo revision because they are subsequently recognized to be inappropriate or too ambitious or because other events or crises in the client's life have brought to the fore a different set of pressing problems and needs. Changed objectives may well entail changes in the help given. For example, in her study of the Open Door accommodation project, which offers emergency accommodation to young homeless people, Lyon (1989) has documented how the introduction of changes in the social security legislation for 16- and 17-year-olds changed the focus and content of work with young people in the hostel. This point can be further illustrated in an evaluation by Fuller (1988) of the M.A.R.S. project, a voluntary sector initiative which offers a service to (mainly teenage) children deemed to be at risk of serious breakdown. The Chatfield family (a pseudonym) had been referred by a hospital social worker and consultant psychiatrist. Mrs Chatfield, a single parent, was having difficulty controlling her two children, aged 8 and 10, and was believed to need help in parenting skills of a practical kind for which sessions with the psychiatrist were proving ineffective and inappropriate. There was concern that Mrs Chatfield's deteriorating parental capacity would result in the children being received into care. The M.A.R.S. objective was to work directly with the mother to help her learn better ways of handling the children.

The M.A.R.S. involvement had lasted 17 months by the end of fieldwork and was continuing. It contained several phases, and is an example of the original objectives being superseded by others. At first the family had regular sessions, in the form of an evening meal, including preparation, eating and clearing up, designed to provide practical help to Mrs Chatfield, through example and direct suggestion, on how to control the children's behaviour, to set boundaries to it and stick to them during the week, and to involve them constructively in the domestic tasks. While this over a period of months was progressing successfully, so that the disintegration of the family was no longer felt to be a real possibility and Mrs Chatfield's general morale had improved, highs and lows nonetheless occurred, and a particular domestic crisis over an act of theft by Kim [her daughter] led to an explicit change of role. This new orientation, described as a counselling role, involved a deeper exploration of the family dynamics, in terms of Mrs Chatfield's history and previous relationships, their effect on her self-image, and her identified tendency to scapegoat Kim. Though the mealtime sessions continued, the new objectives were implemented through additional individual sessions with Mrs Chatfield and Kim, and developed a more strictly therapeutic character, with the deeper issues being explicitly sorted out rather than avoided. This stage was felt to have been made possible only through the earlier work (Fuller, 1988, p. 103).

In this example, the original objectives of intervention have been superseded as a result of unforeseen changes in the client's circumstances. Frequently, though, multiple aims and objectives will be defined at the outset, or a single objective may be pursued by means of a number of different social work methods. The existence of multiple objectives or, more especially, methods of working, may present particular methodological challenges to the evaluative researcher. Not only must it be determined that a given outcome or objective has been achieved, but ideally (if rarely possible) an attempt should also be made to disentangle the various strands in the process of intervention to ascertain which aspects were responsible for the achievement (or avoidance) of particular outcomes for clients.

The process of intervention does not simply consist of a series of activities and interactions which correspond to an objective reality. As the clients in Mayer and Timms's (1970) study only too clearly showed, clients' understanding and interpretation of the process and outcomes of intervention may vary markedly from those of their social workers. Sainsbury *et al.* (1982) similarly showed how clients and social workers differed in their assessments of which types of casework were most helpful:

> Social workers (compared with their clients) overestimated the relative helpfulness of insight work, the use of authority and giving of advice, but underestimated the helpfulness experienced by clients as a result of material and financial help and negotiations with other agencies on their behalf (Sainsbury *et al.*, 1982, pp. 19–20).

Clearly, an attempt should be made, where possible, to document the experiences and attitudes of both clients and of social workers when describing and documenting the social work process: reliance upon the interpretations of social workers alone would potentially misrepresent the significance and impact of the intervention for their clients.

The social work process and its significance for clients is thus neither unidimensional nor unchanging. Nor can it be separated from the responses of other individuals or agencies charged with a responsibility to provide services for, or in some other way meet the needs of, social work clients. The researcher must recognize this and must recognize, too, that the social work process consists of both interpersonal contact and the provision of concrete services, with either being accorded the greater significance by clients depending on the nature, purpose and context of the intervention.

Assessing programme integrity

The assessment of the extent to which programme integrity has been maintained can be considered a special instance of the study of social work process. The latter endeavour is concerned primarily with establishing precisely what was involved in an episode of intervention, including: the content, frequency and context of meetings; the types of services provided; and contact with other agencies or service providers. The issue of programme integrity requires that the analysis is taken a step further. Here the interest is not only with what actually happened but also with how closely what happened corresponded to what had been planned. Thus information about the social work process gathered by means of the techniques or methods discussed in Chapter 4 needs to be related in a systematic way to some objective statement of what the intervention should have comprised.

It is not necessary to look very far to find numerous examples in the research literature of instances where the reality of intervention fell far short of expectations. In the IMPACT study (Folkard *et al.*, 1974, 1976) which aimed to provide a more intensive, situationally oriented service to probationers, as many as 40 per cent of the experimental probationers received no help in addition to that with which they would normally have been provided. Those who did received help mainly in relation to marriage and family issues, rather than work, accommodation and leisure, the types of problems believed to be particularly relevant to a situational approach. Other studies in the probation field that have attempted to provide high levels of supervisory contact and service provision have similarly failed to do so (see, e.g. Latessa, 1987; Petersilia and Turner, 1990) and reductions in caseloads have been found to result in probation officers spending more time on administrative tasks and relatively little additional time on providing direct services to clients (Clear and Hardyman, 1990; Petersilia and Turner, 1990). The message seems clear: interventions which are too ambitious or complex are less likely to be implemented in full. It is consequently difficult for researchers to reach clear conclusions about the effectiveness or otherwise of interventions which might or might not have been effective if they had been implemented as planned.

Quay (1977) has argued that researchers should take into consideration the nature of the service delivered, the characteristics of the staff responsible for implementing the intervention, and the relevance of the intervention in relation to the characteristics of the clients for whom the intervention is provided. Assessment of service delivery or intervention should include a detailed account of what actually happened, the duration of the intervention (in terms of the length of time during which the process of intervention continues and the number and frequency of contacts during that period) and the intensity of service provision (as measured by the duration of individual sessions). Staff variables which might have some influence on successful implementation include degree of expertise, the amount of training provided and the quality and quantity of professional supervision. As Gendreau and Ross (1979, p. 467) have suggested, researchers should routinely ask:

To what extent do treatment personnel actually adhere to the principles and employ the techniques of therapy they purport to provide? To what extent are treatment staff competent? How hard do they work? How much is treatment diluted in the correctional setting so that it becomes treatment in name only?

Clearly, though, a detailed assessment of programme integrity will be more relevant in some circumstances than in others. It will be of particular value, for instance, in the evaluation of innovative services or in ascertaining the conditions under which the effectiveness of a given method of intervention can be maximized. In the Centre's study of homemakers, whose service was established to give intensive but usually short-term practical help to a wide range of clients, it was found that they were, indeed, particularly effective in situations requiring such intervention. These included, for example, settling homeless young people into their own accommodation. Such referrals were, however, a minority. For the most part, homemakers found they had to provide a combination of advice, practical help and emotional support, over long periods, to people with many chronic and often serious problems. In this largely unplanned context, homemakers were able to achieve small reductions in the number and seriousness of problems in most cases. The service could therefore be described as effective, although with a range of work and interventions which were not all originally intended (Cheetham, 1991).

In other studies, the social work process itself provides the primary focus of interest. In the Centre's ongoing comparative study of service delivery to elderly people as a function of team organization, a number of important definitional questions arose: were individual specialists those workers in a team who took on the bulk of the elderly work? If so, were their caseloads specialized in the sense of consisting in the main of elderly cases, or did such cases still comprise a minority of their work? In the case of specialist teams, marked differences may exist between individual social workers in terms of their experience, their reasons for specialization and their methods of working. These differences may temper or mask any variations in practice between teams that are directly attributable to differing organizational structure. In order to ascertain, therefore, whether specialists across different settings had things in common, in their ways of working, which distinguished them from non-specialists, it was important to establish what they actually did.

Recently, attempts have been made by researchers to measure the degree of integrity in projects and in programmes of intervention (see Salend, 1984, for a definition and discussion of behavioural treatment integrity). Scheirer and Rezmovic (1983) noted that a variety of techniques had been employed to measure the degree of programme implementation or integrity across such diverse areas as education, health, mental health, social services, criminal justice, employment and industrial technology. They argued that in many studies the techniques adopted were, when used in isolation, of questionable reliability and validity. Most studies employed multiple measuring techniques (for instance, interviews plus observation plus use of documentary material) but the data from different sources were rarely compared. Scheirer and Rezmovic suggested that if the components of interventions were fully described, measuring tools could be developed for each component and an aggregate implementation index could be devised. They failed to illustrate with a practical example how such an analysis might proceed, although the need for an overall index of implementation would appear less pressing than the necessity of understanding clearly the extent to which individual components of the planned intervention had been achieved.

Quay (1977) has argued that if methods of intervention can be clearly conceptualized and have a firm empirical basis, then the more likely it is that the intervention can be successfully implemented and the easier it is for others to replicate the procedures involved. The replication of apparently successful social work techniques (and even of apparently unsuccessful ones where there is reason to believe that programme integrity might have been breached) is wholly dependent upon the availability of detailed information about what the intervention actually entails.

Relating social work processes and outcomes

Happy is the person who could understand the causes of things.
                                                                   Virgil: *Georgics II*

One of the greatest challenges in evaluative research is to demonstrate that any measurable effect that has been observed following social work intervention is, indeed, a product of that intervention and not of other extraneous but nevertheless relevant factors. Suppose, for example, we find that a group of young offenders who have participated in a community-based probation programme instead of being sentenced to custody have a lower reconviction rate after two years than another group of offenders who receive custodial sentences. We need to rule out a number of possible explanations for this finding before we can be reasonably sure that participation in the community-based programme was responsible for, or at least contributed to, the reduced level of offending among this group. If the community-based group were older than their counterparts who were given custodial sentences, for example, then we might suppose that maturation ('growing out of crime') may be responsible for the differential levels of recidivism observed. Similarly, if the offenders who were imprisoned had a more extensive criminal history and, therefore, a greater *a priori* likelihood of re-offending, this factor alone may have produced the differential reconviction rates that were found.

Even if we could be certain that the two groups were identical in all relevant respects, we might still have considerable difficulty accounting for the differences in recidivism between the two groups. If, for the purposes of illustration, a third identical group of offenders were introduced who received no intervention or sentence whatsoever, and this group was found to have similar reconviction rates to the offenders in the community-based programme, we might have some reason to suspect that the different reconviction rates across the three groups were attributable to some negative effect or effects of imprisonment rather than to the positive influence of programme involvement. If, on the other hand, the reconviction rate for this third group was higher than that for the offenders in the community-based programme and identical to that for the group who were in custody, we might reasonably assume that the probation programme did, in fact, have a positive effect on subsequent offending.

This hypothetical example contains many presuppositions and assumptions and relatively clear-cut comparisons of this kind are usually beyond the realms of possibility in the evaluation of social work effectiveness. Even if such an analysis were feasible, however, we still would not know what it was about the community-based programme that had an impact upon re-offending among its participants, a point amply made by Smith (1987, p. 406) when he asserts that 'research which is exclusively concerned with outcomes rather than process suffers from the serious limitation that it is impossible to tell what the outcomes were outcomes of'. The community-based young offender probation project evaluated by Roberts (1989), for example, contained elements of offence-related group work and problem solving, the development of social skills through drama and role play and introduction to purposeful activities. Additionally, the offenders had weekly individual contacts with their probation officers and were encouraged to become involved in activities, such as voluntary work, which would serve to establish longer-term links with the local community. The project was found to have a positive impact upon re-offending among participants (and particularly those deemed to have a higher *a priori* risk of recidivism), but it was not possible to identify which particular features of the programme or combinations of features were associated with success.

Thomas (1984) has suggested that institutional research, such as studies of residential care, has been relatively fruitful in comparison with other types of evaluative research in the social work field, since the services being evaluated are more self-contained and more readily specified. Otherwise, he contends that given the 'wide spectrum of services and other help which may be directed at a person or problem, it is often difficult to describe that help, let alone trace the relationships between inputs and outcomes' (pp. 13–14). Clarke and Cornish (1972), on the other hand, dispute the assumption that the relationship between process and outcome can be more readily documented in an institutional setting, at least through the use of randomized experimental design.

For the purpose of illustration, the study by Clarke and Cornish warrants further description. The aim of their research was to evaluate the effectiveness of a therapeutic community that had been introduced in one of three separate units or houses in an approved school for boys aged between 13 and 15 years. During the experimental period, the boys who were assessed by the staff in the therapeutic community as being suitable for that unit were randomly allocated (through the toss of a coin) to it or to a second house (the control house) that employed a traditional 'adult-oriented' approach. The boys who were deemed unsuitable for the therapeutic community regime were allocated to a third unit whose approach resembled that of the control house.

In addition to examining the impact of the experimental and control regimes on various measures of outcome (such as reconviction and job performance), Clarke and Cornish also paid considerable attention to the behaviour of the boys while in the school, and a detailed study was made of the therapeutic community and traditional regimes, which went beyond the subjective accounts by staff or other interested parties that are more commonly reported in the research literature.

Although the school agreed in principle to introduce the random allocation procedure, in practice this was found to be difficult to implement and sustain. Of more direct relevance for the present purposes, though, were Clarke and Cornish's observations concerning the generalizability of the results they had achieved through the random allocation experiment. The detailed examination of the regimes in operation in the school served to underscore the uniqueness and complexity of each regime, which precluded the findings of the study being generalized to other approved schools. Nor was it possible to identify those factors or processes in each regime that were important determinants of the subsequent social adjustment of the boys. As Clarke and Cornish (1972, p. 15) concluded: 'contrary to what was hoped for initially, the main effect of the study of process was simply to make clearer the very many ways in which the houses differed in addition to preferred treatment technique, and therefore to proliferate possible alternative explanations for any differences in results'. The differences between the experimental and control units included, among other things: the experience, personality and attitudes of staff; the length of time the boys were resident in the school; the numbers of boys in each unit; and different policies for dealing with boys who were unresponsive to training.

The task of explaining differences in outcome is no less daunting (and may be even more so) when social work intervention outwith the institutional or residential setting is the focus of attention. Here there is an even greater likelihood that other factors, unrelated to the intervention, may have contributed to the outcomes obtained. And even if these extraneous variables can be controlled, the multifaceted nature of intervention can present formidable difficulties for the interpretation of results.

Given the complexity of the social work process, how then might we design research studies in such a way that it is possible to disentangle the effects of different components of intervention on the lives of social work clients? One possible approach might be to design a series of controlled studies in each of which the intervention or services provided to two groups of randomly allocated, or otherwise closely matched, clients differed only in one important respect. To examine the relevance of different components of intervention, the differentiating variable could be varied systematically from study to study which would, in theory at least, allow each of the important or contributory factors to the success of intervention to be identified.

The nature of social work is such, however, that to conceive of such an approach is to enter into the realms of fantasy. Even if the conditions necessary for an adequate experimental design could be fulfilled, an enormous number of experimental comparisons would be required to identify the effective components of intervention. A more realistic and practical approach is to ask the recipients of services for their opinions as to which services or aspects of the intervention they found most helpful and the impact that they had (see, e.g. Sainsbury et al., 1982). As Wallace and Rees (1984, p. 75) have argued: 'Client evaluation is perhaps the most useful means of documenting those aspects of services, needs and appropriateness of services to those needs, which contribute to judgements about a service's effectiveness, cost effectiveness or efficiency'.

Another promising approach (although one which by its scale and complexity is likely to be of limited utility to practitioners who are keen to evaluate the effectiveness of their own work with clients) is the cross-institutional research design whose salient features have been described in Chapter 3. It has been asserted that this method can bridge the gap between evaluative studies, which tend to focus upon outcome with little explication of the actual processes that contributed to the observed results, and descriptive studies, which typically provide a detailed examination of the processes of intervention with little or no regard to the effectiveness, *vis-à-vis* specific outcomes, of one approach in relation to another. The cross-institutional design, it is claimed, enables researchers to 'tackle the twin problems of the identification and explanation of effects' (Sinclair and Clarke, 1981, p. 101).

The cross-institutional design has also been criticized, however, on the grounds that it cannot deal adequately with issues of cause and effect. Even if a particular component of intervention is found to be related to outcome, it is by no means certain that an assumption of direct causality can be made. Fuller (1987a) questions whether the problem of drawing causal inferences from correlational data is unique to the cross-institutional design and has suggested that 'the loss of a degree of (theoretical) explanatory certainty is offset by the richness of strong explanatory suggestion that comes from studies of several naturally occurring examples of the institution in question' (p. 20).

To place too heavy an expectation on causal explanation is, moreover, to misunderstand much of the nature of social welfare evaluation. It should be clear from much of the argument to date that to expect to draw definitive conclusions as to cause and effect is to place on many of the research designs an inappropriate burden. Indeed, the cross-institutional design may be distinctive among methodological strategies not for its failings in this respect but for the extent to which causal inference is attempted.

In much of the evaluative research that is undertaken, the nature of the statements that can be made about causality are of the order of 'plausible hunches'. Some studies will focus primarily on outcomes in the form of a traditional 'black box' model; others will devote considerable effort to addressing details of the process as outlined above. It is rare, however, for the designs that are commonly adopted to allow definitive causal explanations to be attempted. In practice, though, this is less of a handicap than might first appear. Very often the balance of probabilities suggests a fairly high level of certainty, and one that for the process under scrutiny is at least acceptable and often more than adequate.

Thus in the study of supported accommodation (Petch, 1990, 1992) it cannot be stated with absolute certainty that living in the supported projects was the explanation for the outcomes that were observed, that the support available caused or brought about these primarily favourable outcomes. Moreover, the nature of the support was identified only at a fairly global scale and was not subject to detailed scrutiny at individual project level. The instability in the majority of lives prior to the placement, however, together with the many positive comments directed towards specific features on the projects themselves, allows one to conclude that it is more than likely that the supported accommodation has played a significant role in the creation of the current state. Indeed, some may argue that if the outcomes are positive in terms of the provision of a facility of this type, it becomes of less importance to demonstrate conclusively that the outcomes are without doubt a product of that facility.

Similar arguments hold true for many of the Centre's studies. With the exception of the particular case of the cross-institutional design, the majority of studies have to be content with informed assertion rather than confirmed causation. Thus, in the M.A.R.S. study, for example, largely favourable outcomes for the people referred to the project could have been put down to maturational rather than therapeutic effects. Partly for this reason, the therapeutic processes were documented (as described earlier), but in addition a specific methodological experiment was undertaken, designed to answer the otherwise unanswerable question of what could have happened to the young people if they had *not* been referred to M.A.R.S.

This was the prediction exercise described by Fuller (1989). Case histories of a sample of M.A.R.S. referrals, with details up to the referral, were selected. These were shown to a panel of experts knowledgeable about the local child care scene, who were asked to predict likely outcomes given conventional social work resources only, i.e. if they had not been referred to M.A.R.S. These predicted outcomes (without M.A.R.S. involvement) were then compared with actual outcomes (with M.A.R.S. involvement), in order to devise a measure of the difference made by the intervention of the project. The validity of this exercise, involving what might be termed as a hypothetical control group, is not fully tested, but it added to the evidence on which causal inferences might be based.

The difficulties of tracing relationships between process and outcome are by no means limited to social work research. Sechrest *et al.* (1990) provide a detailed discussion of contemporary thinking on causal interpretation of non-experimental data in the health sphere. The challenge of establishing relationships between process and outcome will remain for the evaluative researcher, but just as clarity about process is essential to this endeavour so is clarity about outcomes, the subject of the next two chapters.

6

SERVICE-BASED
OUTCOMES

In the dime stores and bus stations
People talk of situations,
Read books, repeat quotations,
Draw conclusions – on the wall.
Some speak of the future
My love she speaks softly
She knows there's no success like failure
And that failure's no success at all

Bob Dylan (1964) *Love Minus Zero – No Limit*

Evaluative research is critically dependent on the selection of outcome measures. Without the identification in some form of attributes of a service or individual which can serve to indicate outcome, the assessment of effectiveness is not possible. The selection of the outcomes to be studied, however, and the means of their measurement is no simple task. To recap from earlier chapters, the outcomes of important social work goals may be relatively intangible; the different parties involved in social work intervention may differ in their views of the significance of its various aspirations, activities and effects; and there are different views, too, about what in evaluative research should count as an outcome.

Some of the most tricky distinctions to be drawn concern those between social work process and outcome. The previous chapter has shown how crucial a study of social work activities is in evaluative research. But in some respects these activities, the help given and the manner in which it is delivered can be viewed as an outcome of the service, fulfilling for example the objective of providing domiciliary care for elderly people or counselling and advice for parents on the verge of separation or divorce. It is a perfectly legitimate research task to examine, as outcomes, the content and manner of service provision and the fit between what is intended and what is actually delivered – and some studies are confined to this task. Such an approach may be justified, for example, when there are generally accepted assumptions that services are required by certain groups, there is some consensus about their appropriate quantity and type, but no clarity about whether such help is actually being delivered or to whom.

This approach has been adopted in the Social Work Research Centre studies of old people's homes and fieldwork services for elderly people. The first study has examined the quality of facilities and care provided in a large number of homes in the private, voluntary and statutory sectors. The costs of their provision have also been compared. The items examined are largely those about whose importance there is a substantial measure of professional or resident agreement, and the study also tests further the strength of this agreement. The study of a range of fieldwork services, organized in different ways, adopts a similar approach but examines as well the fit between re-quest for service and service provided and the time taken to respond to requests for help. In neither study was the impact of the services on elderly people measured, although the opinions of the users were sought. The principal aim of the research was to explore, in contexts where there is much myth and speculation about the type, quality and quantity of service provision, and little sound empirical data, the help and resources actually given.

There are, however, larger ambitions for evaluative research in which the interest is not simply in who received what service but in its effects, for good or ill, on the different parties involved. Thus the focus is on the out-comes for recipients of services; and the recipients could be direct users, those kin or friends who support them or the personnel of other services whose own good practice depends on collaboration or co-ordination with social work.

The distinction which most readily appears to capture these two somewhat different endeavours is that between service-based and client-based outcomes and this is the one that the Centre has adopted both for its own studies and for the purposes of this argument. Studies may, of course, address both types of outcome: the study of organization and outcomes, for example, includes both outcome measures which address the process of service delivery and others which explore the client perspective on that delivery.

It is useful to locate this definition against others which are in circulation. Much of the Personal Social Services Research Unit's work adopts the distinc-tion between intermediate and final outcomes, the former 'indicators of performance, service or activity rather than indicators of effect, influence or impact', the latter addressing 'changes in individual well-being compared with the levels of well-being in the absence of a caring intervention' (Knapp, 1984, 31–2). The substance of the distinction seems similar to that argued here, the one concerned with the care services themselves, the other with the individual. The terms adopted, however – intermediate and final – are felt to be unhelpful, a product perhaps of an undue reliance on the economic input–output model. An intermediate outcome in one sphere may become a final outcome in another; an intermediate outcomes implies a progression to a final outcome which may be inappropriate. Measures of quality of care, for example, may in some instances be the final outcome for any particular study; in a different context, they may function as intermediate to further work which pursues the impact of the quality of care upon the individual.

Whereas intermediate and final are second-order 'constructs', service and client are first-order constructs and relate to real-world practicality. The preference of this volume, therefore, is to pursue the definition between service-based and client-based outcomes.

The other commonly cited distinction is that which pertains to the division between process and outcome evaluations *per se* (see, e.g. Robèrtson and Gandy, 1983), the former attempting 'to identify – normally through use of "soft" methodologies like participant observation – what seem to be the most important elements contributing to the outcomes of any given programme, and the way these elements relate to each other within the policy or treatment programme itself' (p. 249), the latter 'to assess the effects produced by policies or programmes, and the extent to which such results measure up to programme "goals"' (p. 246). What is important here is that conceptually the distinction needs to be recognized between the sequence of intake, process and outcome, and the outcome measures which may address the process itself. Outcome measures are thus a feature of both process evaluations and outcome evaluations.

It is obviously extremely valuable for policy makers and practitioners when research identifies both service-based and client-based outcomes and the relationships between them, but such studies present complex challenges and usually demand substantial resources. Since the comprehensive evaluation of social work cannot be achieved at a single stroke, the identification of service-based outcomes is an important building block. They are crucially related to, and sometimes synonymous with, the process of social work and, as Chapter 5 has argued, without some knowledge of process there is little point, in policy-related research, in knowing about effects on clients.

A further reason for focusing on the process of service delivery, already discussed in the previous chapter, is that the usually highly personal context of social work service can mean that for their recipients the manner and means by which help is offered can be regarded as important or even more important than its identified ends or outcomes. Numerous studies which have taken account of clients' views testify to the value attached to sensitive patient understanding – friendliness, reliability, regularity of contact, attention to detail and openness – in short, to the significance of the presence of a caring person (Sainsbury, 1975; Rees and Wallace, 1982; Sainsbury *et al.*, 1982; Glendinning, 1986; Petch, 1988). In some cases, these studies have been able to determine little positive change in clients' circumstances, although the clients themselves say that they valued the intervention. Such judgements should not be ignored and this example demonstrates the difficulty in evaluative research of a simple dichotomy or of too rigid an adherence to a single outcome dimension.

Thus for the purposes of planning and describing a research study, clarity can be achieved by distinguishing between service- and client-based measures as this chapter now does. To recap, the former focus on the nature, extent and quality of what is provided, the latter on the effects of a provision on its recipients. Three forms of service-based outcomes will be explored in further detail: basic services measures, outcomes measured by the achievement of objectives and measures indicative of quality of care.

Basic service measures

There is a danger that once the evaluative mode is adopted, the search for sophistication leads to relatively basic and straightforward data being overlooked. In many instances, knowledge of the outcomes of a project or activity can be greatly enhanced through the routine accumulation of measures which record basic service delivery, and which are potential performance indicators. Very often these will be derived after the event from examination of case files or other recording devices such as case reviews or project reports. The types of measures which may provoke interest include indications of the speed of response, basic counting of, for example, the number of visits, or less finite assessments of the type of social work intervention intended.

The preliminary phase of the Centre's study of organization and outcomes is a good example of this basic service measurement. The sample comprised those cases (in four teams) where an assessment had been made for either residential, respite or day care. Information relating to some 30 variables was extracted from case records and transferred to a specially designed datasheet. This included basic personal data, referral and allocation, assessment, service provision, details of continuing involvement and re-referral. Thus, counts were made, among others, of the different sources of referrals, of the problem at referral, of the time between referral and allocation, of the number of assessment visits and of details of the service requested and received. Commentary could then be made both on the nature of the service delivery and on the variation which was to be found between different teams.

If this type of data is taken from case files, an important consideration is that it can be critically dependent upon the quality of the record, a factor which may not always be capable of validation. Can it be assumed, for example, that all visits between a client and worker are recorded? There may be no reference in the file to contact with another agency, but can it therefore be assumed that no such contact exists? Is the method of recording the dates of interventions sufficiently consistent for judgements of response rate to be based upon them? Although not immune from such considerations, collection of data on a prospective basis may often allow a closer specification of exactly what is to be measured. This may take the form of a monitoring exercise and the collection of basic service measures in this way will be addressed in Chapter 8.

Somewhat less 'basic' are measures such as client destination and receipt of services. How many children referred to social services have entered care, and how long have they remained in care? Have children entered residential or foster care? Have children attended school, or come to police notice for offences? Have elderly people remained in the community? Have they received home care services, and of what intensity? What proportion of cases are re-referred after closure? Clearly, measures such as these provide only indirect indicators of the outcomes of intervention for clients, but they may themselves reflect certain kinds of service objectives, for example those which seek to increase the priority given to a client group and hence the amount of professional time devoted. The characterization of a measure as 'service-based' (which may not as in the case of truancy be unambiguous) should also include those instances where the objective is system change. This has perhaps been most clearly evident in the work of the probation service and in the field of juvenile justice where attention shifted during the 1980s to an increased concern with influencing sentencing and disposal practices towards the greater use of non-custodial options and the better targeting of intensive forms of supervision on those offenders deemed to have a high risk of detention or imprisonment.

This takes us closer to what should be a guiding principle throughout, that outcomes should be considered in the light of objectives. What follows develops a particular application of the principle of studying the effects of intervention by close reference to its initial aims, addressing some of the problematic features of social work identified in the opening chapter.

Outcomes measured by the achievement of objectives

In principle, of course, the aims of intervention can be couched in terms that are both service- and client-based, and in so far as they fall into the latter category, the relevant outcome measures are more properly the concern of the next chapter. They are dealt with here partly because managers and practitioners appear to find it easier to articulate objectives in service terms, and partly because the concept of an 'objective' is itself rooted in professional thinking.

In her much-praised study of a New York programme to prevent foster care, Jones (1985) used a series of measures of outcome. This was a carefully controlled study of a programme designed to provide preventive services to children and families at risk in order 'to eliminate the need for foster care and prevent its recurrence'. Cases were randomly allocated to an experimental group which would receive the preventive services and a control group which would not; the two groups were compared in respect of numbers entering foster care, timing of entry and length of time in care, the selection of these as measures of outcome being based on the researcher's interpretation of the programme objectives. An additional measure reflected an objective seen as 'implicit', that maintaining children at home should not jeopardize their safety: numbers of reports of child maltreatment were compared. (Certain more client-based measures such as worker reports of family functioning were also available for the experimental group only.)

In this instance, a self-contained major programme was established with a firmly declared aim, something which characterizes the American scene to a greater extent than the British. Nevertheless, the main measures used here, and other similar ones, can be found in numerous studies, particularly in the child care field (Rowe, 1985).

These measures are probably most legitimate in two kinds of context. First, it may be assumed (with or without empirical justification) that certain characteristics of service delivery are strongly associated with good or bad practice or with desired or undesired outcomes for clients, and may thus be treated as proxies for client outcome. This has been most obviously the case in child care studies, where, say, admission to care itself is construed as a negative outcome, or when moves in care once admission has happened are likewise assumed to be best avoided (Millham *et al.*, 1985). Secondly (and the two categories may often coincide), certain service outputs may themselves be the paramount service objective. Examples here might be those kinds of service where new arrangements are made for the integration or co-ordination of services previously identified as damagingly unco-ordinated, often the case for example in the child protection field (Birchall and Hallett, 1991). In this instance, evaluative research may well focus on the extent, characteristics, and composition of inter-agency meetings, or on the participation of clients in case conferences. This approach is not necessarily a superficial or 'head-counting' exercise: the achievement of good and productive relations within and between agencies might be explored by in-depth interviews with professional staff.

Studying multiple objectives

This having been said, such measures have obvious limitations, though of course they may be combined with others in individual studies, ideally if perhaps unrealistically with quality of care and client-based measures. There is, however, another kind of objection which has been referred to in the introductory chapter, namely that the diversity, heterogeneity and sheer intractability of the kinds of problems typically taken up by social work casts some doubt on the realism of over-arching service objectives. With institutional care in all its forms having fallen into disfavour during the 1970s and 1980s, it has become common for the objective of 'preventing admission to residential care' to be adopted for services to client groups ranging from children to old people. In day-to-day practice, however, it becomes apparent that such overall objectives may need the qualifying clauses which are often inserted, such as 'according to need', or judicious or question-begging use of the term 'inappropriate'. The optimum outcome may simply be Utopian for many clients whose lives are beset by problems on which social work can make only marginal impact. Furthermore, any sample of actual cases is likely to contain individuals whose circumstances differ markedly from each other; they are at different stages of involvement with a number of agencies, and their problems are often interlaced and competing for priority; during any period of sustained intervention, new developments are constantly occurring. Once 'problems' are disaggregated, so too are potential solutions.

A researcher has two options in this situation. One is to seek rigorous specification, in the construction of a sample, of the problems being tackled, to ensure that a global outcome measure or measures is appropriate. The second is to accept the heterogeneity and to seek a solution to the technical problem that this produces; namely, that the detailed objectives of intervention will be to a significant degree tailored to the circumstances of each individual, and hence non-standardizable. This issue has arisen especially, for example, in research which has sought to study the effectiveness of assessment processes, where outcomes clearly cannot be looked at without taking account of the differences between individuals which are identified in assessment (Fuller, 1985). A response to this can take the form of measuring the achievement of distinctive objectives set in individual cases and adopting some means of aggregating these to obtain an overall effectiveness rating for the service under investigation.

This was among the methods used by Rowe *et al.* (1989) in their study of patterns and outcomes in a large sample of child care placements in six local authorities. Thus as well as measuring the length of placements, the researchers obtained social workers' judgements on whether placements had lasted as planned, less than planned or longer than planned; whether they lasted as needed, less than needed or longer than needed; and to what extent, on a four-point scale, they had achieved the 'primary aim' of the placement (e.g. 'temporary care', 'treatment', 'assessment', 'bridge to independence'). Somewhat tentatively, the researchers go on to derive a composite measure of overall placement 'success': a placement was deemed successful if it was rated as lasting as long as needed *and* met the aim fully or in most respects. This may then be analysed in terms of age groups, placement types, area, placement aims, and so on, in order to suggest differential success ratings for different kinds of work, different kinds of setting and different kinds of client.

This is admitted to be a crude undertaking, yet it enables a degree of disaggregation in a sample likely to be composed of widely differentiated sub-groups. One problem, however, is that Rowe *et al.*'s method permits only a single 'primary' objective to be selected for each case, lending an unrealistically unidimensional character to the professional input. In a study of preventive work carried out at the Centre, with a small sample which facilitated a more qualitative approach, a method was developed of analysing outcomes of the multiple and shifting objectives which often characterize the most challenging kinds of social work with children and young people (Fuller, 1987b, 1988). The subject of the study was the work of the M.A.R.S. Project, a voluntary sector child care unit.

The project received referrals primarily from the social work and education departments; rather like the New York programme, its single overall objective was to prevent breakdown in the living and schooling arrangements of the high-risk children and families referred, or put simply to avoid admission to residential care or schooling. It would thus have been possible to take a sample of cases and establish whether, after a period of time, they had entered care. On closer examination of the way the unit operated, however, two things swiftly became clear. The staff worked intensively with children and families over a long period, and much of their effort was devoted to the pursuit of a wide range of objectives, which although they might initially be seen as subsidiary or instrumental to the overall aim, were subject to development over time and had an autonomous life of their own. Secondly, some of the unit's cases actually did enter care, and staff continued to work with them after this had occurred. Therefore, to take the criterion of admission as the only outcome measure would have incurred the risk of misrepresenting and even trivializing the work of the unit.

The central feature of the study was an attempt to use a typology of preventive objectives as a basis for assessing the project's effectiveness, and a

Table 1   Typology of preventive goals

	Ranked first	All
1 Entry into care	1	5
2 Entry into custodial care	1	2
3 Neglect or abuse of children	2	2
4 Harmful effects of poor parenting	1	5
5 Disadvantage (homes/communities)	–	1
6 Long stays in care	–	1
7 Isolation in care	1	1
8 Rejection by professionals	3	4
9 'Professional muddle'	–	6
10 Behavioural – child	2	6
11 Behavioural – family	–	3

sample of 12 cases was studied in detail. A seven-fold set of objectives derived from Holman (1988) was discussed first at a general level with the M.A.R.S. staff. This resulted in clarification of the meanings of individual items and the suggestion of additional ones. The revised list is shown in Table 1. The initial discussion would produce, it was hoped, consistent understandings among staff of all those goals that were now to be included. It will be seen that these preventive goals belong to different dimensions. They include, for example: service objectives (prevention of entry into care); objectives aimed at the professional response (rejection by professionals); and client-centred objectives (the behavioural goals). The goals are not, therefore, mutually exclusive, and include some closely related to each other; this is inconvenient from a research point of view, since totals may be artificially boosted when goals are aggregated. It did prove, however, to be a reliable reflection of the practice goals actually adopted by the team, and it was clearly envisaged that more than one goal would be considered for each case. Indeed, the exercise was explicitly designed to reflect the evident multiplicity of work within each case, and to avoid the error of forcing work into a single category.

The next step was to discuss in detail each individual case in the sample with the staff, and allocate goals to cases. Following this in-depth interview, the staff were asked to rank the goals for each case in order of priority. Although it was expected that this process would reveal many complexities, this particular group of staff found it relatively straightforward. There arose the problem of goals changing over time. How this should best be handled by the researcher depends to a certain extent on the model of social work in question: is the intervention structured and finite (one with a 'beginning, middle and end'), or is it an open-ended, adaptive and 'maintaining' style of involvement? M.A.R.S. had elements of both, with some cases planned with a specified time limit, and others more open-ended. It was decided, however, that the latter was sufficiently prominent for the question of 'time', rather arbitrarily, to be dealt with by stipulating that all objectives pursued over a six-month period should be included.

The next step was to ask the project staff to rate, on a five-point scale, the success or failure of the intervention over a six-month period in respect of the first three preventive goals specified for each case. Self-rating by practitioners in this manner has its dangers. In this instance, the ratings of project staff were then checked against material from interviews with the referrers and with clients or families, and a considerable degree of congruence emerged.

It would, however, be perfectly possible for the rating of 'success' to be carried out solely or initially with clients or with other parties, or with certain objectives to be done by means other than through perceptions. The finding was that approximately three-quarters of the preventive objectives had been achieved with complete or partial success. Within this overall rate, there was some tendency for objectives directed at parenting behaviour to be less successful than work concerned with preventing admission to care, with influencing the approach of the statutory agencies and with preventing deterioration in children's behaviour.

This was an exploratory study carried out with a very small sample, in a setting where time was explicitly devoted to the rigorous identification of detailed objectives. In mainstream social work practice, unless, say, task-centred approaches are clearly established, there might be more difficulty in identifying objectives with the requisite explicitness, as Brown (1989) reports in her testing of the approach in the statutory sector. There are also a number of problems on which pragmatic decisions have to be made in the context of individual studies. These include the presence of a hierarchy of linked objectives, the differences between the short and the long term, the dilemma about how specific to be in studies which seek to investigate large samples. As carried out in this example, there are issues of validity in the way the success ratings are obtained, which makes it desirable that some form of triangulation be attempted. From the point of view of time, it would be useful if the process of eliciting objectives and then obtaining success ratings (by whatever method and from whatever source) could be carried out in a fixed-choice, self-completion mode rather than through the labour-intensive interview method. Brown's study makes some progress in developing standard typologies of preventive objectives which might be applicable to client groups other than children.

There are, then, some drawbacks, but the approach remains a promising if modest evaluative tool, which is adaptable to different circumstances and relatively simple for practitioners to understand and carry out themselves (Coyle, 1988).

Quality of care

The essential components of a service may be addressed in a monitoring exercise which records, for example, the presence or absence of a service or the frequency and duration of service components. A more comprehensive evaluation, however, will address not only the pattern of service provision but the quality. It will seek to identify outcomes which can purport to measure aspects of the quality of a service. The extent to which such measures must be considered as proxy will vary according to the service under scrutiny.

Quality assurance is, of course, very much a concern of the moment (see, e.g. Clifford *et al.*, 1989). Nurtured by the new language of the contracting culture, a greater emphasis has been laid on the provision of quality. Quality forums, quality circles, total quality management – each has its own particular focus and its own advocates in terms of achieving quality assurance. Quality of care addresses most directly the elements of service delivery and is often most readily understood in the context of some form of residential provision, an arena where the creation of a total environment allows for careful scrutiny of aspects of the quality of care. In exploring the measurement of quality of care, we will give particular attention to residential care for the elderly and community provision for those with mental health problems, contexts in which the work of the Centre has been concentrated.

Addressing aspects of quality of care requires, first, the identification of relevant dimensions and, secondly, the selection of appropriate criteria through which these dimensions are to be addressed. Consideration must also be given to the mechanism through which the individual criteria are to be aggregated. As with all measures of outcome, there must be a realistic assessment in any context of the extent and complexity of measurement that can be accommodated. If the focus of the study is elsewhere, scrutiny of a small number of factors may suffice; if quality of care is the key component, a more comprehensive listing may be attempted. For certain dimensions, direct measurement may be attained; for others, proxy measures may have to be adopted.

Bland and Bland (1990) discuss their development of a composite measure of the quality of care in old people's homes. Previous research had identified dimensions whose influence was generally agreed; these tended to express the extent to which the various components of the social environment gave individuals the opportunity to exercise control over their lifestyle, while at the same time having health and social care needs met in a sensitive fashion. As part of a pilot study addressing the relationship between quality of care and cost of provision, nine sets of variables were identified, each group focusing upon a particular dimension. The nine dimensions ranged from the building, procedures and regime, through medical care, the promotion of continence and the care of dementia sufferers, to the services provided to residents, staff qualifications and staff development. One hundred and one items were identified across the nine dimensions, ranging from four addressing care of dementia to 23 relating to the building itself. The inclusion of the promotion of continence is thought to be unique among quality of care measures. Within each dimension, a number of variables was selected to pinpoint what have been shown to be key factors. The particular merit of this measure of quality of care is that it addresses the totality of the residential home experience, acknowledging the equal import of both health care and social care for individual well-being.

An indication of the type of variables which were selected for each dimension should provide a flavour of the practical aspects of measuring quality of care. In terms of the building, for example, one criterion was the distance from local facilities (with a quarter of a mile as a maximum), another the extent to which a 'homely' atmosphere was evident. This in turn was a product of size, of furnishings and of staff–resident interaction, for each of which a direct or proxy measure was selected. Under the regime dimension, particular emphasis was laid on the component of choice, with detail of the system for waking and going to bed, for the timing and menus for meals, for the management of individual finances.

The potential influence of aspects of the quality of care upon the quality of life of the individual (to be explored in Chapter 7) should not be over-looked. This can be demonstrated from the dimension in the Bland *et al.* (1990) study, which recorded through a group of ten variables the services available to residents. These include the availability of a hairdresser, of alco-holic drinks for purchase and of opportunities to go shopping or on holiday. The presence or absence of such facilities is more than likely to affect the quality of life as experienced by residents. Indeed, Bland and Bland (1990) cite the concept coined by Avebury (1984) of the 'quality of experience'.

The measures of quality of care cited from this pilot study (Bland *et al.*, 1990) have been refined further in the large study of the quality of care and costs of 100 old people's homes in the public, private and voluntary sectors. A possible criticism of examining so many dimensions of quality of care is that if each is treated equally, homes might achieve a high quality of care through an aggregation of features (e.g. a visiting hairdresser) which, while impor-tant, would generally be considered less essential to residents' well being as, for example, single rooms. If homes score highly on all aspects, so that the aspects are correlated, the weighting of items will not affect the ranking of homes. If aspects are not correlated, so that a home may score high on one aspect and low on another, the weightings will make a difference.

Data analysis has therefore included various attempts to isolate or weight items considered especially important. In the preliminary study which dealt with 12 homes (Bland *et al.*, 1990), the researchers equally weighted the scores for each section of the schedule and obtained a total score for each home. The intention was to determine whether homes which scored high and low on the raw scale performed similarly on the adjusted scale. There was a high congruence between the two scales. In the second and larger study, a further analysis was carried out that weighted 20 key items which included single rooms, lifts, lockable storage facilities, heating that could be controlled by residents, contracts for residents, a complaints procedure, the use of key workers and the possibility of trial stays for potential residents. One problem with such an exercise is that the weightings must, to some extent, be arbi-trary. Although research has shown some items to be particularly valued by residents, opinions will differ among social workers, managers, relatives and residents about the importance of others. Such an analysis, however, makes explicit the weighting given and it is, of course, possible for the data to be re-analysed with different weightings. This weighting exercise had little impact on the rank order of the homes' quality of care. Homes which had achieved a high quality of care in the analysis of all items remained in the top band. This suggests high internal consistency between the various dimensions examined and the items within them (Bland *et al.*, forthcoming).

Professional judgement about some components of good quality of care may well differ from those of residents and their relatives. This study, therefore, sought the residents' and their relatives' opinions about such generally accepted matters of good practice as preparation for entry to residential care, the existence of care plans and key workers. The residents and their relatives were also asked to give their opinions through questionnaires and interviews about other aspects of home life such as food, activities, privacy, and so on. They were also invited to suggest changes they would like to make. It is important to include such opportunities to balance the high levels of satisfaction questionnaires commonly prompt (Gutek, 1978). The questionnaires and interviews in this study showed that the residents' of old people's homes could give information about aspects of the care provided which was useful for the research and could also contribute to regular internal and external reviews of homes' practices and quality. In particular, the residents' responses showed considerable ignorance and lack of clarity about such professionally cherished practices as key workers and care plans.

In the area of child care, an array of measures is deployed by Colton (1988) in his study of the characteristics of caring regimes in residential and foster care. Here the point of departure is less a concern with quality *per se* than an attempt to compare practices in two broad placement types in order to determine whether family placements are (as has often been assumed without empirical evidence) more child-centred than institutional settings. Drawing on the pioneering work of King *et al.* (1971), Colton developed a number of scales to measure the caring practices of a sample of residential and foster placements.

By a mixture of lengthy structured interviews with care-takers and detailed observation, the study included an exhaustive scrutiny of factors (many of them comparable to those covered in the work cited above on old people's homes) which might be thought to bear upon the variable 'child-centredness'. These included admission procedures, bedtime and mealtime routines, access to parts of the home, treatment of personal possessions, social activities, outings and contacts outside the home, sanctions for controlling behaviour, and many others; the instrumentation covers many pages. From these, Colton derived four separate scales for the assessment of child care regimes which he termed, respectively, the Indices of Child Management, Community Involvement, Physical Environment, and Controls and Sanctions. No attempt in this case was made to weight the individual items in each scale. If the thrust of the findings was unsurprising (the institutional settings were indeed more 'institutional'), the study demonstrates again the possibilities of delineating in structured form aspects of quality of care in great detail, given firm operationalization of key variables. It also raises interesting questions about the quality of care provided in 'normal' family life.

In the mental health field, quality of care has been a consideration both in hospital- and in community-based settings. The concern may be not only with a quality deemed to be satisfactory, but with an environment demonstrated to be effective. An early example of such an approach is the comparative evaluation by Apte (1968) of 25 halfway houses. The Hostel Hospital Practices Profile (HHPP) contained 65 items addressing a range of quality of care issues, a higher return rate to the community being demonstrated from permissive rather than restrictive sites. The use of the modified 52-item version of this schedule in the study of long-term psychiatric care in Camberwell is described by Wykes *et al.* (1982). Again the emphasis was on the extent of restriction across the different types of residential and day provision. In the selection of dimensions to be addressed, there appeared to be a mix of the research-based and the value judgement. This is an issue common to much of the quality of care debate. While there would be little disagreement on basic norms, other areas can generate different arguments for good practice. Is it, for example, acceptable to monitor the movements of individuals outwith a residential provision or is this an unacceptable infringement on the individual? – an argument pursued by Hewett (1979). To what extent, indeed, must the standards for quality of care be differentially interpreted according to the needs of the individual.

Much of the early work in this area was undertaken by Moos (1974) – for example, the Ward Atmosphere Scale (WAS) and the Community-Oriented Programs Environment Scale (COPES) – and his influence extends through a number of the more recent strategies. Segal and Moyles (1979), for example, in exploring the relationship between management style and dependency in California's sheltered care facilities, use items from the COPES as the basis for distinguishing operational style as client-centred or management-centred.

These various approaches to the assessment of quality of care in psychiatric settings have been classified by Lavender (1987a) into three broad categories. An attitudinal approach assesses quality of care through staff attitudes, various treatment orientation scales for example having been devised. The 'ecological' approach, as exemplified by Moos, attempts to measure the quality of care by assessing staff perceptions about specific aspects of (ward) life, while the 'objective measurement' approach attempts to assess practices and conditions either through direct observation or questioning of staff. The HHPP and Wing (1982) exemplify this approach.

Lavender argues that none of these approaches is ideal for the psychiatric setting. The aim of the Model Standards Questionnaires he therefore developed is to provide a comprehensive measure which will address quality of care from a number of perspectives. Thus, five schedules are involved, concerned with treatment practices, staff resources, ward management, community contact and physical resources. Each schedule defines a number of measures on which information must be collected for the unit under study. An attempt to act upon the information gathered from these schedules in order to improve the quality of care on rehabilitation wards through the provision of feedback is described by Lavender (1987b).

Although Lavender speaks of the adaptation of these schedules for use in community settings, their primary focus is on the ward environment. A number of the studies monitoring transition to the community have devised schedules which under various labels record what are primarily aspects of quality of care. The Personal Social Services Research Unit's evaluation of the Care in the Community Demonstration Projects, for example, has what is termed an 'environment' questionnaire, with alternative versions for hospital, residential and day facilities. Items to be recorded include the details of bedroom, living room and bathroom provision, the facilities available to residents, and the details of staff provision. Considerable attention is given to the details of daily living, including the extent of individual choice in key areas, e.g. the opportunity to keep a pet. The opportunities for social contacts and community links are also recorded. These detailed responses are supplemented by an environmental checklist which allows for ratings in key areas. Similar dimensions are addressed in the environmental index devised by O'Driscoll, and used both by the Team for the Assessment of Psychiatric Services (TAPS) in their evaluation of reprovision from Friern Hospital, and by Le Touze and Pahl (1991) in the study by the Health Services Research Unit at Kent of individuals moving from psychiatric hospital in Medway. Scores are allocated in relation to activity, possessions, meals, health and hygiene, residents' rooms, services, homeliness and staffing.

The growth of the inspectorial function and of the concern with quality assurance is likely to lead to a greater emphasis on the measurement of quality of care. A lead has been given by the work for the Social Services Inspectorate Report, *Homes are for Living In* (DoH, 1989). Indeed, the models devised in this exercise address the two components of quality – the quality of care provided, the concern of this section, and the quality of life experienced. The former focuses on what is actually provided in the way of care by the agency, e.g. measures indicative of privacy, of choice or of independence; the latter picks up how for any one individual those features were actually experienced. This juxtaposition points neatly to the focus of the next chapter, with quality of life as one of a number of client-based measures of outcome.

7

CLIENT-BASED
OUTCOMES

The previous chapter has addressed those outcomes, characterized as service-based, which attempt to convey the essence of what is being provided. In this chapter, we turn to a different stage of the evaluative process, to the attachment of outcomes to the individual client. Having been in receipt of a particular service, what has been the effect on the individual? The dimensions to be targeted in any study will depend on the focus of the study and the specific research questions which are being addressed. The aim is to select as client-based outcomes features which measure the impact of the intervention on the individual. Three sets of client-based measures of outcome which are commonly applied, overlapping but distinct, will be outlined. These are measures of client state, judgements on quality of life and measures derived from user response. The last, being a broader category which can in practice embrace elements of the other two, will be addressed first.

It is inevitable that a chapter of this type will resemble to some extent a catalogue of disparate measures, but a broad indication of their type and range will be offered, together with discussion where appropriate of the issues to be confronted when making choices between them. The objective of this chapter is to indicate the nature of the different types of measures that are available, and to reassure through examples that their application can be readily achieved in practice.

User response

There is, rightly, much contemporary concern with reflecting the perspective of the user of services and it is therefore appropriate that this set of responses be accorded separate treatment. If the objectives of any service include the delivery of a product which is deemed reasonably acceptable to the recipient, some assessment of this outcome must be in order. This is not to imply, however, that this category does not overlap with other client-based measures of outcome. There can be a tendency to speak loosely of the user response being itself an outcome measure when more correctly what is required is a specification of the measures through which the user response will be codified. Thus, aspects of the user response may be reflected in certain measures of client state, while outcomes designed to assess quality of life will almost certainly be dependent to a greater or lesser extent on the expressed opinions of those in receipt of services. None the less, a focus on those outcomes which address the user perspective *per se* allows for a wider remit before the focus later in the chapter on these more specific measures.

The logic for the association of the user response with more qualitative research methodologies has already been presented in Chapter 3. Caution has to be exercised in respect of global expressions of satisfaction which merely replicate the 80 per cent figure commonly found. Care has also to be taken in adopting simple dichotomous or pre-coded categories that the absence of detail does not detract from the interpretation. Attention must be paid as well to the possibility that individuals may express satisfaction with the outcome *per se* but have very different responses to the process by which that outcome was achieved. The measures most likely therefore to feature in this area are those which extract from more narrative responses to less structured questioning. Although these may contribute to a generally positive or negative set of outcomes, they are likely to be expressed more in terms of collective themes or ranges of responses rather than as a single dichotomy.

The interviews conducted for the supported accommodation study illustrate the type of outcome measures that can emerge from user interviews (Petch, 1990, 1992). Certain of the outcomes fall into the category of client state, e.g. Cantril's Ladder and the extract from the Psychosocial Functioning Inventory (PFI). Others are direct quality of life outcome measures as derived from seven-point scales for various domains. There remain, however, a set of responses which both elaborate on these other measures and which summarize across a wealth of interview data. In terms, for example, of the support that is received or the extent that outside activities are pursued, there are a range of responses which speak to the effect that intervention has had on the individual and which allow for generalizations to be drawn in that particular area. Methodological issues raised earlier have, of course, to be borne in mind; the desire to exhibit certain outcome measures should not be pursued to the extent of forcing complex qualitative data to respond to inappropriate categorization. Bailey's (1987) sensitive evaluation of a mental health centre shows how this can be avoided.

As was argued in Chapter 3, there may however be certain situations that allow the outcomes representing user response to be derived from relatively straightforward structures, the postal questionnaire or the standardized interview. The best examples from the Centre's work are to be found in the community service studies; for example, the attitude to the work undertaken by those sentenced to community service functions as an important outcome measure which can be related to other measures such as absences from placement and attitudes towards further offending. The subjective experience thus adds explanation to the more objective record of how many completed their sentence. Similarly, in the study which examined the attitudes of individuals and agencies towards work carried out on their behalf by offenders on community service orders, satisfaction was expressed in terms of the perceived quality and usefulness of the work and the recipients' willingness to have further work performed by offenders on orders.

Developing from work on evaluating mental health services, it has been suggested that satisfaction might be measured through three short questions: 'to what extent has our program met your needs; in an overall general sense, how satisfied are you with the services you received; and if you were to seek help again, would you come back to our program?' (Berger, 1983). The extent to which these questions may prove robust in a different area is currently being examined through their inclusion in the interviews with elderly service users in the centre's organization and outcomes study.

An important consideration when user response outcomes are used in conjunction with other outcome measures is how the different sets relate to each other. How do satisfaction levels equate with scores of, for example, client state? American evidence in the mental health field suggests low to moderate correlation between consumer satisfaction and other measures of outcome. What must also be addressed, however, is the expectation, for example, of change on client state scores compared to the individual's evaluation that the conduct and delivery of the service was satisfactory. As we have argued above, the process of service delivery in social welfare may be regarded as important as the end-product: 'Client satisfaction has evolved into a viable outcome measure . . . satisfaction data present a dimension of the outcome of therapy as viable as symptom reduction' (Berger, 1983, p. 77).

Client state

The diversity of measures which could be harnessed to indicate client state or well-being is potentially enormous. Moreover, the assumptions implicit in the adoption of any particular measure may be considerable (McDowell and Newell, 1987). Discussions in other chapters, for example, have outlined the circumstances in which one must aspire to longitudinal studies and the extent to which any change in client state can be attributed to aspects of process, and Chapter 4 has highlighted the critical questions which should be asked in the selection of such schedules. We will concentrate in this section on the measures of client state that have actually been adopted for Centre studies. In doing so, it should be borne in mind that instruments can be both research- and practice-based. Those which can be of value to practice may hold a particular attraction in offering spin-offs to the practitioner for their participation in the research.

The arguments advanced for addressing client state include the importance of a base line measurement. This can afford an opportunity both for comparison with other studies which have adopted similar measures and for the examination within any one study of comparison between groups and of change over time. An additional concern may be to reach a particular audience through the use of measures with which they are familiar.

Practical considerations may often dictate choices. An initial distinction for example is between assessments of client state which are completed by some third-party, often a key worker or other individual with close know-ledge of the person under study, and those which record the response of the subjects themselves. Likewise, client state measures, whether from the subject or a third-party, may be sought through verbal interview or through a self-completion questionnaire. They may refer to the immediate present or they may seek recall over a shorter or longer period. They may be rapidly completed within five or ten minutes or they may demand a lengthy period of interview or form filling.

Considerable attention should be given to such practical concerns when alternative choices are being considered and time should be reserved for adequate piloting of the potential choices. Such piloting is for the benefit of both parties. Realistic judgements should be made of both interviewer and respondent tolerance and measures should not normally be adopted with which the interviewers themselves are uneasy. Such discomfort, however, should be taken in context; interviewer reticence to discuss, for example, suicidal behaviour should be weighed against the 'normality' of such discussion in certain contexts.

The researcher in search of measures of client state may be overwhelmed by the range of potential alternatives. This may especially be the case when the focus of the study is fairly general (e.g. organization and outcomes of services for elderly people), yet there has been a considerable history of detailed measurement. Specificity may be rampant at the expense of a good general measure. This danger lurks particularly when the field of research fringes upon other disciplines and above all on psychiatry and psychology. It must also be recognized that a particular phenomenon may be multi-dimensional and that it may be appropriate to employ different measures to record different dimensions. In her discussion on measuring outcomes in mental health, for example, Renshaw (1985) identifies seven domains: symptoms; behaviour and social functioning; morale and satisfaction; engagement in activity; social contacts, friends and outings; significant events; and personal presentation.

The response adopted by the Centre has been to assume that in most circumstances it is far better to work with an existing validated measure rather than to embark on the long process of innovation (Streiner and Norman, 1989). Such a strategy should provide at least some guarantee that the instrument does indeed measure what it purports to do (face validity), and that measurement is not unduly influenced either by varying conditions over time or by the individual carrying out the measurement (reliability). Of major consideration also is that the use of a standard measure provides norms for comparison with other studies. It may also be possible in certain circumstances to capitalize on the use of a particular measure for both re-search and practice purposes. This may involve the researcher encompassing a measure already adopted as routine in the particular practice environment, or it may lead to the practitioner being persuaded of the value of incor-porating into the agency a particular measure initially proposed for research purposes. The current flurry of activity in preparation for the new specification of assessment procedures may, particularly in respect of elderly people, lead to more examples of this type.

Those embarking on the Centre's studies in the mental health field were confronted by the embarrassment of alternative measures, and indeed by the perennial arguments over the extent to which measurement of specific state is attainable (see, e.g. Platt, 1981). Even if this hurdle is crossed, there may be doubts as to the adequacy of available measures (Hall, 1979). As indicated above, the detail and specificity of available measures may be problematic for the social work researcher seeking a more general, global response, with the detailed differences between adjacent measures cumbersome rather than enlightening. The tendency in such situations may be to opt for the familiar and widespread, say the General Health Questionnaire (GHQ) developed by Goldberg *et al.* (1970), yet the very generality may, as with the use of this measure with a population with long-term problems (Benjamin *et al.*, 1982; Stanley and Gibson, 1985), be a contraindication. Even if circumstances might indicate the GHQ, a choice has to be made between a number of potential alternatives – the full 60-item version (Goldberg *et al.*, 1970), the scaled 28-item form (Goldberg and Hillier, 1979) or the interval version which selects 12 items and compares responses over time (Surtees and Tansella, 1990).

Having selected the dimensions of client state to be measured, it can be daunting to be in the position of casting around for an appropriate scale or schedule. Very rarely is one in the position of an optimal selection from the total set; more often a satisficing solution is reached. A trawl is made of studies in similar areas; the more familiar and frequent is selected in preference to the recent innovation. A factor in the choice may be a desire for the proposed study to bear comparison with others which have adopted a similar measure or, while perhaps privately sceptical about the measure itself, there may be pragmatic reasons of credibility or consistency which speak to its use. A specialist medical audience, for example, may be attuned to certain traditions of client state measurement. It is important, as for any outcome measure, that the rationale for the use of a standardized measure of client state has been thoroughly argued. As Wing (1977, p. 515) and colleagues maintain in their exploration of the Present State Examination (PSE): 'if a less structured, less classifiable and less communicable description of "mental state" is required it would probably be best to avoid standardised interviews altogether and adopt the questionnaire approach'.

Selection of the measures of client state to be used in the Centre's study of supported accommodation for those with mental health problems went through several of these stages. A broad trawl was made among the most readily accessible of the measures used to scale for psychiatric status and for social well-being. Inevitably, this could only touch the surface of what is a vast literature (see, e.g. McDowell and Newell, 1987; Freeman and Tyrer, 1989). Many subsets are found within the general area: 29 ward rating scales for example are reviewed by Hall (1980), 15 measures of social adjustment by Weissman (1975). Inevitably, there are fashions, preferences and different interest groups and whenever possible the views of expert colleagues should be sought. This may not necessarily lead to clarification, but it does provide the confidence of the expert umbrella!

A major consideration in the psychiatric field, however, was that the chosen scale(s) could be administered by the non-specialist. Certain scales that are commonly used in this area require either a psychiatrist or a trained interviewer. An example of a scale which can be used by a non-specialist is the standardized psychiatric interview developed for use in community surveys by Goldberg *et al.* (1970) and whose role in the evaluation of a GP attached social worker is described at Cooper *et al.* (1975). The Psychiatric Status Schedule, on the other hand (Spitzer *et al.*, 1970), is an example of a client state measure which requires a medical specialist. In the study of rehabilitation at the Royal Edinburgh Hospital conducted by the Social Work Research Centre, the availability of sessional input from a research psychiatrist enabled the Scale for the Assessment of Negative Symptoms (SANS) (Andreason, 1984) and the Schedule for Affective Disorders and Schizophrenia (SADS) (Endicott and Spitzer, 1978) to be adopted as two of the research instruments. Use could also be made of the scale developed by Krawiecka and colleagues (1977) for the rating of chronic psychotic patients.

Also to be considered is whether there is scope in any situation for the use of self-report scales. An advantage commonly cited for the self-report strategy is that the individual may communicate more 'truthfully' with a piece of paper than in verbal dialogue. Weissman *et al.* (1978), for example, discuss the use of a self-report scale (SAS-SR) to measure social adjustment in both a community sample and three psychiatric outpatient populations. This scale has subsequently been used in the series of reports on the Nithsdale schizophrenic population (McCreadie and Barron, 1984). In general, however, self-report is considered to be most reliable with a non-psychotic population.

Yet a further consideration is the origin of the scale and in particular the extent to which modification or adjustment has been made for cross-cultural variation. Cooper *et al.* (1982) report on their modification of the original United States SAS for use with a UK population. Its wording was made more appropriate for the UK and the rating scale was standardized throughout the questionnaire. Again, common sense should prevail: no-one should attempt to deliver a schedule which feels alien to them or in which they are uncertain of the meaning of key phrases.

Given the emphasis in the supported accommodation study on the attainment of satisfactory levels of functioning within the community, it was decided that this aspect rather than a solely symptomatic profile should provide the focus for client state. The project staff, therefore, were asked to complete two of the community assessment schedules devised by the National Unit for Psychiatric Research and Development (NUPRD), now Research and Development in Psychiatry (RDP). These schedules were the Social Functioning Questionnaire (SFQ) and the Problems Questionnaire (PQ), not dissimilar in form to those developed by Wykes (1982). The SFQ focuses not so much on symptomatology *per se* but on the extent, if any, to which social functioning is impaired. Across 40 items ranging from personal finance and medication to various domestic and community skills, the informant is asked to select which of four statements best describes the functioning of the individual. Likewise, the PQ seeks to highlight the limitations to community living imposed for the individual by the particular configuration of problems. It was considered important, in addition, to have a measure of client state which was familiar in the psychiatric world. The scale selected for this purpose was the Morningside Rehabilitation Status Schedule (MRSS) (Affleck and McGuire, 1984), an instrument devised to address in particular the outcomes of the rehabilitative process. In designing the scale – four dimensions scored on an eight-point rating (dependency, inactivity, social integration and effects of symptoms) – particular attention is given to scores above which survival in the community becomes difficult. The authors stress also the necessity as ever of selecting the requisite outcome measure dependent on the objectives of the evaluation.

These measures of client state for the supported accommodation study all rely on the observations and reports of staff members. Within the interview with respondents, however, elements from another measure were incorporated, the Psychosocial Functioning Inventory (PFI) of Feragne and colleagues (1983). The PFI is a multi-scale measure comprising 12 different scales which builds on and extracts from many of the earlier instruments. The Centre studies employ only one of the sub-scales, that on morale which asks how often over the previous month people have experienced a range of emotions, e.g. boredom, restlessness, anger. In doing so, they echo both the PSSRU and the Pahl studies referred to above.

These latter studies of community provision share in common a tendency to assemble a fairly eclectic selection of outcome measures from a variety of sources. The PSSRU evaluation of the care in the community demonstration projects, for example, adopted the approach of building eclectically around the SPS as a central core. Additional items have been added from REHAB, the Clifton Assessment Procedures for the Elderly (CAPE) (Pattie and Gilleard, 1979), the Adaptive Behaviour Scale (ABS) (Nihira *et al.*, 1974) and the Disability Assessment Scale (DAS) (Holmes *et al.*, 1982). There would appear to be a certain irony in selecting specific scales on the basis of reliability and validity, only to prune and amplify with apparent abandon. It is difficult to conclude that the original integrity of a measure can be retained when it is used in this apparently cavalier manner.

We have chosen to look in some detail at the assessment of client state in the mental health studies. The vigorous (and avowedly rigorous) tradition of such measurement in psychiatry provides a sharp focus for the argument. Similar detail could be advanced, however, for many of the other fields of study. For elderly people, for example, the extent of the literature detailing different measures for client state rivals that of the psychiatric domain, with interest particularly at the current time in the most appropriate measures for use with those suffering dementia. A useful overview of this area, which focuses in particular on measures of dependency, is that by Wilkin and Thompson (1989). They cite only UK measures and examine in detail the particular strengths and weaknesses of nine specific measures, including the Crichton Royal Behavioural Rating Scale and the Clackmannan Model of Dependency. A preliminary discussion highlights the different dimensions of dependency, the distinction between performance and capacity, and issues of scaling and of validity and reliability.

A popular measure for use with the elderly, and one included in the Wilkin and Thompson review, is the Clifton Assessment Procedures for the

Elderly (CAPE), developed by Pattie and Gilleard (1979) to provide an assessment of cognitive and behavioural competence. This can be of value, for example, in identifying individuals for rehabilitation or more independent placement or in evaluating the effects of specific interventions. Two different scales relate to these two different aspects, the Cognitive Assessment Scale (CAS) and the Behaviour Rating Scale (BRS), the latter measuring four principal areas of behavioural disability: physical disability, apathy, communication difficulties and social disturbance. For example, four of the 18 items on the BRS ask

1 When bathing or dressing, he/she
   requires
   — no assistance
   — some assistance
   — maximum assistance

7 If allowed outside, he/she would
   — never need supervision
   — sometimes need supervision
   — always need supervision

14 He/she is objectionable to others
   during the day (loud or constant
   talking, pilfering, soiling furniture . . .)
   — rarely or never
   — sometimes
   — frequently

18 His/her sleep pattern at night is
   — almost never awake
   — sometimes awake
   — often awake

The CAS is administered to the subject while the BRS is completed by a staff member or carer. The scores are entered on the CAPE Report Form and are then compared with a five-point grading system indicative of the varying degrees of impairment. A recent development of CAPE is the less detailed Survey Version, designed for use in more rapid screening and assessment surveys. A single form provides measures of orientation and of physical disability and allows for a rapid overview of a particular population. The grading system developed for the fuller version applies also to this shorter form.

More detailed social and behavioural functioning is addressed in the Problem Checklist developed by Gilleard (1984) for use with carers. For a problem checklist of 35 items, information is sought from the carer on both the frequency of occurrence and the extent to which the item is regarded as problematic. Although developed initially for use with those with dementia, the checklist has more recently been employed for elderly people without dementia and with parents of children with learning difficulties.

For elderly people, the other major area for which client state measures are sought is psychological well-being. Again the potential choice is wide and we can do no more than highlight a few of the measures which have gained common currency. A useful review is to be found in Davies and Knapp (1981), while a more comprehensive handbook is provided by Kane and Kane (1981). A cluster of studies have sought to rate life satisfaction, the rating being by an assessor other than the elderly person him or herself. Considerable attention has been given to the Life Satisfaction Rating Scale of

Neugarten *et al.* (1961) which analyses well-being into five constituent components. To offset the requirement for a lengthy interview with a professional demanded by the rating scale, two shorter, self-report Life Satisfaction Indices (LSI-A and LSI-B) have subsequently been developed, although it is only the first of these that has been widely used. In terms of widespread use, mention should also be made of the Philadelphia Geriatric Center Morale Scale, developed by Lawton (1972, 1975) and currently in use in a number of the studies at Stirling University. Consisting of 22 items which seek a positive or negative response, the attraction of the PGC Scale is in its relative simplicity compared to many of the more elaborate devices. It can be embedded in a more wide-ranging interview or can stand alone for more rapid screening. A fuller discussion on aspects of the validity of the measure can be found in Davies and Knapp (1981).

There has typically been less use made of measures of client state in studies which have evaluated the effectiveness of services for offenders. Here, more attention has generally been paid to behavioural outcomes such as re-offending, academic achievement or vocational adjustment. The Mooney Problem Checklist, used among others by Folkard *et al.* (1974, 1976) and Raynor (1988), elicits clients' perceptions of their problems and difficulties on a self-report basis. It has been used on a before and after basis to assess whether self-reported problems have increased, decreased or remained unchanged over the period of intervention. In the USA, a 'positive adjustment scale' has been developed by researchers at the University of Ohio to assess offenders' social adjustment in the community. The scale, which was designed to measure several parameters generally considered to demonstrate 'acceptable societal behaviour', has been used by Latessa (1987) and Latessa and Vito (1988) in conjunction with recidivism measures in their evaluations of intensive supervision with high-risk probationers. The nature and seriousness of social, family and personal problems experienced by offenders and their levels of social adjustment may also be taken as indirect indicators of the risk of continued offending.

In the child care field, research on social work intervention has likewise made less use than might be supposed of the plethora of standardized measures of child state or level of functioning available from disciplines such as psychology and education. The service-based measures described in the previous chapter predominated, for example, in the studies summarized by Rowe (1985), together with non-standardized measures based on social workers' perceptions of, say, family functioning.

Important exceptions, however, are to be found in studies of pre-school intervention and of adoption and fostering – see Ferri (1981) and Tizard (1977) for examples of the use of standard measures of cognitive and social/emotional development – and in some studies of children reared in care, especially if carried out by psychologists. The behavioural questionnaires developed by Rutter (1967) for completion by teachers and parents (the 'Rutter A and B scales') have been extensively used by their originator and his collaborators in various studies of the impact of care and/or other experiences on the behaviour and adjustment of children (see, e.g. Rutter *et al.*, 1983). Attempts to measure what is probably more correctly located in the following section as the quality of life in familial or institutional settings have been more elusive. They include a number of specially designed instruments like that of Sylva *et al.* (1980) for distinguishing the quality of play observed in their study of childminding, and such methods as that devised by Quinton *et al.* (1976) for assessing the quality of marriage, used by some child-care researchers on the grounds of the known association between marital discord and children's problems.

Another approach, and one more centrally geared to social care, is represented in the recent work of Parker *et al.* (1991). This develops in systematic form a large and elaborate array of outcome indicators suitable particularly for use with children and young people receiving some form of public care. These indicators, although designed primarily for periodic use by practitioners, may have considerable research potential. They appear in the form of a series of assessment and action records, each related to specific age groups (from under one year to 16+), and covering several domains or 'key areas of development' (health, education, identity, family and social relationships, social presentation, emotional and behavioural development, and self-care skills).

The outcome indicators themselves cover a number of types, ranging from the service-based ('has the child seen a dentist in the last six months?') to measures of children's behaviour, relationships and developmental state ('can the child tell you who his/her special friends are?'). The records also incorporate for each domain a set of questions which elicit from the person completing the forms (a social worker or, in the case of older subjects, the young person in question) an estimate of how far 'aims' have been achieved. These aims are not specific to the intervention episode, but rest rather on consensual views of normal or healthy child development at the relevant age point and are assumed to be the objective of any professional action.

Since population norms are not built into the various measures, the instruments are likely to be most useful to researchers comparing one group with another or, by focusing particularly on the 'aims' sections, comparing one group over different points in time. Although work remains to be done on the validation of the instruments, they offer a notably comprehensive specification of potential indicators of children's progress.

An area of increasing interest in recent years has been the response of carers, specifically in this particular context the development of measures of carer state. Again such measures can be completed through self-report or can be administered verbally, perhaps in the context of a more qualitative interview. As with any of these measures, care must be taken not to make assumptions as to causality. Individuals may differ from the group norm or specific groups may show markedly different results from a general population; the explanation for such variation may, however, be somewhat complex. A good example of such a measure is the Malaise Inventory originally developed by Rutter *et al.* (1970) and discussed at some length by Quine and Charnley (1987). The Malaise Inventory focuses in particular on the measurement of stress among carers and is valuable both for evaluation before and after an intervention and for comparison among different carer groups. Scores are available from studies among others: parents of children with severe learning difficulties (Burden, 1980), parents of disabled children who had applied to the Family Fund (Bradshaw and Lawton, 1978) and elderly carers of adults with learning difficulties (Kurkowski, 1989).

A particularly attractive feature of the Malaise Inventory is the relative ease of both administration and scoring. The respondents are asked to answer 'yes' or 'no' in response to 24 items, symptoms they might have experienced in the last few weeks. The number of affirmative answers is taken as the total score. The questions include:

- Do you feel tired most of the time?
- Do you usually wake unnecessarily early in the morning?
- Are you easily upset or irritated?
- Do you suffer from indigestion?

The questions can either be asked face to face or the respondent can be asked to fill in the inventory, perhaps at a natural break in a more qualitative interview. Experience suggests that this can be useful both as a breathing space for both parties and as a means of ensuring transition from one phase to another of a perhaps complex interview. The Malaise Inventory is currently being used with carers in the evaluation of the EPIC project (Hudson and Dobson, 1991) while Levin and colleagues (1985) completed the GHQ with carers of individuals with dementia in an attempt to determine the influence of home help assistance on carer well-being.

The Nottingham Health Profile (Hunt *et al.*, 1980, 1981) has similar attractions to the Malaise Inventory in terms of ease of administration and understanding, although it is designed for self-completion rather than verbal response. Part I of the questionnaire provides a profile of perceived distress in the areas of pain, physical mobility, emotional reactions, social isolation, sleep and energy. Respondents are asked to tick 'yes' or 'no' to a range of statements such as 'I lie awake for most of the night' or 'I feel there is nobody I am close to'. Part II gives a rough guide as to how far such distress is affecting the activities of daily living. A particular advantage of the questionnaire is that since it does not ask directly about health problems, it can therefore be used with samples of respondents who do not consider themselves to be ill. It is appropriate for the evaluation of medical or social interventions in a pre-/post-test design and as a method of monitoring change in subjective health.

The profile was one instrument used in a study of the effectiveness of homemakers (Cheetham, 1991). The small sample size precluded any statistical analysis, but the completed forms were used both by homemakers and their clients to monitor changes in subjective health and, in cases where there were measures of problems and client state at three or four different points, to judge whether the changes in clients' problems and their seriousness were reflected in their own assessment of their health. The clients in the study found the profile easy to use and there were several expressions of interest as they looked back to record changes in their health. There were also such comments as 'oh, this makes sense', 'yes, that's just how I feel'. These responses reflect the care the authors of the instrument took to ensure its ease of use and its acceptability to different population groups.

This overview of a handful of client state measures for a limited range of applications has tried to provide an indication of both the potential and the limitations of such devices. Discussion of the merits of their use in social welfare research can provoke considerable passion among different parties. Decisions as to their desirability for any such study must depend upon the specific research questions under investigation, on the research design and its underlying theoretical assumption and, ultimately, on the preferences of the individual researcher.

Quality of life

'Quality of life' as a term has been used with such abandon as to bring into question its continuing status. Some give the concept a medical orientation amenable to sophisticated statistical manipulation in the quality adjusted life year (QALY); others perceive a subjective experience whose complexity and richness they would be loathe to reduce to a summary measure (Baldwin *et al.*, 1989). As with quality of care, there is a basic attractiveness to the concept of quality of life: an intimation of a superior service. Indeed, it is perhaps the very nature of the construct that has led to its ubiquitous spread: 'As an evaluation criterion, quality of life has an intuitive appeal, capturing concisely the notion that the ultimate concern of all health and human services is the well-being of people' (Lehman, 1983b, p. 143). There would, however, be general broad agreement that quality of life is a multidimensional concept, one that seeks to encapsulate the totality of an individual's life.

It is helpful to distinguish probably three somewhat different approaches that have emerged in the quality of life debates. Much of the initial discussion in this area originated in the concerns with mental well-being (Beiser, 1974; Cherlin and Reeder, 1975; Campbell, 1976) and the attempts to separate out the different psychological components. Subsequently, the rather different strands started to evolve. One, less commonly followed in the social welfare area, seeks a single indicator and is exemplified in the discussion by Kind (1986). The definition here is of 'a composite of those health-related aspects of life which are subject to change by the provision or withholding of medical treatment'. The focus is very much on health outcomes, with the underlying consideration, the allocation of limited resources between individuals. A natural outcome of such an approach is the work – for example, at the Centre for Health Economics at York – on quality-adjusted life years (QALYs) (Williams, 1985; Gudex, 1986).

In much of social policy, however, it is considered important to extend the remit of quality of life measures beyond those which are primarily health-related to those that reflect on basic social conditions (Levine, 1987). For example, in a review article, Flanagan (1982) outlines the derivation of 15 components from the reporting of 6500 critical incidents. In the US context, the five dimensions most frequently described as important comprised health, children, understanding oneself, work and spouse; the five dimensions where needs and wants were least well met were participation in government, active recreation, learning and education, creative expression and helping others. The five dimensions correlating most highly with reports of overall quality of life were material comforts, work, health, active recreation, and learning and education.

In adopting this broader definition of quality of life, it is important to recognize that there can be both subjective and objective dimensions to quality of life measurement and it is these which we would cite as the second and third of the approaches in the quality of life debate. In assessing the quality of life of carers of those with dementia, for example, a simple (objective) measure termed, perhaps, 'independence' might be the number of times in a day they could walk out into the garden. The more subjective dimension on independence would explore for any one individual to what extent they felt they were independent of their caring burden.

For both objective and subjective dimensions, there are measures which focus on specific areas of life (domain-specific) and others which function as global indicators of well-being (e.g. Cantril's ladder). In considering an individual's social network, for example, there can be both a qualitative and a quantitative component to this domain-specific indicator, and the one might not accord with the other – 'lots of buddies rather than real friends'. Although for the purposes of this argument we are primarily concerned with outcomes at the individual level, the quality of life concept can also be applied on a community basis, commonly drawing upon a range of social indicators (Zautra and Goodhart, 1979).

Many of the dilemmas of quality of life measurement are particularly germane in the mental health field. Quality of life has become a major focus in discussion of policy for those with long-term mental health problems, with particular attention (see, e.g. Huxley, 1986) to the extent to which subjective responses may be influenced by factors such as mood, a tendency to give socially desirable responses, temperament characteristics or symptomatic disturbance. Huxley argues that on discharge from hospital physical health is likely to be a major determinant of quality of life – health status imposing, he suggests, a ceiling effect. Such dimensions overlay certain well-documented demographic correlates of quality of life. Satisfaction, for example, has been shown to increase steadily with advancing age, whereas reports of happiness tend to diminish. However, a careful analysis by Lehman (1983b) demonstrates that, save for health domains, the presence of psychiatric symptomatology does not significantly alter the response to quality of life assessment.

The work of Lehman and his associates (1982; Lehman, 1983a) has been of particular impact in the determination of quality of life in the mental health field and elements of this work have been adopted for two of the Centre's mental health studies. Lehman devised a special Quality of Life interview in order to interview residents of board-and-care homes in Los Angeles. Objective measures of life conditions and subjective assessments of satisfaction were sought in eight areas (life domains): living situation, family relations, social relations, leisure activities, work, finances, safety and health. For each domain, comparisons were made with the general population (satisfaction being lower). The interview devised for this study was structured in format and took about an hour. Seven-point 'delighted–terrible' (D–T) scales were used for the rating of satisfaction with the different domains and with general well-being. These subjective measures of satisfaction were shown to correlate appropriately with objective indicators of life conditions. However, Lehman argues that the relatively low level of these correlations suggests that, although related, the objective and subjective indicators are measuring rather different aspects of quality of life. He suggests that it is appropriate, therefore, to use both types of measures in quality of life assessment.

Elements from Lehman have been incorporated in a number of British schedules, e.g. the E QUAL-C measure developed by Huddersfield Health Authority (Harris, 1988) and the Lancashire Quality of Life Instrument assembled by Oliver for use in that county's social services department. Objective measures for each domain are sought before the individual is asked to select his or her subjective response from the D–T scale. Comparison was also made for this population with the quality of each domain when the patient had been in hospital. A modified version of this approach was used in the quality of life schedule devised for the Social Work Research Centre's study of the discharge of individuals from the Royal Edinburgh Hospital.

The interview format developed for the Centre's study of supported accommodation was less closely modelled on Lehman. It did, however, adopt the convention of the seven-point scale, each area of discussion being summarized by this measure of satisfaction level. Ten domains were evaluated in this way: the house, area and general living situation, daytime and evening activity, family contacts and social life, the financial situation, and project and professional support. The experience of this study was that the interweaving of this more structured element into the more discursive interview functioned well, providing a series of staging points which both allowed for summary and for the drawing of breath.

The argument from the experience of the Centre would be that discussion of quality of life must balance the utility of a scoring device which can allow ready comparison against the evocative account of an individual's own words. Indeed, throughout the Centre's work, the policy is to select the range of devices consistent with the scale and objectives of the particular study. In the final analysis, however, there would be agreement that any reduction from the free expression of the individual experience must inevitably lose in terms of quality; such loss must be deemed necessary for the practical achievement of the evaluation.

The guiding principle of selecting the strategy appropriate to the scale and aim of any evaluation holds true more generally with regard to selection across the range of outcome measures that have been reviewed in these two chapters. The studies that have been accomplished at the Centre to date provide examples of a wide range of different outcome variables and a similarly catholic approach to their measurement. In the homemakers study, for example, basic service measures relating to the problems to be tackled and the tasks to be performed were recorded through checklist devices. The client-based measures included a schedule for assessing the number and seriousness of problems (and their change over time), together with the measurement of client state by use of the Nottingham Health Profile. In the M.A.R.S. study, the primary focus was on the service base and on the measurement of objectives, with the detail of this explored elsewhere in this volume. Finally, the mental health studies, with their focus at the client base, have touched upon quality of care, have made considerable use of client state measures and have explored both subjective and objective domains of quality of life.

8

MONITORING AND EFFECTIVENESS

Here are only numbers ratified.
Shakespeare, *Love's Labour's Lost*

I have often admired the mystical way of Pythagoras, and the secret magic of numbers.
Sir Thomas Browne (1643) *Religio Medici*

Monitoring may be defined for present purposes as a system for gathering information, in principle on a continuous basis, about what happens in day-to-day practice in an agency. There is a potential play on words here. What happens in practice may be different from what happens in theory, and the aspiration on the part of managers, practitioners or researchers who undertake monitoring will often be to establish whether what is actually happening corresponds to what may be thought, claimed, hoped or feared to be happening.

Monitoring is not, therefore, a very precise term, and may refer to (internally established) information systems as well as to the gathering of data for a one-off study. Information obtained from monitoring can be of many different kinds: referral ratios; the state of caseloads; the provision of specific services; occupancy, discharge or throughput in residential or other facilities; use of professional or administrative time; the continuing identification of needs and demands; changes or patterns in client circumstances. The means by which such information can be obtained are likewise various, and might include the use of existing records in 'raw' or summary form, extraction of specific items from records for noting on a data schedule, the use of diaries or forms completed by practitioners, and many others. If in research monitoring has tended to acquire a somewhat narrower meaning, to refer to a means of generating a flow of information about referrals and cases on a case-by-case basis, this is partly due to its leading use in research by the proponents of the case-review form developed by Goldberg and her colleagues at the National Institute for Social Work (NISW) discussed below. This by no means exhausts its possibilities, however, and the growth of computerized management information systems, performance indicators, quality assurance, and the like has seen monitoring become increasingly central to the business of managing the personal social services, and with the development of the managerial requirements of care in the community this will increase.

Departmental monitoring on this sort of scale, managed centrally and covering in principle all aspects of an agency's functioning, is a subject in its own right; where such systems exist, they will be extremely useful to the researcher. This chapter, however, is concerned with the development and use of monitoring instruments as tools for evaluative research. It is possible to indulge in a perhaps rather sterile argument about whether monitoring itself constitutes research, or whether it is 'merely' the gathering of unfocused information. Although it will be suggested that for monitoring to be of substantive significance for research purposes it needs to be accompanied by one or more specified foci, this is not to deny that almost any information about day-to-day activities will raise all kinds of questions, for managers and others, which are relevant to effectiveness.

This itself is a reflection of the extent to which such information is either not routinely available in social work agencies, or available in notoriously crude form; and also, perhaps, of an inevitable measure of invisibility about the very activity of social work. The need for detailed monitoring will be particularly felt by managers and researchers when a newly developed service or the implementation of new legislation is in question, especially when there are anxieties or myths about possible consequences. Whatever the managerial or conceptual framework in which it is assembled, however, the descriptive information generated by monitoring requires skilled collection and interpretation, and has a wealth of uses, as well as some abuses and other pitfalls.

The case review concept

As noted above, the idea of monitoring social work activities has to some extent developed from, and been appropriated by, a specific approach, that of Goldberg and Warburton (1979). Their interest stemmed from the period when statutory social work itself could be said to be an innovative service, in the early days of the Seebohm-inspired departments. It was then common to remark upon the imprecision of terms for describing the activities of social workers, with researchers echoing the lay questions: But what do social workers actually do? What problems are they tackling? What methods are they pursuing? What are they trying to achieve? Despite a greatly increased specificity of terminology since the early 1970s, of which this book is a reflection, these questions often remain real ones; what distinctive activities, for example, characterize preventive social work or community social work? An important point of departure for the need for monitoring in detail social work activities was the lack of an agreed vocabulary with which to disaggregate what Goldberg and Warburton (1979) called the 'vastness and vagueness of the social work task', a feature of the problems of researching social work discussed elsewhere in this book. One might speculate that, at worst, this lexical deficiency created a vacuum into which terminologies of other disciplines such as medicine, believed to be more clearly defined, could move, with debatable appropriateness and in some respects damaging consequences.

A second starting point was the lack of information available in the early days of social services and social work departments that went beyond gross figures for referral rates and caseload size. Without some means of further breaking down and quantifying the spectrum of problems tackled and tasks undertaken by social workers, managers and researchers alike had only hazy knowledge of the relative composition of caseloads in different settings, the time devoted to different kinds of work, the duration of various categories of case – 'who was doing what, for how long, and with whom' – let alone with what degree of effectiveness.

These were some of the problems that the case review system was designed to tackle. The NISW researchers, working closely in an action-research spirit with practitioners in an area office, had two aims:

1 To develop a model information and review system which would enable fieldworkers and managers to monitor . . . activities in order to discover how professional skills and other social service resources are used in relation to different problems presented and to different aims pursued.
2 To encourage social workers to become more explicit about both means and ends of their activities (Goldberg and Warburton, 1979, p. 21).

The approach followed was the development of a standard form, to be completed by social workers for each client on their caseload (see Fig. 1). The form, which is designed for completion in respect of current cases, covers client problems, type of worker involved, services provided, social worker activities, other agencies involved, and future plans, including an estimate of the likely duration of the case. In each of these areas, there is a listing of a number of pre-coded sub-categories, which are to be ticked by the practitioner, who is also invited to supply some open-ended material.

The form is rather daunting in appearance, and makes certain assumptions about the definability of the components of the social work task. It is also in a format which appears rather mechanical and alien to what is assumed to be the average social worker's concern for the nuances of individual situations. The form was, however, created in close collaboration with the professionals who were to complete it, and underwent a number of trials and modifications, some of them suggested by the participating social workers (including, say the authors interestingly, some 'mechanistic' solutions which they would never have dared to suggest themselves). It seeks to record the maximum possible useful information which the capacity of the staff and space on a single sheet would permit.

The results of its initial use were reported in a series of seminal journal papers and subsequently in a book (Goldberg and Fruin 1976; Goldberg *et al.*, 1977, 1978; Goldberg and Warburton 1979). The findings concerned the application of the system to the work of both intake and long-term teams. In the intake team's work, data were analysed to illuminate the characteristics of initial referrals and the nature of help requested, and how different categories of client were dealt with: by immediate provision of information, referral on, passing to the long-term team, and so on, including the duration of contact. For the long-term teams, the researchers again focused on characteristics of clientele and of service provision, drawing attention, for example, to the preponderance of surveillance-type contact, and to the uneven distribution of social work time and resources between client groups.

For the researchers, the main import of the data seems to have been to raise questions for local policy and organization. Was it appropriate for intake workers to deal with such a broad range of enquiries, and were they adequately equipped to do so? In what proportion of the cases was the model of individual casework the most suitable? Is it right that the long-term cases should be kept open solely for the purpose of legitimating an occasional visit? Was it making the best use of resources to close some cases early, at the intake stage, and leave others open? In other words, the data served to reflect in systematic form what was going on, and to ask how that corresponded to either managerial intentions or to a rational deployment of resources – especially, perhaps, when there were differences in patterns (for example of case closure) between the two long-term teams studied.

There were, however, other functions noted by the researchers. These included the system's uses as a practice tool for individual social workers reviewing their work and in supervision. Workers are quoted as commenting that 'the goal-oriented review questions made them realise that they had avoided painful decisions, prolonging well-intentioned support in face of a reality that pointed to the hopelessness of their endeavour'. Another function is said to be that of a research tool 'for exploring possible associations between aims pursued in different problem situations and methods and skills used ... [for] longitudinal studies of client careers and as a sampling frame for *ad hoc* studies' (Goldberg and Fruin, 1976, p. 16). The extent to which such research uses might be of evaluative force is taken up below.

Examples of case review monitoring in research

Once the focus of a study has been clarified, the monitoring form may be more or less freely adapted for particular purposes. The examples which follow all represent somewhat different uses and versions of a case review instrument.

Black *et al.*'s (1983) comparative study of services provided in social work teams located in contrasting urban and rural locations used an adapted case review form as a means of establishing a comparable database of social work practice in three areas. In this case, data was collected on referral and long-term samples retrospectively, so that what was recorded had already taken place, sometimes months previously. The form was completed, once only for each case, by a variety of means, sometimes by the social worker involved in the case, sometimes by the researcher with the aid of a case file, and occasionally by both in collaboration.

The researchers clearly had reservations about the method, especially in the reliability of categorization decisions required by the form, and its mixture of 'reasonably objective descriptions, professional judgements, or self-validating accounts' (Black *et al.*, 1983, p. 12). While acknowledging that these

Fig. 1 Case Review Form
Source: Goldberg and Warburton (1979) *Ends and Means in Social Work*. Reproduced by permission of Allen & Unwin.

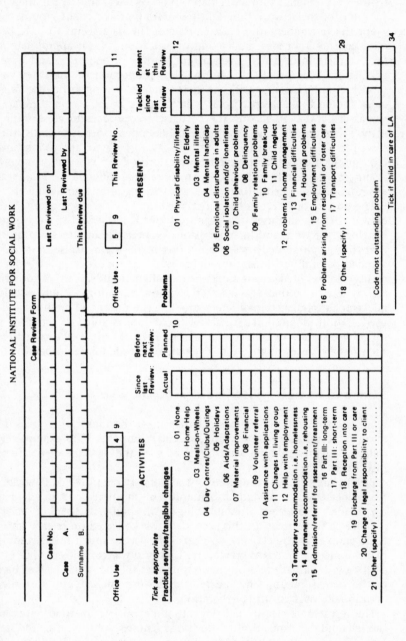

Outside agencies in contact with social worker [31]

01 None
02 General Practitioner
03 Health Visitor/Nurse
04 Psychiatric Hospital/Outpatient Services
05 Other Hospital/Outpatient Services
06 Other AHA (Chiropody, Ambulance, etc.)
07 Child Guidance Clinic
08 Community Homes
09 Educational/School
10 Housing Department
11 DHSS
12 Probation
13 Police
14 Court/Solicitors
15 SSD's in other LA's
16 Voluntary Agencies (clergy, WRVS, etc.)
17 Other (specify) ....

Types of workers [48]

1 None
2 Qualified Social Worker
3 Unqualified Social Worker
4 Social Work Assistant
5 Volunteer
6 Others with specialized knowledge
7 Social Worker plus specialized knowledge

Social worker activities [55]

01 None
02 Exploratory/(re-) assessment activity
03 Information/advice
04 Mobilising resources
05 Advocacy
06 Education in social skills
07 Check up/review visiting
08 Facilitating problem solving/decision making
09 Sustaining/nurturing
10 Group activities

Code most important activity [64]

Estimate no. of contacts [80]

Spare 1   1 2 3 4 5 6 7 8   [80]

Describe present situation/reason for closure ....

Code case status to be [35]

1 Current
2 Dormant
3 Closed
4 Transferred

FUTURE

OPEN CASES What changes are you aiming for? Specify ...... [36]

Code Major Change Area [36]

1 No change intended
2 Major environmental
3 Social/personal environment
4 Social role
5 Behaviour/attitude relationships

Code time before case likely to be closed [37]

1 Up to 3 months
2 6 months
3 1 year
4 2 years
5 3 years
6 More than 3 years

CLOSED CASES Code Reason for Closure [55]

1 Aim achieved
2 Change in circumstances
3 Client died
4 Client withdrew
5 Client left area
6 Contact not achieved
7 Social Worker/Dept. withdraws
8 Referral to other facilities
9 Other (specify) .....

Date of last social work contact [44]
Today's date [50]
Date of next Case Review [56]
Social Worker and Team [60]

Next social worker and team to review (if different) [64]

Spare 2   a b c d e f g h i j k l m n o p   [80]

difficulties may be 'inherent in the process of reducing the intangibles of case-work' to analysable categories, they made selective use only of the case review data, and stressed the advantages of having other sources of data (primarily interviews with practitioners and clients) built into the research design. In fact, the findings of the research were somewhat inconclusive, with practice across the settings, at least as measured by the methods employed, showing more similarities than differences.

Adaptations to the NISW form were in this study minor, and the researchers claim to use it solely for comparative purposes, disavowing any explicit or implicit yardstick of good practice against which to assess results. This, a central dilemma of monitoring, may of course be easier to assert than to achieve.

The monitoring system described by Challis and Chesterman (1985) was part of the larger series of Personal Social Services Research Unit studies of the case management model of service delivery to elderly people. In this instance, the case review form was one of several monitoring instruments, including an 'assessment sheet', which recorded in semi-structured format basic referral details and living and care circumstances; cost forms recording expenditure; and a 'monitoring chart', which represented in visual terms the day-by-day processes of meeting client needs. The case review forms followed procedures somewhat closer to the spirit of the original, but with a perhaps clearer set of research questions. In the context of the case management scheme being studied, which was concerned with the maintenance in the community of frail elderly people, the requirement was for a monitoring instrument which would identify and record what was done for elderly people in the scheme. This included 'the kinds of problems tackled, the activities of social workers, the other agencies involved in the care process, and the resources used' (Challis and Chesterman, 1985, p. 117), and was seen as useful for accountability, and for further clarification of the case management role, still at that point not well understood.

The form included sections for problems and changes achieved, care planning, activities (with categories reflecting the distinctive case management roles), contacts with other agencies, practical services provided as part of a care package, and a 'new' section headed 'resources required but unavailable'. Unlike the previous example, it was completed by the social worker and at several stages of the clients' involvement: after an initial contact, and thereafter at three-monthly intervals and/or on closure, thus giving the opportunity for monitoring changes of circumstances.

The researchers argue that the monitoring system described can provide 'answers to crucial questions which face management and front-line staff concerning any new scheme', such as whether it is reaching its target population. They further suggest that it is well suited to a range of training and self-evaluation uses and for research studies which seek to compare the merits of different organizational structures.

At the Centre, monitoring forms have been used to date in three studies. The first was a study carried out in collaboration with the Social Services Research Group (Scotland) of the impact of the Social Fund on social work departments (1989). The study followed a successful feasibility exercise which was carried out shortly after the implementation of the Social Fund. The study was designed to yield information about those clients of social work departments whose particular circumstances meant they might need to apply for a Social Fund loan or grant and about the help social work departments give these clients. Ten authorities took part and the exercise required close collaboration between representatives of all the participating departments. Enthusiasm and support for the monitoring in part reflected the concern of senior officers about the impact of new social security arrangements and the expertise of specialist welfare rights officers in designing an instrument which was simple enough to allow completion and which would yield information useful for departments which were, at that time, expecting an onslaught of financial problems with which they would not be able to deal. The study added usefully to information about groups of clients with particular financial problems, e.g. sick and disabled and very young people. It also revealed, to the surprise of the participating departments, very little interest or involvement among clients and social workers in applications to the Social Fund. The monitoring, set in the context of other studies of the Social Fund being carried out at the same time (Berthoud, 1991; Stewart and Stewart, 1991; SSRC, 1991), allows some speculation about the reason for this lack of interest, pointing to serious problems in the administration of the Social Fund and to continuing difficulties among social workers in dealing with complicated social security matters.

Smith's (1991a) study of the work of mental health officers throughout Scotland aimed to collect information on each piece of work generated by the Mental Health (Scotland) Act 1984 over a period of 12 months. If collected information relating to both the client – age, living circumstances, diagnosis, case status – and to the particular referral – service, action taken, length of contact, outcome. Involving all local authorities in Scotland, this monitoring study represents a major achievement both organizationally in its collaboration between the Social Services Research Group (Scotland), the Association of Directors of Social Work and the Social Work Research Centre, and in research terms, where it embraced the large majority of appropriate cases over the 12 month period.

The study illustrates a number of characteristic features of monitoring. The form was developed from that used in a similar exercise carried out in England and Wales, thus enabling a measure of comparability between two studies, a potential which the monitoring method shares with other standardized instruments. The choice of self-completion, permitting large numbers, enabled a picture of practice to be developed across an entire region, in relation to a newly instituted set of practices about which even the most basic questions – such as how often mental health officers would be called upon to implement the procedures and how much of their time would be involved – could not be known in advance.

A system of liaison officers in each region was developed, to oil the wheels of form distribution and collection, and to 'nurture' the process of form completion. In addition, considerable attention was given to the process of feedback and dissemination in order to keep the profile of the monitoring high and to reassure individuals that the completion of forms had an end result. This feedback on a regional basis was given after three months and at a national seminar on the six-month data.

As well as throwing light on the questions it set itself concerning the evolution of new practices at a national level, the study demonstrated its usefulness locally in a way which reinforces the claims made for monitoring as a means of enhancing management information. At least one Scottish region decided to continue using a modified version of the instrument after the study had finished in order to maintain the process of service review.

The third Centre study – which is ongoing – takes up the hint of Challis and Chesterman (1985) by using monitoring forms to collect data with which to explore the effects of different patterns of team organization on the delivery of social work services to elderly people. The 'organization and outcomes' study includes 15 social work teams – specialist, generic and community social work – gathering data on samples of referrals by use of a series of forms inspired by the original case review forms. In this study, there are two separate forms completed by social workers: the first immediately after allocation and assessment, and the second after six months and again after a further six months if cases remain open. Cases are thus monitored for a period of up to 12 months.

Together, the forms cover three categories of data. The first records referral details (source and dates of referral and response), together with characteristics of client/carer circumstances and the social worker's assessment of problems, needs and plans. Secondly, the social worker's activities, services provided, and level of contact with the client, carer and other agencies are noted. Finally, the form asks for the worker's assessment of changes in 'problem status' after a period of intervention and the degree to which needs have been met. The forms are thus more ambitious than others that have been cited, in seeking to build in not only process variables but also those which represent the degree of initial need and a range of service- and client-based outcome measures, including workers' judgements as well as services provided, response times and client destination.

When complete, the data will be analysed for differences in both social work procedures and client outcomes between the types of team included in the study. As in Black *et al.*'s (1983) study, there is some triangulation of data collection, with the addition of selected interviews with clients and professionals. In addition to its immediate purposes, the study has the potential advantage of constituting a snapshot of practice in social work with elderly people, which may be usable for comparative purposes in future studies of the major changes that may follow from the introduction of care in the community programmes which are pending at the time of writing.

Some principles and problems

The foregoing examples (and others reported in, for example, Goldberg and Connelly, 1981) raise issues of both the conceptual and practical kinds. Conceptually, there is an apparent gap between the identification of social work problem-definitions, activities and processes, and the assessment of effectiveness. If monitoring in a 'pure' or neutral form is possible, then the information it yields is essentially descriptive. As such, it can certainly raise interesting questions, relevant to effectiveness, after the manner of Goldberg and Warburton (1979), if only in the rather vague form of whether what is found to be happening corresponds to someone's view of what ought to be happening. This is not to deny the exploratory usefulness of monitoring exercises where there is little known about how a particular service operates, which probably was the case in the original case review studies and, partially, in the case management study cited earlier.

The seeming neutrality may, however, be disputed on the grounds that the formulation of categories is itself a kind of structuring which betrays a view of what is significant. Obviously, the design of a monitoring instrument, as with any other, involves a set of decisions about what is to be monitored, whether these decisions flow from specific hypotheses or from certain perspectives on what constitutes 'good', 'bad' or managerially or professionally significant practice.

It is desirable in monitoring studies for these decisions to be made explicit, and not only for the purposes of valid interpretation and general honesty. As has been noted, the development of the case review form as an instrument has its own history, and its originators are associated particularly with the promotion of task-centred casework. This is likely to have had an effect on the way such items as social work activities, goals and problems are categorized, and the typologies originally used (see Fig. 1, pp. 94–5) have recurred in numerous instances of the form in use. There appears to be some danger of the typologies becoming fossilized, so that new perspectives and new categories may not be accommodated; an example, under 'activities', would be the care manager role. A similar issue in a system designed for individual case review is the treatment of client-related activities, other activities not involving client contact and non-conventional activities such as joint working. At this point, it becomes clear that there are differences in the approach to instrument design between monitoring a social work method (such as task-centred casework), monitoring an 'approach' (such as community social work), monitoring the service to a whole client group (elderly people), and so on.

This calls for clarity and explicitness in the purposes of any monitoring exercise. If the aim is to generate material to feed into discussions of effectiveness, this in itself may be sufficient, but if monitoring is built into the design of an effectiveness study, then ideally the additional focus that is required means that one or more of three elements need to be present:

- A comparative dimension, so that different services may be compared (as in Black *et al.*, 1983, and the 'organization and outcomes' work). This may be a comparison between services at the same point in time, or it may be in the form of a before-and-after study. In practice, this requires considerable trouble to ensure that samples are genuinely comparable, which is no easy matter in a case-by-case study, since the processes by which clients become clients and reach a social worker's caseload are both widely various and often rather opaque. The latter point applies particularly in the more informal or patch-based styles of social work, as found, for example, in the variant of community social work studied by Fuller and Petch (1991) in a preliminary phase of the 'organization and outcomes' study.

- A clear statement of service objectives, such as a definition of a target population, specified standards of service, specified patterns of throughput or client destination (as, partially, in Challis and Chesterman, 1985). It has been apparent throughout that this is not always to be assumed in the world of social services, though those varieties of social work which are most likely to be amenable to study through monitoring – those, for example, influenced by the task-centred approach – are also those most likely to have relatively clear objectives.

- Most ambitiously, a building into the monitoring instruments of items that are themselves of evaluative import, such as estimates of problem reduction, as in the 'organization and outcomes' work (see also Goldberg *et al.*, 1985). These, however, are likely to be those variables which are most beset by problems of reliability and validity, and to fall prey to the (self-) criticism of Black *et al.* (1983) of mixing worker judgement with more reliably ascertainable measures. In practice, the choice of monitoring as a method is likely to be settled by the trade-off between the desirable and the feasible with which readers of this book will have become familiar, and by the way a range of practical difficulties can be tackled.

Before turning to these, however, it should be noted briefly that the dearth of management information in the local authority departments, which was one of our points of departure, has over the years been partially remedied. Sharpened by the increasing prominence of value-for-money perspectives, and given further impetus by the 1990 community care legislation which obliges the local authorities to monitor performance in the services they purchase, the growth of thinking about performance indicators and quality assurance has developed its own momentum. As a result, those responsible for designing systems which routinely collect similar data to that sought by evaluative monitors will have considered some of the issues raised above. It is apparent, for example, from the papers edited by Barnes and Miller (1988), that the definition of management information has significantly expanded since the 1970s, and includes such items as statements of objectives, the integration of information on needs and costs with that on more narrowly defined performance, and input from users. There is also a developed awareness of the need for such information to be used productively, and that this involves all levels of a department and will include consultation with users and carers. What this adds up to is an apparent convergence between management information, monitoring and action research, very much of the kind which Goldberg and Warburton (1979) were arguing for as external researchers.

Unfortunately, it is not yet the case that the type of monitoring described in this chapter is unnecessary on the grounds that it is already happening on a routine basis. This may come about in the future, but experience shows that the reality lags some way behind the theory, with fieldworkers frequently claiming to find the picture of their workload that emerges from the departmental computer scarcely recognizable. It is also likely that research needs will often not coincide with those of the management system, though where they do this can be exploited.

What is probable, however, is that the basic grade staff who are the usual source of information in research-based monitoring exercises may already be obliged to complete paperwork that will often bear an irritatingly (from the worker's point of view) incomplete resemblance to monitoring forms. This relates directly to the first practical consideration that the researcher needs to weigh: the prospects of getting the forms completed at all. Assuming that in most cases the form will be for self-completion, it can be an intrusive and burdensome method of assembling data, and the risk is that social workers will decline to cooperate, or worse, will agree and then fail to complete forms fully or with care.

There are a number of things the researcher can do to guard against these dangers; if many of them apply to other forms of cooperation being sought, they are particularly important in monitoring. The exercise must not only be sold convincingly to senior managers, but also to social workers, and perhaps most of all to team leaders (or some other nominated liaison persons) whose active support is likely to be vital in maintaining commitment, ensuring that forms are distributed and collected, and perhaps doing some preliminary quality control. The motivation of practitioners and managers is likely to be increased if the service is an innovation in which they have a vital professional interest, or if the exercise can be seen as one which will give attention to neglected areas or low-priority groups, such as clients with mental health problems.

The form itself, it goes without saying, must be as user-friendly as possible, which involves careful piloting, preferably practitioner-based and -influenced. It is helpful if an estimate can be given of the time the forms take to complete, and guidance given as to whether they need the worker to check records or can rely on memory; this should ideally be discussed at the negotiating stage so that time may be programmed by managers. (The longer of the two 'organization and outcome' forms is said to take about ten minutes.) The researcher will be tempted to supply elaborate notes of guidance, but this must be to some extent held in check lest they make the form appear too forbidding or be themselves too lengthy to keep conveniently to hand.

An important consideration is the timing of form completion. In general, undue reliance on the memory of participants is to be avoided, and in cases where forms are to be filled in more than once, the researcher will often wish to argue for relatively short intervals. The workers, on the other hand, will probably wish to minimize the number of forms, and a compromise may have to be reached. An advantage in practice may be that the forms will lend themselves to use in routine departmental procedures, such as regular reviews or supervision, in which case there is the opportunity for gearing the timing to these cycles.

One issue on which practitioners will need to be satisfied is that of confidentiality, since it may be convenient for administrative reasons for a client's name to appear. One solution to this is the use of self-copying carbons on which the client's name is blanked out on the copy; the carbon can be returned to the researcher while the worker keeps the top copy, a device which has the additional (if two-edged) advantage of allowing the worker to refer back to an earlier form when completing a subsequent one.

The opportunity for the worker to refer back is two-edged because, as well as facilitating completion, it may encourage an undue concern for consistency of response, especially where it is a question of providing data on the outcome of plans or objectives previously specified. This is a specific example of the general problem of how the act of completing the forms might itself influence practice. The researcher might be quite pleased to hear social workers say that filling in the form makes them think more clearly about a case, but at the same time feel some concern about the possibility of a Hawthorn effect. And, conversely, if (as one practitioner in the 'organization and outcomes' study remarked semi-seriously) social workers are reluctant to open doubtful cases because they would have to complete the form if they did, then the researcher would get really worried!

Finally, it is particularly important for the researcher to keep in touch with participants by telephone and visits during what might be a lengthy period of data collection, and to give interim and final feedback as soon as conveniently possible. This is usually something that the researchers will anyway be keen to do, since in a research mode where there is inevitable anxiety about the quality of the data, they will need to reassure themselves regularly that forms are being completed and that commitment is being maintained. It is often suggested that monitoring involves a less intensive research effort than other forms of data collection, even allowing for the intensive negotiation involved in setting up a system. Though there is some truth in this, it should not be overestimated. As well as maintaining contact with the field, the researcher will be constantly concerned with checking forms and numbers as they come in, cleaning the data (which sometimes will involve making contact with workers or liaison people), and possibly in collecting other data by other methods, which, it has been suggested, is often desirable in a monitoring exercise.

These may be thought to represent a daunting set of obstacles to overcome, pragmatic compromises to be struck, or disadvantages to bear in mind. Certainly the limitations of the types of data that can be gathered, akin to those imposed by a written questionnaire but if anything more restrictive because of the lack of space on the average form, make it inappropriate for certain kinds of research use. In fact, the Social Work Research Centre's experiences of monitoring have been happier than might be expected, though there is a certain tendency, to be guarded against, for the researcher to want to believe that the system is working once it has been set up, and consequently to give less heed than is warranted to worrying questions of data quality.

Apart from being fairly obviously best suited to collecting relatively unproblematic service data of the type that practitioners find easiest and least threatening to provide, perhaps the most important consideration in the decision to use a monitoring strategy is that of numbers. The larger the case sample or dataset that any given study is judged on theoretical grounds to require, the less feasible it is for researchers to adopt a direct means of collecting data, and the more attractive will it be to arrange for data to be supplied by practitioners.

9

STUDYING COST-EFFECTIVENESS

We haven't the money, so we've got to think.
                    Lord Rutherford, 1871–1937

In the context of fiscal restraint on welfare budgets and scarcity of social work resources, policy makers and managers must have regard to the economic implications of service provision. The emphasis on efficiency and value for money (VFM) as exemplified by the work of the Audit Commission for England and Wales and the introduction in the probation service of resource management information systems (RMIS: see, e.g. Humphrey, 1991) are evidence of this comparatively recent trend, which none the less seems likely to endure for the foreseeable future.

To a greater extent than before, there is an expectation that researchers engaged in the evaluation of social work services will, in addition, give due regard to the issue of service costs. From the outset, the Social Work Research Centre has acknowledged that it should include, where appropriate, an analysis of the costs of services in studies of effectiveness that it undertakes. Such an approach reflects not only economic and political realities (where, for example, research briefs from central government increasingly stress the need for the integration of information on effectiveness and costs), but also an awareness of the importance for social work managers of the ability to make reasoned decisions about resource allocation and service development in the context of knowledge about both the relative effectiveness of different models of service provision and the economic implications of choices that are made.

The aim of the present chapter is to highlight some of the general principles associated with the costing of social work services and to illustrate with reference to our own and other work how carefully costed studies can, when integrated with information about the effectiveness of services, provide a clearer understanding of the implications of different choices concerning the development and delivery of social work services. First, however, the case for incorporating economic analyses in the evaluation of social work effectiveness, and hence the Centre's rationale for including such analyses in several of its studies, will be considered.

The case for costs

The work of the Audit Commission (previously the Audit Inspectorate) has been extremely influential in focusing attention on the need for social work managers to take account of the relative costs of the services that they provide. The financial analyses conducted by the Audit Commission in the social work field have included the costs of providing residential and community care for the elderly (1985) and the costs of providing care in the community for vulnerable groups (1986, 1989a). Most recently, the work of the probation service in England and Wales has been subject to such a value-for-money review (Audit Commission, 1989b).

The approach adopted by the Audit Commission has been typically comparative in nature: the patterns of service provision within a number of local authorities are contrasted and compared, variations in costs across different authorities are identified, and recommendations are made as to how service provision might be best organized in order that improved efficiency in the use of resources and increased value for money might be achieved.

The costing of social work and other public services is typically greeted with a degree of scepticism, being viewed as the almost inevitable precursor and justification of cost-cutting exercises. The strength of economic argument may outweigh other factors when decisions about service provision are made. Sometimes, the significance of these other factors (such as, for example, quality of service) is down-played. In other instances, where they are compatible with the achievement of cost-driven objectives, their significance may be stressed. This is evidenced, for example, in the development of care in the community for a range of vulnerable client groups and in the development of community-based alternatives to imprisonment.

Researchers, too, may experience some unease when confronting the issue of service costs in evaluative research. This discomfort may stem from concerns that their motives will be viewed with suspicion and their findings misused. Knapp (1984), for example, introduces the subject matter of his book *The Economics of Social Care* in a slightly defensive though not apologetic tone:

> This is not a book inspired by missionary zeal, nor a collection of celestial truths passed down heavenly hot lines. Nor is it one which rides roughshod over humanitarian concerns, nor one which places the minimisation of costs over the meeting of need ... It is a book about economic analysis and its application in the area of social care. It is about scarcity, choice, resource allocation, effectiveness, efficiency and equity (Knapp, 1984, p. 1).

The work of the Audit Commission (and Audit Inspectorate) has been criticized on several grounds (see, e.g. Miller, 1984), but the most notable omission perhaps is the scant attention typically paid to the issue of service effectiveness. In none of the Audit Inspectorate reports (e.g. Audit Inspectorate, 1983a,b) has there been a systematic attempt to juxtapose the costs of the services examined with information regarding their relative effectiveness and to examine the relationship between variations in costs and the quality and effectiveness of the services provided. Instead, cost variations are explained as a function of the varied levels and patterns of provision, regardless of how effective different types or amounts of services might be.

The approach adopted by Knapp and his colleagues at the Personal Social Services Research Unit (PSSRU), on the other hand, is characterized by attention to both the relative costs of services or activities and their relative effectiveness. Such attention to effectiveness is also evident in the work of the Audit Commission, especially in relation to care in the community (1986) and the provision of services to people with a mental handicap (1989a). These analyses and the costing studies conducted by the PSSRU provide more comprehensive data on which to base informed decisions about the allocation of finite social work resources. The value of linking both economic and effectiveness data can be illustrated with reference to a hypothetical example.

Let us suppose that social work managers in areas X, Y and Z, faced with limited budgets, wish to organize the delivery of services by their area teams in such a way as to maximize their effectiveness. The manager in area X knows that the delivery of services by generic social workers is less costly than the delivery of similar services by specialists in generic teams and that both are cheaper options than the creation of specialist teams. In the absence of information about the relative effectiveness (however defined) of the different organizational arrangements, manager X opts for a wholly generic model of service delivery.

The manager in area Y, on the other hand, has no idea what the cost implications of the optional models of service delivery are. He or she does know, though, that the effectiveness of service delivery is likely to be maximized by the creation of specialist teams, while the organization of service delivery along generic lines would be least effective and plumps, therefore, for the former organizational arrangement.

Manager Z has both costed the implications of the three models of service delivery and has commissioned an evaluation which assessed their relative effectiveness. He or she is aware that a fully generic arrangement would be the least costly option, but would also be the least effective. The creation of specialist teams, however, while attractive in effectiveness terms, would be beyond the scope of the available budget. Consequently, manager Z opts for the development of generic teams comprised of individual specialists and in doing so maximizes the potential effectiveness of service delivery within the resources available.

The above example is, of course, grossly oversimplified (and totally hypothetical), but it does serve to illustrate the danger of basing decisions about the development of services and resource allocation on cost or effectiveness data alone. Although compromises will often be necessary, as in the scenario above, in many instances the implications of cost-effectiveness studies will be relatively clear. If, for example, the three models of service delivery were found to be equally effective but were associated with varying costs, then all else being equal the least costly alternative should be the preferred option. If, conversely, the different models were known to have identical cost implications but were found to be differentially effective (according to predetermined criteria whose relative importance had been taken into account), then common sense would dictate that the most effective option be pursued.

What if, as in the example above, the alternatives under consideration are both differentially costly and differentially effective? If the least costly option is also the most effective, then there is little difficulty: it would be the obvious choice. But such neat and convenient scenarios are rarely encountered. If the most effective alternative is also the most costly, or if there is no clear relationship between effectiveness and costs, then the task for policy makers or service managers is to weigh up the anticipated costs and benefits of pursuing different courses of action and reach some informed decision based on the relative importance attached to different outcomes. There is no particular mystique involved in cost-effective analyses. Cost-effectiveness is little more than the juxtaposing of information about service effectiveness and associated costs. And where choices are to made between a range of options, this juxtaposition will greatly facilitate informed policy making and resource management.

At this point, it is appropriate to highlight the distinction between cost-effectiveness and cost-benefit analysis. Sometimes, the two terms are used interchangeably, and inappropriately so. Unlike in a cost-benefit analysis, in the assessment of cost-effectiveness monetary values are not attached to the outputs (or outcomes) of services. Thus, according to Challis *et al.* (1984, pp. 111–12), cost-effectiveness analyses:

> . . . cannot . . . be used to say whether or not the benefits of a project or procedure actually outweigh the costs. What it can do is ensure that a full range of costs is estimated and that measures (but not values) are sought for all relevant dimensions of output. The information thus gathered can then be presented in such a way as to make plain the efficiency and distributional implications of the alternatives under consideration and allow policy makers to make the necessary trade-offs.

The usefulness of cost-effectiveness analyses is entirely dependent, of course, on the accuracy and reliability of the component cost and effectiveness data upon which decisions are based. The various methodological challenges which may be encountered in the evaluation of social work effectiveness have formed the primary focus of the present volume. The costing of services is similarly dependent upon clarity of definition and of objectives and careful consideration is required to ensure that account is taken of each of the diverse factors that might have some bearing upon service costs. Cost-effectiveness analysis is in its relative infancy and certain assumptions will have to be made in estimating the costs of social work or other public services. While some costs may be little influenced by the assumptions made, others may be highly sensitive to these assumptions. By examining the effects on predicted costs (and hence upon cost-effectiveness) of varying the assumptions upon which they are based, the sensitivity of the cost-effectiveness analysis to these assumptions can be assessed.

Although the demystification and increased accessibility of cost-effectiveness evaluation is a central objective of this chapter, it is also necessary to emphasize that the costing of social work and other welfare services should not be undertaken lightly. Where they can be drawn upon, the skills and knowledge of economists and accountants will prove invaluable in obtaining comprehensive and accurate service costs and in the design of the full cost-effectiveness study. Inadequate costings of services can at best be misleading and at worst can result in inappropriate choices being made among a range of service options. For this reason we now turn, before providing practical illustrations of cost-effectiveness studies, to a consideration of the principles that underlie comprehensive and accurate economic analyses of social work services which require the inclusion of all costs (service and other) of caring for particular groups.

Principles of cost analysis

Here the intention is to do little more than introduce the main principles involved in the costing of welfare services and to define some of the various concepts and terms that are referred to in the economic analysis of public services. A more detailed discussion of relevant issues and techniques can be found in Knapp (1984). A forthcoming PSSRU publication (to be edited by Anne Netten and Jeni Beecham) will explore and illustrate the practical application of cost-effectiveness analyses.

The costing of social work services is, as already indicated, appropriate only when decisions have to be made between a range of service options. Is, for example, residential care for the elderly more cost-effective than various packages of community care for a given population? Is service delivery organized along generic lines more cost-effective than that provided by teams of specialists? Are intensive probation programmes more cost-effective than the custodial sentences they are intended to replace?

The following six stages have been identified by Knapp (1984) and by Challis *et al.* (1984) as being relevant to a cost-effectiveness analysis:

1 Separate or define the alternatives to be analysed.
2 List the likely costs and effects (or outputs).
3 Measure the costs and effects.
4 Compare the costs and effects.
5 Qualify or revise that decision in the light of risk, uncertainty and sensitivity.
6 Examine the distributional implications of the alternatives.

With this framework in mind, the following principles for costing welfare or other public services have been outlined by Knapp (1991) and by Knapp *et al.* (1989, 1992). By considering each principle in turn, the potential pitfalls in costing social work services can be illustrated.

1 Costs should be comprehensively measured across the full range of agencies and individuals affected by policy or practice decisions

Frequently, services are costed without due regard to their full costs to society. Often, costs which fall outwith the budgets of social work or probation departments are overlooked, as are the costs to clients, their carers and other family members. In costing services, it is necessary to include both *direct costs*, which fall upon immediate service providers, and *indirect costs*, which are hidden costs or costs to other agencies. The total cost of supporting elderly people in the community, for example, will include the costs to social services or social work departments of providing domiciliary services, social work assessment and support. It will also be appropriate to include where relevant the financial and emotional costs to carers of looking after an elderly dependant and the costs of services provided by other health and welfare agencies.

If costings are to be comprehensive, account should also be taken of the concept of *opportunity costs*. The opportunity costs of a service can be defined as the benefits foregone by providing that service rather than another alternative service. Cost is thus expressed in terms of the value of alternatives or opportunities that have been missed. The opportunity cost to a department of allocating resources to the development of a day centre for the elderly rather than to the provision of a day nursery for disadvantaged children could be the benefits that would have accrued had the latter service been provided. In practice, however, the opportunity costs of providing particular social work services are often far from clear and, in the absence of a more reliable estimate, the observed service costs are usually believed to suffice.

The importance of measuring costs comprehensively can be illustrated by a specific example. The Home Office suggested that in 1986–87, the average cost of supervising an offender on a community service order was £740 (Home Office, 1989), which appears to compare favourably with a weekly imprisonment cost in 1987–88 of £275 (Home Office, 1988). When Knapp *et al.* (1989, 1992) compared the direct costs to schemes of community service orders in Scotland with the direct costs of alternative prison sentences they, too found that community service (at £631 for an average order) was significantly cheaper than custody (£2693 for an average alternative sentence). When the indirect costs of both options (including, for example, court and social work resources) were taken into account, however, a different picture emerged. Thus while community service with an average cost of £1020 per order was still cheaper than imprisonment (which when indirect costs of both options were taken into account averaged £2268), it was not as cheap as previous estimates tended to suggest.

Comparative costings of intensive probation supervision programmes and custodial sentences which purportedly demonstrate substantial cost savings in favour of the former have similarly been subject to criticism (Tonry, 1990; United States General Accounting Office, 1990). Tonry (1990), for example, has argued that failure to take into account the actual rate at which such programmes do indeed divert offenders from prison sentences and the rate at which offenders are incarcerated following the commission of further offences or other breaches of programme requirements, substantially underestimates the costs of intensive supervision relative to imprisonment.

The comparative costing of community service and custody undertaken by Knapp *et al.* (1989, 1992) is based upon an assumed breach rate of 10 per cent. A direct comparison of the costs of community service orders and custodial sentences also assumes, however, that the former has been imposed in lieu of imprisonment. Thus while community service is a less costly option for the 45 per cent of offenders who have been diverted from custody by this measure (McIvor, 1990a), it is a relatively expensive option for the small majority who received their community service orders in place of fines.

The costings of psychiatric provision (Knapp *et al.*, 1990a; Beecham *et al.*, 1991) have similarly taken into account the full range of services that is used by those who have moved to the community. The package of services specific to each client is determined, itemizing elements of accommodation, of day care, of General Practitioner, nursing and social work services and of other professional services such as chiropody or occupational therapists. In addition, individuals' drug costs and income support costs are included.

2 Variations in cost from one part of the country to another or between different individuals served should be noted, examined and 'explained'

Often, when information about the costs of services is provided, it has been unhelpfully aggregated. To quote a single cost for a community service order, for instance, disguises wide differences in the costs of orders between schemes and prevents the identification of operational variables which have an influence upon costs. Community service schemes differ procedurally in various ways. By disaggregating the costs of community service into its component activities and examining the way in which the costs of these component activities vary across schemes, it is possible to explain at least some of the cost variations observed. Knapp *et al.* (1989, 1992) found, for example, that differing hourly costs of supervising offenders on community service orders could be attributed at least partly to the different enforcement practices (and, consequently, average levels of absences per offender) across schemes and to the proportionate use of team and agency placements.

Knapp and Fenyo (1988) have similarly shown how prison costs are influenced by a range of factors such as the size of the inmate population, occupancy rates, security category of inmates, sentence length and number of previous offences per inmate. Each of the relevant cost-influencing factors was taken into consideration by Knapp *et al.* (1989, 1992) to obtain an appropriate costing for the prison sentences that community service was assumed to have replaced.

The characteristics of clients or service users may also have some bearing upon the costs of service provision. In the above example, for instance, prison costs tend to be higher where the prison population is comprised of inmates with higher security classifications and community service orders are likely to be more costly if schemes accept substantial proportions of offenders whose characteristics suggest that they have a high likelihood of breach. All other factors being equal, we might also expect the costs of residential care to be related directly to the dependency levels of elderly people, or the costs of providing supported accommodation for people with mental health problems to be related in some systematic way to their need for support.

Variations in costs between similar facilities or services or between different social work teams offering comparable services clearly warrant explanation.

Do differences in costs reflect characteristics of the client population served, the quality of care provided or the effectiveness of services offered? If they do not, how might the provision of services be modified to minimize their costs, and hence maximize their cost-effectiveness? The work of Knapp and his colleagues (1990a) on the reprovision arrangements from Claybury and Friern looks in detail at potential explanations for the observed variations in cost. For the first 136 leavers, they demonstrated that baseline characteristics alone (gender, age, length of stay, Social Behaviour Schedule score, negative symptoms) explained 38 per cent of the cost variation. Thus, for example, men cost more than women, younger people more than older people and hospital stays over ten years lead to an increase in costs. Males with a larger number of named social contacts and both males and females with fewer negative symptoms cost less. Subsequent work on the TAPS project has revealed the influence both of accommodation type and of provider. Provisions developed by the district health authority, for example, are more costly than those of other agencies.

A comprehensive cost-effectiveness analysis will look beyond the immediate context of the evaluation by providing information about the wider implications of service development. What are the implications, for example, of developing similar projects or services in other parts of the country or extending the availability of a particular service to a wider range of potential users within its existing locality?

3 Comparisons between services, areas of the country, agencies or individuals should be made on a like-with-like basis

Sensible and obvious as this principle may seem, it too is often open to abuse. To return once again to the community service example, the Home Office costings of an average order are frequently contrasted with the costs of other sentences, such as imprisonment, without any account having been taken of the known differences between groups of offenders sentenced to each disposal. Offenders on community service are not directly comparable with offenders serving an 'average prison sentence'. The former tend to be younger than the average inmate, to have fewer previous convictions and to have committed less serious offences. They would be expected to receive shorter custodial sentences and, if sentenced, would likely be assigned a lower security category: the fact that they received community service suggests that they could be trusted in open conditions. The relevant alternative prison costs for offenders on community service will, then, be somewhat lower than the average prison costs which are usually quoted in the literature.

Care is similarly required when comparing different examples of the same service, within or across agencies. It is important to ensure consistency of inclusion and exclusion with respect to which items are included in the calculation of service costs. This is equally applicable in the costing of different services. Here it is also necessary to avoid double-counting: if, for example, the living costs of prisoners have been included as savings in the estimated cost of a custodial sentence, it is unnecessary to include them in the costing of community service. Similarly, inclusion of the costs to carers as a saving in the costing of residential care means that this factor should not be included when estimating the comparative costs of care in the community.

At this juncture, it is appropriate to consider the' issue of *average* and *marginal* costs. The average cost of a service is the total cost of that service divided by the number of individuals for whom it is provided. The marginal cost, on the other hand, is the cost of providing a service to one extra individual. Marginal costs may provide a more accurate representation of the actual costs of service provision and may in certain circumstances equal average costs. As Knapp (1984) acknowledges, though, marginal costs are not directly observable and may be difficult or impossible to compute from available information about total and average costs.

For this reason, economic analyses of the costs of social work services are often based upon average costs. This was the case, for example, in Knapp *et al.*'s (1989, 1992) costing of community service and custody. It is clear, though, that while average costs were employed for comparative purposes, the actual savings likely to accrue from the diversion of offenders from custodial sentences would be less than the sum of the average prison costs for these offenders. A large proportion of prison costs are fixed costs, which will change only if there are large changes in the inmate population. As Tonry (1990, p. 180) has indicated:

> The reality is that one more prisoner costs the state only marginal costs – a bit of food, some disposable supplies, some record keeping. Only when the numbers of people diverted from prison by a new program permit the closing of all or a major part of an institution or the cancellation of construction plans will there be substantial savings.

In applied economics, a distinction tends to be drawn between short-run and long-run marginal costs. Selection between these two mechanisms will depend on the particular policy options which are under scrutiny; though generally for public and social policy purposes, long-run costs are preferable. If the focus of concern is the cost of community care in relation to the closure of a hospital base, it is the long-run marginal costs which should be identified. Early leavers may be able to be slotted into existing services, but in the longer term new facilities will have to be provided for the larger group of discharges diverted from hospital care. Allowance for these capital costs must therefore be included in order that community care costs are not underestimated. Long-run marginal costing is the model adopted by the Friern and Claybury team (Knapp *et al.*, 1990a) with capital costs set at their long-term replacement values.

In the Centre's study of the discharge of a group of patients from the Royal Edinburgh Hospital, it is the short-run marginal costs that are being applied. This is deemed more appropriate when the focus of the comparison is the costs incurred in caring for that group in the community *vis-à-vis* the immediate savings made by the hospital when there is no plan for the closure of units or beds and where only small numbers of people are moving out. In this context, there will not necessarily be immediate additional costs to the GP service, whereas occupancy of a day-centre place is more likely to be a perceptible cost. For any service utilization in the community, the level of spare capacity in each service has to be considered to identify where there are positive marginal costs.

4 Costings should preferably be integrated with findings on outcomes or effectiveness

Had the costing of community service and its alternatives been based upon marginal rather than average costs, community service might have ceased to be such a comparatively inexpensive option and may, indeed, have been found to be as expensive as or more expensive than custody. If this were the case, then on cost grounds alone, there would appear to be little justification for encouraging the increased use of community service by the courts. Were the relative effectiveness of the two penal options to be taken into consideration, however, then so long as community service was not found to be vastly more expensive than imprisonment (and this seems highly unlikely), it would be preferable as the more cost-effective sanction. There is no reason to suggest that community service is any less effective in preventing further offending than imprisonment (Pease *et al.*, 1977), but it does produce considerable benefits to the community and to the offenders themselves (McIvor, 1990b, 1991a).

Another illustration can be drawn from the cost-effectiveness analysis conducted by Knapp *et al.* (1989, 1992). In this study, breached community service orders were shown to be substantially more expensive than successfully completed orders as a result of the staff time involved in the follow-up of absences and the processing of the breach, and the costs associated with subsequent court appearances and alternative sentences. The provision by community service staff of advice and support to offenders who experienced family or personal problems would increase the supervision costs and hence the average cost per order. But if such support could enable some offenders who might not otherwise do so to complete their orders without recourse to revocation and breach (McIvor, 1991b, 1992b), then the additional costs could be offset by savings resulting from the reduced necessity of returning offenders to court as a result of failure or inability to comply with the requirements.

The relationship between outcomes and costs in the DoH Care in the Community demonstration projects (Knapp *et al.*, 1990b, 1991) varies with client group. For people with mental health problems, higher costs were associated with greater achievements in the promotion of client well-being. For individuals with learning difficulties, higher expenditure appeared to produce favourable outcomes in terms of maladaptive behaviour but no difference in skill levels.

Judgements about service provision or development based on cost information alone are likely to be misguided. Only when information about the relative costs of services and their relative effectiveness can be considered in tandem will optimal decision making result. The outcomes of intervention may be service-based (where, for example, the aim of the study is to compare the cost-effectiveness of different approaches in providing a given level of service to clients) or client-based (where cost-effectiveness is examined in relation to desired or expected changes in clients' well-being, functioning or quality of life). Effectiveness should also ideally be defined in relation to all individuals, such as carers or other family members, likely to be affected by decisions concerning the allocation and deployment of social work resources and whose assumptions about the value of different outcomes may differ from those held by social work managers or service providers.

Correlational techniques may be applied to examine the relationship between costs and effectiveness. A significant positive correlation would indicate a direct association between increasing costs and increasing service effectiveness. A lack of correlation suggests the absence of a clear relationship between effectiveness and costs. In such instances, regression analysis can be applied to establish whether the relationship between costs and effectiveness varies as a function of differences in client characteristics and features (such as quality and quantity) of the services provided (see, e.g. Beecham *et al.*, 1991).

In utilizing the cost and effectiveness data, it is incumbent on those responsible for policy decisions and service development to decide whether higher costs associated with a particular option are outweighed by its greater effectiveness. As well as 'supplying the missing valuations' (Knapp, 1984, p. 136), the policy maker should take into account the longer-term implications of the existing options; whether, for example, a model of service delivery which is less cost-effective at present will become more cost-effective over time. This type of consideration may be particularly relevant when newly developed or innovative services are being evaluated.

Studies of cost-effectiveness

The application of cost-effectiveness analysis to the field of social work can be best illustrated by the provision of practical examples. In each of the following studies, attempts have been made to integrate the costing of services with information regarding their effectiveness, and to highlight the implications for policy and practice. The examples have been selected to reflect a variety of approaches to the assessment of cost-effectiveness, to illustrate how such analyses can be applied across a range of social work services and to indicate some of the problems or pitfalls.

1 Community service by offenders

An important objective of the Centre's evaluation of community service schemes in Scotland was to examine the extent to which community service was being used by the courts as an alternative to custody and to examine the relative cost-effectiveness of community service orders and the prison sentences they replaced. The manner in which these alternative options were costed and the conclusions drawn have been discussed in some detail in the previous section. The focus here will therefore be upon that aspect of the evaluation which sought to establish whether differences in practice between schemes had some bearing upon the completion rates achieved and the levels of unacceptable absences sustained by offenders during their orders. The associated costing of schemes was used to determine whether different approaches to practice were differentially costly and to examine the relationship between cost variations and effectiveness across a range of procedures such as the assessment of offenders' suitability for an order, the matching of offenders to placements, the supervision of orders and the procedures instituted in the event of breach (Knapp *et al.*, 1989, 1992).

Community service organizers indicated how much of their time was spent on each of the component activities outlined above and this information, combined with a range of service-based measures such as number of assessments undertaken, enabled the costs of each component to be calculated for each scheme. By disaggregating the costs of orders in this way, it was possible to highlight cost-influencing factors and to explain differences in costs between schemes as a function of practice, staffing levels, and so on. The linking of this data with knowledge about the relative effectiveness of different approaches to practice, enabled informed recommendations to be made regarding the most efficient use of community service resources and indicated the implications for both costs and effectiveness of potential changes in policy and practice.

For instance, the costs of some activities (such as assessment and matching to placement) are fixed, whereas others (such as supervision costs) vary according to the length of order. It was thus possible to provide separate costings for short (40-hour), average and long (240-hour) orders per scheme and to examine the cost-effectiveness implications of, say, increasing the maximum or minimum hours which could be ordered by the courts. The evaluation had suggested that longer orders were no more likely than shorter orders to result in breach, so long as the offenders were able to complete their orders within a reasonable period of time. But although longer orders were no less likely to be completed than shorter orders, they were found to be proportionately less costly than orders comprising smaller numbers of hours. Longer orders were more costly overall than shorter orders, but with longer orders the fixed costs of assessment and matching were spread over a greater number of hours, resulting in a lower total cost per hour. On this basis, it was possible to conclude that longer orders were more cost-effective than shorter orders and that a reduction in the minimum number of hours which could be ordered would lead to an overall reduction in the cost-effectiveness of community service schemes. The cost-effectiveness of community service would, conversely, be increased were the courts able to impose orders of more than 240 hours, so long as these orders could still be completed within a reasonable period from the order being imposed.

2 Intermediate treatment

The cost analysis of intermediate treatment (IT) conducted by Martin Knapp and Eileen Robertson at the PSSRU (Knapp and Robertson, 1986; Robertson *et al.*, 1986; Robertson and Knapp, 1987) addressed similar issues to their study of Scottish community service schemes, in that it was concerned with establishing whether IT was more cost-effective than its alternatives. The methodology employed was, however, somewhat different. Costings were obtained for individual packages of IT and compared with the costs of the most likely alternative sentences or services: community home with education, community home, supervision order and detention centre:

> Youngsters receiving IT during the year ending 31 March 1985 were allocated to one of four groups according to what would have been the most likely alternative for each of them. A 'representative' youngster was selected from each group, and both the IT 'package' and the alternative package were costed (Roberston and Knapp, 1987, p. 136).

The analysis revealed that while IT was less costly than residential care or detention centre training, it was more expensive than a supervision order. On the assumption that IT was at least no less effective than the other options it could replace, the researchers supported the increased use of intensive IT as an alternative to care and custody, but cautioned against the use of this measure instead of non-residential supervision. The latter usage would be both less cost-effective and would place young people at risk of being pushed further up the sentencing tariff than was justified by their offence (Knapp and Robertson, 1986; Robertson and Knapp, 1987).

Clearly, though, the conclusions and policy implications that flow from the costing of services are more persuasive (and meaningful) if the costs are related to actual effectiveness data, rather than to assumptions, however reasonable, about the relative effectiveness of different responses to offending by young people. The costing of IT and its alternatives was conducted as part of a broader evaluation of IT in England and Wales. The first phase of this research – a national survey of intermediate treatment policy and provision – is reported in Bottoms *et al.* (1990). The second phase – which includes an examination of the impact of IT on young people in four local authorities – remains unpublished at the time of writing.

3 Services for people with mental health problems

The costing of mental health services is in its infancy. In their review of the state of the art in 1988, O'Donnell *et al.* (1989, p. 19) conclude that 'there is little evidence on the efficiency of alternative programmes of mental health care'. Indeed, they go so far as to characterize the traditional reliance in choosing between services on received wisdom and custom as both 'unscientific and unethical'. At that date, only seven studies in the UK which had addressed the costs and effects of alternative forms of mental health care could be cited.

The Centre's unsuccessful attempt to include a costing component in the study of supported accommodation illustrates a potential pitfall of collaborative ventures between social work researchers and economists. Here, the different perspective of the economists and their lack of detailed knowledge of the subject matter resulted in the inappropriate costing of the supported accommodation provisions. This is potentially a general problem for such studies and points to the need for considerable efforts to clarify and agree the terms of reference and objectives of the evaluation.

The approach to costing which was adopted took as a key variable the variation in individual contact between client and staff over time. Data were collected from three projects, which for three days of each of 12 months recorded the differing patterns of contact between individual residents and staff members. Some limited details were also collected of the number of contacts with outside services. The length of such contacts was not, however, recorded; moreover, contacts for any week were assumed typical for each week of that month.

The economists' particular interest in the variation in individual contact over time centred on two main issues. One suggested that initially high levels of support may reduce over time and, therefore, in cost terms the first months after discharge should not be regarded as long-term (see, e.g. Buckingham and Ludbrook, 1989). The second argued that staffing may have to adjust to peak rather than average demand.

Although the Centre was initially content to accord with the logic of this approach, in the light of broader experience the argument became less convincing. Staffing is the least flexible and most costly component of revenue costs. However, in the nature of the projects under study, there need not necessarily be a direct relationship between the needs of the individual and the length of time that is spent in staff contact. Some may be merely more sociable or more voluble. Much more variable, and of more significance in terms of marginal costs, are the resources which individuals consume outside the projects. Particularly when there is a debate about the relative costs of hospital-based and community-based care, detailed attention must be paid to the additional components of community support that individuals consume outwith the accommodation.

This latter approach has been adopted in the Centre study of the discharge of long-term patients from the Royal Edinburgh Hospital. Collaboration here has been with the Centre for Health Economics at the University of York. Details of service utilization have been obtained from respondents at 1 month after discharge, 4–5 months' post-discharge and at the end of the 12-month follow-up period. Where this data could not be obtained from clients, an alternative source was approached, either the service provider or a friend or relative. As detailed above, the principles of short-run marginal costing are being followed, the primary emphasis being the immediate costs within the community of caring for this group.

This approach differs in practice from the long-term marginal costing adopted by Knapp and colleagues at the PSSRU in their studies both of the DoH Care in the Community Demonstration Projects (Knapp *et al.*, 1990b, 1991) and of the reprovision from Claybury and Friern hospitals (the TAPS project: Knapp *et al.*, 1990a), though the same underlying principles apply. Eight of the demonstration projects were for those with mental health problems and for each different type of placement the relative cost contributions of the different elements of community care were assembled (similar comparisons are available for the other client groups). In all instances, from residential home to supported lodgings, the community cost is found to be lower than the cost in hospital. Accommodation and associated staff support costs account for the largest proportion of costs, followed by the costs attributable to day-activity services. The care packages for individuals who were more dependent on staff and other support for daily living activities were shown to be more costly. Additionally, all other things being equal, higher costs were shown to be associated with a higher level of client well-being.

The likelihood of increasing costs for those of greater dependency discharged at a later date is being explored in the TAPS project. Knapp *et al.* (1990a) report the development from the data on those already outwith the hospital (£136, with weekly costs ranging from £47 to £568 per week) of a prediction equation for those yet to leave. This demonstrates, they argue, that community costs will remain lower than hospital costs not just for the first cohort of leavers but for others also as the hospitals are closed. Although these predictions should perhaps as yet be treated with caution, they conform in their development to what are cited as the four key rules in the costing of health or social care services. Costings should be comprehensive, incorporating each service component from the package of care. They should acknowledge and explore the variations which occur between different areas, different facilities and different clients. They should be wary of direct cost comparisons unless like is being compared with like. And, finally, as is the argument of this chapter, data on costs should be integrated with outcome measures relating to effectiveness.

4 Residential care for elderly people

The Centre has collaborated with colleagues in the Institute of Public Service Accounting Research (IPSAR) at the Universities of Stirling and Edinburgh on two studies aimed at examining the relationship between quality of care, costs of care and effectiveness in residential homes for the elderly. The results of the first feasibility study are reported in Bland *et al.* (1990) and the second, much longer study was nearing completion at the time of writing.

The purpose of this research is to add to the understanding of the costs of providing old people's homes and the quality of that service. Earlier research (see, e.g. Darton and Knapp, 1984) had established no clear relationship linking the costs and characteristics of homes with their quality of care or outcomes for residents. A major purpose of the feasibility study was to combine an examination by research accountants of the actual costs of homes of different size, an analysis of these homes' quality of care in the seven domains described above (pp. 70–1) and a detailed account of the dependency of these homes' residents. It is thought that these analyses are the most detailed to have been conducted so far, and they yielded important research questions with implications for the provision of adequate levels of care and good management, including financial planning and control. For example, it was clear from the case studies that similar care tasks are performed in different homes by staff with different gradings (and sometimes qualifications). This can greatly influence the costs of homes, while the implications for the quality of care provided is less clear.

The second study, in progress at the time of writing, deals with 100 homes from the private, voluntary and statutory sectors (Bland *et al.*, forthcoming).

Again research accountants are making a detailed study of the actual costs of homes, including the likely significant variations between the sectors. For example, in private homes, capital costs are likely to be a major preoccupation of their owners. Furthermore, homes of between 40 and 50 beds, the most efficient in the public sector, are a rarity in the private sector; this could have implications for both costs and quality of care. This study also examines quality of care. It includes a detailed analysis of the use of staff time and an exploration of residents' attitudes to certain aspects of quality of care (e.g. the use of key workers or regular reviews of resident progress) which have an important place in professionals' notions of good practice.

The study therefore addresses major issues of policy, and practice and public expenditure, for the provision of residential care for elderly people, a subject which raises strong emotions and provokes political rhetoric. The hope is that the research will throw some light on questions which too often are debated with more passion than information: How do the costs of the homes in the three sectors compare? Could the market provide for an expansion in residential care? Do the three services cater for similar groups of elderly people? What variations in quality of care can be found between and within the sectors? Can individual components of quality of care be costed? What is the relationship between costs and quality of care? What are the characteristics of homes, in the three sectors, which often give quality care at a reasonable cost?

The above examples illustrate ways in which the cost-effectiveness of social work services can be examined and the types of information that such analyses can provide. The Centre has also included a cost-effectiveness analysis in its evaluation of two innovative pre-prosecution reparation and mediation schemes (Knapp and Netten, 1991; Warner, 1992) and the integration of cost and effectiveness data is planned in a Centre study of bail information and accommodation services and in a large programme of research in community care also being undertaken in the Centre.

The application of cost-effectiveness analysis in social work research is still a comparatively recent phenomenon and one which will no doubt continue to be refined. As knowledge of the costs of service provision is accumulated over time, cost-effectiveness studies should be able increasingly to draw upon information about the actual costs of providing social work services rather than on estimates as is at present so often necessarily the case. Much cost-effectiveness analysis will, however, be context-specific, so that 'off-the-shelf' costs are of limited utility. This is not to undervalue the contribution currently made by cost-effectiveness research. So long as those engaged in the study of cost-effectiveness are aware of the assumptions upon which their analyses are based and the limitations that these assumptions impose, evaluative research of this kind can vastly improve the quality of data upon which reasoned judgements regarding resource allocation and service development are made.

10

DISSEMINATING THE RESULTS OF RESEARCH

'What is the use of a book', thought Alice, 'without pictures or conversations?'
Lewis Carroll (1865) *Alice's Adventures in Wonderland*

What is written without effort is in general read without pleasure.
Samuel Johnson, 1709–1784

Potential consumers of research are a wide and disparate group who, it sometimes seems, are divided between cynics and naive optimists. For the cynics, research is commissioned by managers with suspect motives, and its messages are rarely to be trusted. They may also regard research as hopelessly inconclusive or providing self-evident answers to last year's questions. Optimists, on the other hand, hold expectations that research can resolve all manner of problems of policy and practice: studies of need will enable agencies to argue for more resources and target existing resources more efficiently; studies of effectiveness will identify successful and unsuccessful working methods; investigation of alternative models of organization or practice will unerringly pinpoint the best option; and so on. When the Seebohm Report recommended that the new social services departments should employ research staff, it was widely believed that this was part of a new era of social policy management, mirrored in other contemporary fields of public administration, in which rationality and the information revolution would prevail over prejudice, habit and disjointed incrementalism in the development of policy.

Neither of these stereotypes is without foundation, and it will be the task of this chapter to identify the kinds of influence research may have and the most effective ways of achieving it in the process of dissemination. After some brief introductory remarks, some of the particular techniques that have been found useful in giving feedback to participants and in wider dissemination will be reviewed, before underlying issues are discussed.

The rationale for dissemination

Pace the cynics, it is a truism that those who commission or fund research, those whose activities are researched and those who carry out the studies have a vital interest in the results. While their various interests may well not coincide, all of the parties are entitled to expect that the results and findings should see the light of day, in usable form and without unconscionable delay. Yet there exists the familiar cliché of bulky research reports unread and gathering dust on shelves.

The reasons for proper attention to dissemination scarcely need labouring. Research in the social work field will almost always be in some sense 'applied'; which is to say that, if sensibly conceived and successfully carried out, it will contain some truths which have a purchase at some level on policy, management or practice. There is therefore a need to feed conclusions of studies into debates, in the various locations at which they take place, about policy and practice. More than this, there may be lessons to be learnt, and an opportunity afforded by research findings specifically to educate, persuade or otherwise influence policy makers, managers and practitioners towards more effective organization and practice.

A subsidiary but none the less important purpose for dissemination is the scope it provides for achieving publicity for the research enterprise. In a hard world where research must defend its claim for resources against competing activities, researchers cannot afford to neglect opportunities for demonstrating the usefulness of their craft. Nor (researchers will argue) is this consideration confined to research self-interest: the interests of policy makers do not lie in the under-valuation of research.

It has become a commonplace in discussions of the influence of research to observe that 'the facts do not speak for themselves': the impact that research can make on the wider world needs to be worked for through presentation, interpretation and argument. Indeed, researchers would in many cases dispute the implication that research findings consist entirely or even mainly of 'the facts'. What needs to be got across are the ways in which 'facts' should be interpreted, the assumptions which underpin them, and the commentaries that may be developed on the basis of findings.

These dissemination activities should really be seen as part of the research process itself, but it is an aspect of that process which has in the past been somewhat neglected. There are a number of reasons for this. With academic research undertaken chiefly on a fixed-term contract basis, the final stages of a study are often rushed and the researcher's mind is at least half focused on the next job. Those who do research in their 'own' time – whether academics, managers or practitioners – are even more pressured. Furthermore, dissemination has only recently entered the culture of both researchers and funding bodies. An example of this is Richardson *et al.*'s (1990) significantly entitled *Taking Research Seriously*, commissioned by the Department of Health, which assembles a battery of recommendations for improving the utilization of research which is directed at research commissioners and consumers in government departments as much as at researchers. Time for dissemination has not always been built into funding periods, and effort has not always been expended on producing reports in a style which different audiences find accessible. Indeed, the question of time is itself a problem, given the tendency of research questions to be formulated in terms of today's issues and the equal tendency of research to reach fruition tomorrow; researchers will sometimes find that they have an interesting story to tell to an audience which has long since departed.

Underlying these well-known obstacles to adequate dissemination is a range of complex intellectual issues revolving around a problematic relationship which might be variously expressed as that between research policy, between theory and practice, between fact and value, or between knowledge and power. It is not simply that research may be used or ignored. It may also be abused, and the manner in which it is disseminated is likely to have an impact on its uses for good or ill.

Feedback to participants

Although a form of dissemination, the process of feeding back results to those who have participated in research raises issues of its own. 'Participants' here will usually include those whose activities are studied, their managers, those in the organization who have either sought or volunteered agency participation in a study, and (many would argue) service users.

Researchers have special obligations, recognized in codes of practice issued by both the Social Research Association and the Social Services Research Group, to ensure that such parties are adequately informed about findings at appropriate times. This will often be in the form of interim or progress reports during the course of a study, as well as after completion but before the results reach a wider public. Since this exercise, especially if a study has involved a number of different sites, requires a significant investment of time, it needs to be carefully planned, and it is important to agree with the participants in advance the stages and manner in which it will take place. Such agreements, which cover the kinds of information that will be revealed at different stages of the research process, may well include some prior discussion of likely sensitivities, such as the way in which any potentially negative findings would be handled. It is here that such issues as the anonymization of individuals and locations should be clearly agreed – particularly in studies of smaller agencies where unrealistic assurances of professional anonymity should not be made glibly.

As well as simply informing participants, the feedback stage usually has the specific research function of 'respondent validation' (McKeganey and Bloor, 1981). In addition to giving subjects the opportunity to correct factual errors, it is likely that discussions of preliminary findings or draft reports will produce a detailed exploration of matters of understanding and interpretation, which the researcher, in the standard formulation, will 'take account of' in revising drafts. In the case of interim presentations, it may in some cases be thought desirable that the researcher should exercise a degree of reticence, in case practices which remain to be studied should change as a result of early feedback. This situation, which implies the kind of research design in which rigorous control of the process variables is essential, is in practice rather rare in the research discussed in this book, though should it arise it will form part of the advance agreements. At the opposite end of the spectrum is the special case of action research, when the feedback loop is specifically built into the design. In this case, it is explicitly intended that practice should be modified in the light of stage-by-stage reports of findings, with the ensuing changes forming the basis for the next stage of the evaluation.

No matter how carefully all these matters have been prepared in advance, it is likely that difficulties will be encountered which will make demands on the tact and integrity of both researchers and subjects. For the latter are in a delicate situation. On the one hand (especially front-line practitioners), they have run certain personal and professional risks in exposing their activities to research scrutiny, sometimes without great control over the way findings are used; on the other, their perspectives may have influenced to varying degrees the way the study has been carried out.

Simply to state these points is to identify a range of possible pitfalls. It is common for researchers to be taken aback at the vehemence of responses evoked by reports to participants, when, for example, small reservations are seized upon in the midst of more favourable messages, or even when messages researchers themselves believe to be favourable are construed the other way. The researcher may interpret this as hypersensitivity, though researchers are also capable of professional *amour propre* and have their own investment in their results. What is important to bear in mind, however, is that once researchers enter the dissemination arena, particularly in local research sites, the agenda is broadened to include managerial and political considerations of which researchers cannot assume they are aware: the participants may be happy to discuss problematic areas as long as the dialogue is between themselves and a researcher, but be understandably wary of managers or agency funders being party to the same discussions.

Techniques of wider dissemination

Traditionally, the main instrument of dissemination has been 'the final report' made to commissioners or sponsors of the research. At its best, the final report is a systematic, concise, but contextualized account of the questions addressed by the study, the means by which they have been addressed, the relevant data collected in the process, the answers that have been arrived at, and a discussion of their significance and implications. At its worst, however, it can resemble a particularly indigestible answer to one of those examination questions which asked candidates to write down all they know about a topic. Researchers differ about the status of the final report. The usefulness of the whole story, including discussions of competing theoretical, methodological and analytical issues, being contained in a single if lengthy document, is partly something for researchers themselves, partly a resource for fellow researchers or the most motivated of other readers. Against this should be set the possibility, even probability, that relatively few might read something whose assembly has consumed a great deal of time and effort which might have been devoted to producing more focused documents with less delay. Whatever the merits or demerits of this debate, the final report can by its nature make little genuine contribution to dissemination among non-research audiences.

One solution to the 'final report problem' is that adopted for the Centre's supported accommodation study. In this case, the first publication was a summary report (Petch, 1990), compiled after the main analysis had been carried out but before lengthier or more academic documents had been written, and produced in an eye-catching format which picked out the main findings and supplied illustrative material. The speed with which this appeared and its attractive style evidently contributed much to the impact it was reported to have made on audiences who might not otherwise have encountered the study.

As this example suggests, it is no longer considered adequate for the results of research to be allowed to 'filter down' in some unspecified way from scholarly publications into the general consciousness. Researchers can write papers for scholarly journals, so that their work may become part of mainstream educational and research literature and may be subjected to rigorous scrutiny (or so it is said) from their academic peers; often, indeed, this is a condition of continued existence for those seeking academic credibility or funding from bodies like the research councils which set store by an academic track record. It is perhaps ironic that this kind of production is more widely recognized by at least some key holders of the purse-strings than those dissemination activities which might reach wider audiences with more direct interest in the implementation of findings. Alongside scholarly output, then, researchers have become used to responding to demands for reports in summary and accessible form for a variety of audiences, an activity given inadequate recognition in career terms, which none the less involves significant investment of time. Furthermore, the rapid growth in recent years of technologies for producing documents in attractive and different formats has presented opportunities which have only begun to be exploited.

In most fields, there are a number of possible outlets for these more popular versions of research accounts: one-off or free-standing short accounts or pamphlets which may be widely circulated; articles in the general social work press; articles in the numerous professional journals that are widely scanned by practitioners; newsletters; the mass media, including press releases and briefings for journalists. Each of these various forms of publication will present their own challenges for targeting particular audiences and emphasizing different kinds of relevance to the intended readership. There are, of course, costs in time and materials involved in all this, and depending on resources decisions have to be made about priorities, which can act as a healthy spur to clear thinking about the precise purposes of a study.

Communication in written form has the disadvantage of being one way. The oral presentation of research findings not only allows researchers to hear feedback themselves and to keep in touch with practice perspectives, but also provides a potentially enriching opportunity for discussion to develop about the consequences of adopting particular methods, the meanings of particular findings, or more general research-derived insights. As will have become apparent throughout this book, social work research is full of open questions, which no amount of attempted intellectual rigour can or should completely foreclose. When findings are summarized, it is not always easy, with an audience which may be disposed to grasp at straws, to convey some of the qualifications and uncertainties that may cluster around methodological choices or the interpretation of conclusions. Many researchers lament that they are pressed to present findings as 'the answers' when they are more appropriately seen as an invitation to dialogue.

Thus it is important for researchers to seek out opportunities at conferences and at specially convened seminars or meetings. While audiences at conferences are likely to be mixed, seminars may be organized for very particular groups – whether practitioners, managers or policy makers – often in particular settings, which together with an oral presentation probably allows for a more refined targeting of content and style.

So diverse are these various activities, and so labour-intensive some of them, that dissemination could well become a full-time job in itself. Dissemination strategies clearly need to be carefully planned in advance, potential audiences identified for both written and oral presentation, and time duly allowed. While encouragement from research funders to take dissemination seriously and to include dissemination time in research proposals is welcome, it often seems unrealistic for these activities to be confined to a finite period.

One model that has not been widely practised but which may become more common as research in social work accumulates is that of the specialist disseminator, or 'research interpreter' (Richardson *et al.*, 1990), who publicizes the results of a number of related studies. This may be done through a series of seminars (Hevey, 1984) or, most ambitiously, in the form exemplified by Rowe (1985). Rowe was specially commissioned by the then Department of Health and Social Security (DHSS) to review nine studies of decision making in child care, some themselves commissioned as part of a linked programme of studies, others coincidentally coming to fruition at the same time. The resulting large-format booklet (the so-called 'pink book') contained brief summaries of each study, together with the author's reflections on their cumulative import and a batch of exercises designed to enable professionals to scrutinize their own practice in the light of the findings. This publication was supported by a series of regional conferences. This was clearly a major undertaking beyond normal resources, which might none the less be imitated on a more modest scale.

Among the advantages claimed is the disseminator's detachment from the research: audiences are freer to be critical of the studies without distracting issues of politeness, and the presenter is less likely to be seen as having a personal stake in putting across a message. Indeed, there are real dangers of researchers being so associated, with a proselytizing message in their own minds as well as in those of others, that they become uncritical of their own work and fail to encourage a critical response in others.

Underlying issues

This hint at the contentious question of 'objectivity' points towards some closer scrutiny of the range of issues which underlie the dissemination act; indeed, an enumeration of dissemination techniques is likely to appear bland without such further discussion, which will necessarily raise questions about the *purposes* of research. These in turn lead on to consideration of the varied *settings* in which research takes place, and the implications of these for the relationship between research and policy. It will be suggested that although these two factors influence the ways in which dissemination dilemmas mani-fest themselves, they do not necessarily determine how dissemination devel-ops in practice.

The pressure, already noted, for at least some audiences to demand 'the answers' sits uneasily with the well-known tendency for researchers to query the questions, sometimes, indeed, for them to appear more interested in the ways in which questions are formulated than in the possibility of there being answers. By the same token, some researchers are sometimes uncomfortable about providing summaries of complex findings, fearing over-simplification and wishing to insist on the importance of context and method. The exist-ence of different audiences, each with their own expectations not only of what is to count as relevant but also of what is to count as research, points to subtle pressures on researchers to select certain kinds of evidence and argument according to their perceived credibility with particular groups.

Some of this may safely be put down to intellectual self-indulgence, be-longing to an era less hard-headed about the need for research to be 'useful' or 'relevant' if it is to justify its existence. Researchers should no doubt avoid an unduly squeamish attitude towards popularizing their findings: the art of producing summaries in the form of key statements which do not over-simplify is an important and legitimate one. It is, however, possible for simplified messages to be over-learnt: witness the debate, in the 1980s and persisting, about how the adverse findings about statutory care as a depriv-ing experience for children may have led to the damaging consequence of entry to care being seen as a last resort. To summarize over-briefly, the world of research is characterized by 'rationality' (or at least the aspiration towards it), whereas the arena in which practice and policy develop and change is one in which values and politics jostle with 'rational' argument. This ground has been extensively worked over, notably by Bulmer (1982, 1987) and Bulmer *et al.* (1986), but see also Etzioni (1968) and Booth (1988) for a range of perspectives on the relationship between research and action and on ways of characterizing their respective assumptive worlds. Not all would agree on the way the above dichotomy is put and the extent of its influence: it is not difficult to show, for example, that research-based analysis is itself permeated with values and politics, whether in the selection of issues, in the credibility of analytical procedures, or in the highlighting of interpretations. Although it should not be overdrawn, however, many if not all researchers would probably agree with Lindblom (1980) that there exists a dilemma in the relationship between the researcher's dispassionate analysis and the changes in policy or practice which could be argued to flow from it. Once the analysis and findings have been delivered, is it legitimate that the researcher should become involved in the process of making recommendations and discussing changes? Or should that be left to the 'real-world' decision makers in whose province (it might be thought) such matters properly lie? Are there dangers of an unholy alliance between researchers with axes to grind and ambitious politicians, or even in benign alliances between researchers and politicians committed to the expansion of welfare as may have occurred in the 1960s? Researchers often bemoan their lack of influence, but do they really want the responsibility and should they? And what *kind* of influence is in question: that of the acknowledged policy adviser, the grey eminence or the independent commentator?

There is no single answer to this question, just as there will rarely be any automatic or axiomatic relationship between research findings and the question of what should be done. This partly reflects the ambivalent nature of many research findings, and perhaps a general lack of fit between social research and the demand for precise policy recommendations. This is neatly illustrated by Cooper's (1978) comment in her review of studies of the outcomes of fostering placements: these tended to produce a 40–50 per cent success rate, which, she argued, 'provides fertile grounds for ideological loyalty rather than scientific support' for the extension of fostering. But it also reflects the nature of the incrementalist and negotiated processes of policy and practice change.

Models of the research–policy relationship

As Booth (1988) comments, 'social science research has percolated into policy only in diffuse ways'. The literature identifies a number of different models and a number of different typologies of the relationship between empirical research and policy. A recent review (Smith and Smith, 1992, partly following Bulmer, 1982) suggests four:

1 The *engineering model*, whereby research 'is seen as a technical process, investigating solutions to specified problems' identified by the commissioner, usually a policy maker.
2 The *political arithmetic model*, where the starting-point for the researcher is a contemporary social problem and the intent is consciously reformist. It seeks to marry the researcher's value-laden choice of issue with objective methods of data collection, in order to influence the policy area in question.
3 The *enlightenment model*, in which research does not influence policy directly but rather promulgates insights which in time affect the ways policy makers conceptualize problems and solutions.
4 The *value-critical model*, which does not recognize a split between policy/action and research, and seeks to uncover the latent assumptions and values which determine both, in order to test and amend the paradigms on which policy and a 'knowledge-for-policy' are based.

Of these four models, 'political arithmetic' is most closely associated with the style of research engagement seen, for example, in the Educational Priority

Area studies (Halsey, 1972). The 'value-critical' approach, perhaps not one likely to commend itself to policy-making research funders, seems to belong to a tradition of independent academic scrutiny and criticism not at the time of writing in particularly good health. While both of these may be present in the motivation of researchers, it is the first and third models which are probably most relevant to the perspective from which this book is written, certainly in the sense that they are likely to form the framework of the debate.

As suggested in Chapter 1, the evaluative enterprise is one which starts from inside the world of the policy maker or manager, with the objectives of intervention, which itself might seem to point towards the (rather pejoratively named) engineering model. This was the approach given formal endorsement by the Rothschild Report (1971) in the form of the 'customer–contractor principle'. The language of the latter, together with its seemingly ever-increasing array of research-management procedures (Richardson *et al.*, 1990), still obtains in the research-commissioning branches of government departments: 'the customer says what he wants; the contractor does it (if he or she can); and the customer pays'. This is despite widespread scepticism about the assumptions behind the model among researchers who have had experience of the negotiation processes involved, most of whom are probably more attracted to the enlightenment approach.

Some of the reasons for their scepticism will already be clear. There may be doubt about the capacity of policy makers to identify researchable issues, or to accommodate the lessons which might already be clear from previous research. As Cornish and Clarke (1987) remark, the customer usually gets rather more than he bargained for. A particular problem is that of clarifying the difference between the long- and the short-term research task. For non-researchers to think in research terms is itself something of a difficult imaginative leap, as is shown by the unsatisfactory nature of 'research agendas' which are compiled without the participation of experienced researchers. At a level above the pragmatic, however, important distinctions between the various models lie in the relationship each bears to the treatment of values, or to the implicit assumptions on which existing policies and practices may be based. The engineering model, at least in its most extreme forms, more or less obliges researchers to take as given perspectives which professional self-respect urges them to challenge. Research as enlightenment, on the other hand, distances the researcher from the values of the policy world, absolves them from the sordid task of political engagement, and – as Smith and Smith (1992) point out – might even enable them to have the last word, thus satisfying self-esteem as well as integrity. The intellectual or political attractiveness (for some) of this stance, however, should not be confused with evidence for the empirical effectiveness with which ideas 'percolate'. Other than a few case studies (see, e.g. Thomas, 1985), empirical data about the influence of research, its extent and manner, is elusive.

At first sight, there appear to be clear implications here for the targeting of dissemination. It is important not to create straw men, however, and as noted above, the different approaches are not mutually exclusive. The kind of models described above tend to be empirical generalizations; on-the-ground experience of research dissemination tends to show a spread of less neatly differentiated activities. Before illustrating the variety of ways in which dissemination can make an impact, it is worth noticing a further set of distinctions which may be thought to influence the kind of impact that may be made.

Research settings

Research actually takes place in a variety of institutional settings, at varying removes from the policy process. There is academic research, whether in university departments or in relatively free-standing research units staffed by academics; research carried out in-house in government departments or local authorities; the activities of private sector or freelance researchers; the research that develops from longstanding involvement between researchers and practitioners in the voluntary sector. From whatever setting, most studies will be in some sense 'commissioned', or at least negotiated with an eye to policy relevance, if only as the price rightly paid for access.

It should not be assumed that in-house location necessarily produces closer alignment between research and policy thinking of a kind that would make the engineering model workable; or that organizational distance goes automatically with remoteness from the policy process in a way that would favour 'enlightenment' rather than direct influence as the goal. It was not easy, for example, for social services and social work departmental managers to learn how best to use an in-house capacity, and Bowl and Fuller (1982) in a study of in-house research found that researchers themselves were the most common source of initiatives for specific projects. Conversely, in-house researchers in local authorities have opportunities denied to outsiders for day-to-day contact with managers, which may well be conducive to a discussion of underlying issues rather than truncated communication of headline findings. And, in turn, Thomas's (1985) study of the impact of research on policy suggests that the cultural gap between policy makers and externally funded researchers, though real, is less wide than might be supposed, and that both sides may be committed to cultivating close links.

However close these links might be, it remains more likely in general that the kind of engagement with policy-making machinery that potentially goes with in-house location makes for greatly increased credibility in the art of making recommendations for policy on the basis of research. This, an area where researchers often feel that they are damned if they do and damned if they do not, can be a hazardous undertaking. Existing policies and practices are embedded in organizational history, geography, personalities, and intermeshing sectors. Unless researchers are intimately acquainted with such particularities, and this is hard to achieve from outside, their recommendations can look merely naive.

The institutional base of the researcher, then, may make some difference to the influence exerted by research, but will not necessarily be decisive. To sceptics who might doubt that research makes any impact at all, examples can be cited (see the opening chapter), with perhaps a few cases of excessive impact. What is extremely rare is the kind of triumph of rationalism that would be represented by the spectacle of new theories, supported by research evidence, successfully challenging old and discredited ones. If there are signs of this in the way the case management approach has found its way from research findings through reports and a white paper into legislation, there are also signs on the one hand of political contingency, cost-cutting and a degree of muddle, and on the other of ideological choices being made which research may inform but does not determine (Sinclair, 1990).

This is to some extent as it should be. Like Booth's conclusion cited earlier, this scenario is often taken as a reason for pessimism. While pessimism may sometimes be justified, it might be argued that a world in which changes in policy and practice were obvious and easy to achieve would be an odd and not wholly attractive one. What it rather suggests is that the results of research dissemination should not be judged by standards that are inappropriately high and arguably smack of the technocratic – inappropriate in that they ignore the role of both contingencies and politics in determining changes.

Dissemination and impact: a case study

This having been said, the obligation of the researcher remains one of using skill and judgement in the techniques, targeting and timing of dissemination, whether the effect of research is direct or through more subterranean influences on the attitudes of key actors. The variety of ways in which dissemination can make an impact, and something of the mixed character of that impact, can be illustrated by the example of the studies undertaken at the Centre relating to community service for offenders (McIvor, 1989).

As initially devised, the evaluation of different operational arrangements in community service schemes (McIvor, 1989, 1992b) was intended to inform practice at both the local and national level – community service staff were attempting to introduce a degree of standardization of practice across the country. Shortly after the fieldwork began, however, the Scottish Office announced its intention to assume responsibility for the full funding of schemes and to introduce national standards and objectives for the operation of community service in Scotland. The proposed timing of the introduction of these national standards created an opportunity for the research to be linked directly to the policy development process.

The dissemination of the research results was pursued in a number of ways and for a variety of audiences with different purposes in mind. In addition to a lengthy and comprehensive research report, a summary report was produced to make the findings and conclusions more accessible to practitioners and managers. Copies of both reports were circulated to all community service schemes in Scotland. The implications of the research for practice were highlighted in seminars aimed at community service staff and through contributions to staff training programmes. Consultation with community service staff in the development of the research and as part of the fieldwork process had ensured that issues of relevance to practice had been addressed by the study.

The focus of the research upon identifying effective practice meant that the findings were similarly relevant to the development of policies aimed at standardizing the operation of schemes in such a way that optimal practice could be retained. After an early initial discussion with representatives of the Scottish Office at which the potential contribution of the research to the development of national standards was discussed, the preliminary findings were made available to the consultation group responsible for the development of the standards prior to the issuing of the consultation document. Subsequent discussions with policy makers centred around possible future developments, such as changes to the maximum or minimum number of hours which could be ordered, which did not form part of the National Standards but which might be implemented at some later date and which could be informed by the results of the research.

A key issue for the Scottish Office concerned the likely impact of the National Standards upon sentencing practice. While the document had no formal status with sentencers, the hope was expressed that the organizational changes resulting from the implementation of the National Standards would enhance the credibility of the community service order with the Scottish courts and encourage its more consistent use as a direct alternative to a custodial sentence. Since the earlier research had suggested that community service had replaced imprisonment for slightly fewer than 45 per cent of offenders on orders (McIvor, 1990a), the Centre embarked upon a further study (Carnie, 1990) aimed, among other things, at assessing the likely impact of the new arrangements on sentencers' use of community service orders and for which funding was provided by the Scottish Office Home and Health Department.

This research, which involved interviews with sheriffs, high court judges and lay justices in the district courts, confirmed that the National Standards document had had a minimal influence upon sentencers. When the interviews were conducted, some three to four months after the publication of the standards, only three of the 21 sheriffs who were interviewed had received a copy and none had had an opportunity to digest the contents. The sheriffs were adamant that their sentencing practices would not be influenced directly by the National Standards and were unanimously opposed to the introduction of sentencing guidelines or other legislative changes which would limit their judicial discretion. Concerned by the inconsistent use of community service by the Scottish courts and aware that the National Standards in themselves would have little impact upon sentencing practice, the Scottish Office amended the existing legislation. The changes which were instituted by the Law Reform Miscellaneous Provisions (Scotland) Act 1990 required sentencers to impose community service orders only where the offender would otherwise be dealt with by means of a custodial sentence.

The Centre's third community service study (McIvor, 1990b) examined the experiences of individual members of the public and of voluntary and statutory agencies who were the recipients of community service work. The willingness of community service schemes to participate in this further study (schemes in eight of the nine mainland social work departments readily agreed to take part) was, it is believed, influenced by the wide dissemination of the previous research and its perceived relevance to local policy and practice, even if some of the findings had not been particularly welcomed by all community service staff.

The completion of the three studies enabled the identification of wider issues of relevance to the various groups involved in the community service process – community service staff, sentencers, offenders and beneficiaries of the work. The Scottish Office agreed to host a seminar to facilitate and encourage discussion by representatives of the different interest groups concerned of the wider issues highlighted by the research. The seminar provided an opportunity for the exchange of ideas among participants and served to stimulate wider debate regarding the future operation of community service schemes.

This series of studies indicates how effective dissemination strategies which are linked to the needs of different audiences can maximize the impact of research on policy and practice and can facilitate the generation and development of further research. The processes of consultation and feedback to practitioners (including those not directly involved in the research) influenced positively their willingness to participate in further research. The close links developed with policy makers facilitated the development of ideas for further studies which would be of direct value to subsequent policy development. Within this process, the researcher has an obligation to interpret the research findings and convey their limitations lest inappropriate conclusions are drawn and embraced. The more relevant the research is perceived to be to policy and practice development, the greater, perhaps, is this risk. While instilling a necessary degree of caution or restraint, the researcher is also well placed, however, to direct attention to some of the wider issues which, though not addressed directly by the research, may be informed or at least identified by it and in so doing stimulate wider debate.

This illustrates a number of dissemination themes. A developing programme of research successively prompted and was prompted by a carefully planned dissemination programme. The dissemination took place by several different means, and engaged audiences at different levels. By a mixture, no doubt, of luck and judgement, the researcher was able to capitalize on the subject having acquired topicality in the policy agenda after the initial ideas were conceived, and through the dissemination processes began to develop good relationships with key policy-making actors.

This is a piece of research which appears to have made a significant contribution to policy and practice, and in ways which are difficult to characterize in terms of the models discussed earlier. If in the end there were identified 'customers' awaiting the outcome of the research, the studies were not initially contracted; their impetus stemmed rather from the researchers' understanding of critical issues in the field, developed and reinforced by contact with central policy makers. As such, it should give some heart to those who believe that the baby of rationality should not be thrown out with the engineering-model bathwater, and that fruitful partnership between research and policy, however elusive, is not impossible.

11

CONCLUSIONS: CURRENT PRIORITIES AND FUTURE CHALLENGES

> As often as a study is cultivated by narrow minds, they will draw from it narrow conclusions.
>
> J.S. Mill (1865) *Auguste Comte and Positivism*

This chapter has two purposes: it draws together the potential and priorities for the evaluation of social work effectiveness in the mid-1990s discussed earlier in this volume, and it looks forward to the terrain still to be crossed and the complicated research questions this will present. An important conclusion of this book is that it is right to travel hopefully in the difficult journey of social work evaluation. During the next decade in Britain, the major changes planned for the delivery of community care services and the reassertion of the importance of preventive services for vulnerable children will present great opportunities and demand for evaluative research. The challenge and excitement of these developments will require renewed efforts to tackle the research problems which are inevitable in attempts to evaluate large, worthwhile and at times contentious aspirations, the very scope of which both stretch the competency of social scientific analysis and demand its most stringent application. Not just in Britain but throughout the world the last decade of this century and the beginning of the next promise major, even revolutionary reassessments of the old questions which lie at the heart of social policy and social work: How do individuals best cope with personal disaster and social misfortune? What are the proper limits of public intervention and private responsibility? How should dependency be recognized? What are the rights and obligations of families and individuals? In this maelstrom the still, small voice of evaluative research must be heard, and the lives of its researchers will certainly not be dull.

In the immediate future in Britain, this optimism about the demand for evaluative research is consistent with contemporary social policy interests in user rights and choice and in the quality of services. In such a climate, evaluative research which focuses on the outcomes of intervention and responses to them is essential if policies are seen to be more than rhetorical. This research can be conducted through large and elaborate studies lasting several years which seek to analyse the policies of many agencies. It can also be pursued in much smaller studies, and some of these can be conducted by individual practitioners who are curious about the impact of their work. There is now a sufficient history of both approaches to encourage their continuation and the further exploration of research designs and methods which seek to capture the complexities of social work tasks, the multiplicity of interventions and their impact, and the responses of the many constituencies who have interests in social work.

Principles for evaluative research: prerequisites and priorities

There are four prerequisites for evaluative research; there are also several priorities for research design which are either essential to the endeavour or so important that they should neither be disregarded while plans are being formulated nor lightly discarded. The first prerequisite is clarity about the questions the research is to address; the second is judicious flexibility in the choice of research design and method; the third is clear recognition of what can and cannot be achieved in the studies judged to be feasible, that is the limitations imposed by the necessary research designs. So far, so conventional; the fourth prerequisite, of a rather different order, is to retain, in every study, a clear view of the significance and ordinary meanings of the matters being studied for those who give and receive social work services and to eschew narrowing of focus which, in the interests of precision in data collection and analysis, distorts these realities.

The principal argument of this book is that researchers must understand social work as a complex interaction of responsibilities and expectations which may conflict, of tasks which frequently change as the work progresses and to which standardized responses are rare and usually inappropriate, and of resources which are often inadequate. This understanding, which should be seen as a challenge rather than a deterrent to evaluative research, must provide the context for choosing a research focus which can illuminate certain questions, in full recognition that others for the present must be ignored, although they may be pursued in later studies. Evaluative research will thus be incremental. At this point, when researchers are presented with the complicated questions that arise in everyday social work, it is more important to think how a reasonably respectable (and repeatable) evaluative study could be designed than to be paralysed by its inevitable imperfections. The priority is to encourage, at all levels of social work management and practice, evaluation of both routine and innovative work. The understandable aspiration for the best must not be the enemy of the good or, worse still, *any* attempt at evaluative research.

The research designs and methods that are feasible are unlikely to be equal to all the intriguing questions which arise whenever evaluation is seriously considered. However, if this is to become an established component of agency practice, and if research which evaluates effectiveness is to increase beyond the one-tenth of research effort in the field of social work which Jenkins (1987) estimated it has occupied in the United States, then ways must be found of accommodating the small sample sizes, the heterogeneous clientele and workers, the varied care and help provided and the shifting time-scales which are the reality of day-to-day social work. Thus, and this may be contentious for researchers from some traditions, the context of social work services and the nature of practice will, to a substantial extent, determine research design and method. To act otherwise, by designing studies which control the agenda and methods of social work, will greatly limit the amount of evaluative research undertaken. Furthermore, studies of services specially designed for research purposes, studies which therefore impose rigid constraints on social workers' practice, may prove counterproductive if practitioners come to see the needs of their clients as pre-eminent and not met by the research protocol. In such circumstances, social workers may, with greater and lesser degrees of openness, disregard the requirements of research in favour of their professional priorities. It is thus extremely unwise to design a study in which the actual process of social work may differ greatly from what the research had both expected and required.

Since selection and adaptations of research methods, unusual in some scientific traditions, and recognition of the ensuing limitations are endemic in the study of social work, it may sometimes be argued that this very activity is pointless and wasteful of resources. The opposing arguments, espoused by the authors of this book, are that the importance of social work's sphere of operation, its varied manifestations and the large questions it invokes do not simply justify evaluative research, they demand it. The tension between complexity of subject matter and precision of research method is by no means confined to social work, as Polanyi shows in his exploration of the scientific enterprise in fields as far apart as evolution, atomic physics and the identification of intelligence. The research challenge, and the fourth prerequisite of evaluative research, is thus to devise methods of enquiry sufficiently rigorous to throw light on important elements of the subject without so narrowing the focus as to trivialize matters which have ordinary and important meanings. 'The existence of animals was not discovered by zoologists, nor that of plants by botanists, and the scientific value of zoology and botany is but an extension of man's pre-scientific interest in animals and plants.' (Polanyi, 1958, p. 139). Likewise, suffering, welfare, help and human kindness, the very stuff of social work, are the daily experience of us all. Worthwhile evaluative research enlarges this understanding, albeit slowly and step by step, by studying the ends and means of social work services with sufficient precision and rigour to allow comparisons and informed commentary while not distorting, beyond the reach of general understanding, the needs and responses which are a recognized fact of ordinary life. Progress comes through a combination of rare creative leaps and dogged persistence with careful, detailed description and analysis. An example of the former are the first studies of the recipients' views and experience of social work and, indeed, of other human services which when they were published, despite being subject to all sorts of methodological criticism, were recognized as a long overdue essential component of the study of health and welfare. The labours of countless researchers have enhanced the precision and expanded the horizons of this research, and further work is required, but it was the bold and innovative studies which established the understanding of recipients' experiences as part of the canon of evaluative research.

With these prerequisites providing the essential backcloth to evaluative research in social work, what are the priorities for research design which those who carry out studies and those who read their reports should expect to be carefully considered, even if they cannot be incorporated?

1 The identification of outcomes

The first and essential research priority, highlighted in Chapter 2 and discussed at length in Chapters 5 and 6, must be attention to outcomes. There can be no determination of effectiveness without information about the impact of services, and there can be no serious evaluation without knowledge about outcomes and effectiveness. The identification of outcomes can focus on the content and context of the services delivered or on their impact on clients, e.g. improved resources, morale, health, capacity for daily living, behaviour, and so on. Since services are intended to benefit the recipients, such outcomes should be given central importance. Their determination may, however, require substantial research resources in the administration of questionnaires and other instruments or the observation or tracking of behaviour. 'Quality of life', which now has an established place in the language of social policy and welfare, can be a particularly elusive state to identify with any precision.

The identification of service-based outcomes can be more straightforward and may provide important information about, for example, the type, amount and continuity of services provided, their relationship to what was requested by the applicant or referrer or to what is generally regarded as desirable. Quality of care has become both a fashionable and a proper preoccupation and a worthwhile focus for research; but there is one important caveat. Quality of care is not a synonym for quality of life. Such a statement of the obvious may be surprising, but sometimes a combination of muddled thinking and the presumptions of policy makers and practitioners engender such a confusion, and perhaps especially in residential or institutional establishments. This confusion is not a recent phenomenon. The workhouses of the nineteenth century provided, according to the standards of the time, excellent standards of care: cleanliness, discipline, honest labour, an orderly way of life. It was left to Dickens to highlight the dreadful gap between this excellent 'quality of care' and the inhabitants' quality of life.

The selection of outcomes to be studied and the methods of so doing may depend, in part, on the intended research audiences. These can include those who pay for the research, those responsible for the service, pressure and consumer groups, and those practitioners or associated personnel whose attention is judged to be important. These groups may have different priorities, their preferred familiar scientific traditions and different professional languages and preoccupations. The researchers' choice of research design and instruments must try to take account of these different expectations if studies of the effectiveness of social work services are to be taken seriously by the several audiences whose attention must be caught.

2 Pluralist perspectives

A second important research priority is attention to the experiences or perceptions of the different parties involved in social work. Indeed, these may be regarded as one kind of outcome. Users' responses to and understanding of the services they have received must usually be a key preoccupation; but in complicated situations, the social workers' perceptions of the problems and their intentions are an important context for users' reactions. 'Users' may include those who receive services directly and their carers who, with differing degrees of intention, are expected to be indirect beneficiaries. The intentions of policy makers and managers which can significantly influence the context, form and content of services may also be an important focus for research. Chapter 3 discusses how these various perspectives should permeate the identification of effectiveness but, as Chapter 2 argues, it is not enough to know simply that people have different perceptions of services and their impact. Policy and practice usually require some judgement as to whether greater consensus is either possible and desirable and, if not, some further judgement of the consequences, in planning services, of according priority to different views which may reflect conflicting value systems and thus a range of different rhetorics. This is central to the evaluation rather than simply the identification of effectiveness.

3 Identifying the social work process

A third priority, and one too often neglected, is attention to the process of social work intervention. This goes beyond the identification of service-based outcomes and may involve careful description of the congruence or otherwise between the theoretical or intended content and form of the intervention and its actual delivery. It may also include careful analysis of the manner in which help is given, including the relationship between those who receive and those who offer help, and the style and characteristics of the helpers, all of which can be important influences on users' perceptions of the usefulness of the service. As Chapter 5 shows, without such attention to process and the careful description of the services given, it is impossible to know how to repeat an apparently successful service or avoid an unsuccessful one. And when outcomes appear to be the opposite of what might be expected from an avowedly high-quality service, the integrity of the actual service, that is its consistency with its theoretical base and planned delivery, must be addressed.

4 Identifying the costs of effective services

The identification of the costs of services, in the context of their effectiveness, has to be a priority for policy makers and managers who have to make choices about the best value to be obtained from limited resources. Increasingly, practitioners will also have to make such choices as their responsibilities for assembling 'packages of care' and for purchasing services increase. It is therefore sensible when first considering the outlines of a possible study to think what place the analysis of the costs of services might have. This may, for example, be particularly significant when the effectiveness of innovative and more traditional services are being compared or when comparisons are being made of different methods of dealing with similar problems. Without some comparator, the identification of the costs of a service will not be helpful.

In a cost-conscious climate, there can be much uncritical citing of sums of money which, on their own, have little meaning. It is also common, as part of the rhetoric of managerial or political argument about service provision, for there to be much ill-informed or poorly calculated comparison of costs. A frequent example is the cost of a bed in some form of residential institution with an alternative community service. Not only is it usual for the full costs (including the costs of any informal family care) of the community service to be ignored, it is also frequently implied that any difference between these costs is actually saved if a person does not enter a residential establishment. Real savings will only be made when so many people are directed from residential or institutional care that establishments are either wholly or partially closed.

It is not difficult for researchers and readers who are largely innocent of economics and accountancy to fall into such traps. It also seems common for there to be far less critical scrutiny of data preceded by a pound or dollar sign than of other information yielded by a research report! At least at present, the paraphernalia of the market sometimes appear especially potent, and perhaps especially when the public provision of health and welfare is being discussed. It is therefore extremely important that researchers do not allow a simplistic or ill-informed analysis of costs in their studies. It is also essential for any analysis of services' costs to be integrated with the analysis of their effectiveness, so that policy and practice choices are not simply made on grounds of expenditure but in the light of their comparative effectiveness. The best value is often not the cheapest service.

Whereas all researchers are able to identify outcomes and processes and incorporate different perspectives in their research designs, only a very few are equipped with the skills required for thorough analyses of the costs of services. These should therefore only usually be included when it is possible to collaborate closely with accountants or economists. This means sharing the design and planning of the study so that data collection for the identification of costs and effectiveness can, where appropriate, be congruent and analysis of and commentary on the relevant data carried out jointly. Experience shows that such collaboration enlarges the understanding of the different disciplines involved and allows increasingly sophisticated and informed commentary on both the efficiency and effectiveness of social work services.

5 Dissemination

No research should be planned without thought being given at the outset to the different forms of dissemination which are essential to its successful completion and are a necessary (but not sufficient) condition of its being read, heard and having some impact. This early review of dissemination strategies must also include consideration of those tasks which the researchers themselves must carry out as part of the study and those which can be done only with more resources or in collaboration with those who provide or manage services.

Some dissemination with expert audiences of early research findings may well be necessary before conclusions can be drawn about their accuracy or significance. At this point, the comments of those centrally concerned with services, including recipients, may well help researchers in the final presentation and discussion of their conclusions. All this may be an important component of the evaluative task. It will also help in reaching conclusions about the implications of the research for policy and practice. Researchers are not necessarily the best qualified for this task, particularly in judging where it is more or less realistic to suggest the changes which might emanate from their studies.

The form of the various research reports required for the different audiences with interests in the subject must also be considered when the study is first planned, to allow for sufficient time and resources, and again in more detail when the study is in its final stages. At this point, too, possible media interest must be explored and, at the appropriate point, managed.

The previous chapter has touched on the usually complex combination of circumstances which are required for research to be seen as influencing policy and practice. In social work, and probably in most other forms of human services, it is highly unlikely, and probably inappropriate, for a set of research findings to have an immediate and significant impact on practice. Established practice, training and agency tradition militate against such sudden transformation of the heard or written word into practice; appropriately so or services could become a succession of new or fashionable fads. Furthermore, and equally important, given the usually complex interaction of human needs and social work service, it is rare for research findings to have simple, unequivocal implications for practice. These, as has been suggested earlier, must be teased out and agreed with those close to the delivery and receipt of services. When this has been achieved, changes or developments in policy and practice can be pursued in ways which take account of the relevant agency, management, educational and political traditions. Here researchers may have a collaborative role, but this must not be confused with that of policy makers, managers or teachers.

Conceptual conflicts and research aspirations

> Though this be madness, yet there is method in't.
>
> Shakespeare, *Hamlet*, Act III Scene ii

Thus far, the emphasis of this concluding chapter has been optimism about what can and should be attempted in the evaluation of social work effectiveness by pragmatic and eclectic means. The argument is that this is a proper stance as the art and science of evaluative research evolves. It is an argument, however, which takes philosophical and scientific risks and which has to balance, often precariously, the gains of the modest research endeavours with an appreciation of what should be expected of research which gives adequate attention to the complexities of the demands on social work and of the delivery of its services and which, most important of all, can identify relationships between outcome and intervention.

Research in the social sciences has for decades been subjected to criticisms and exhortations of philosophers' and scientists' conflicting views about the meaning and status of objectivity, truth and knowledge and therefore about the proper nature of scientific enquiry. Within social work research, these debates have been manifest in assertions, on the one hand, about the pre-eminence of experimental studies rooted in the traditions of positivism, and, on the other, about the primacy of interpretive approaches which challenge the overriding salience of any single intervention or outcome. As Fuller and Lovelock (1987, p. 689) remark, we face here a familiar chasm:

> ... between those approaches (which following popular but inadequate usage we have termed positivist) which aspire to imitation of the methods of the natural sciences and those which reject them, not merely pro-visionally (through some belief that the methodology of social science is 'as yet imperfect'), but on the grounds that the nature of the social world – and particularly, perhaps, that of social work – makes such methods categorically inappropriate. There really do seem to be stark choices here. One position implies a belief that the social sciences, while methodologically imperfect, are perfectible, and would lead to an ever more rigorous specification of variables, outcome measures, process measures, experimental conditions, and so on, with the promise of eventually being able to derive findings of both explanatory power and generalisability... The interpretative opposition, while embodying its own version of 'rigour' and at its best being no less intellectually demanding, would point in different directions, towards a more context-bound and situation-specific mode of evaluative research, one which offers accounts of and arguments from the particular situation under study.

This volume may appear innocent of such debate or crassly inconsistent in its apparent determination to live with and draw from different scientific traditions. Its authors' defence is precisely that it is possible to do this, and not only possible but necessary if knowledge about the impact of social work is to accumulate step by step. Thus we give a positive answer to the question raised by one of us early in the Centre's life: is a synthesis of different approaches possible? (Fuller and Lovelock, 1987, p. 687). This commitment to pragmatic eclecticism in research design and method is not new. It is encouraged by Smith (1987), and it has been acknowledged with ambiva-lence by Sheldon (1986) and Thyer (1989) as a *faute de mieux* and a step to more exclusive reliance on research approaches dominated by positivism. Although it is impossible to predict with accuracy the shape of evaluative research in social work during the next two or three decades, the Centre's experience so far leads us to believe that eclectism of design and method is not simply a transitory phenomenon, a confusion of paths to be trod before a clear and simple route can be identified. Rather, it is the only way in which substantial progress can be made in exploring and evaluating, in any depth, the impact of social work. The accompanying conceptual tensions are therefore not to be seen as simply unavoidable and embarrassing handicaps; they are necessary to the illumination of the different, often conflicting, and often complex elements which make up social work and to the debate about their significance.

Long-term research challenges

This cautious enthusiasm for the merits of a pragmatic and eclectic approach in contemporary evaluative research in social work must not be confused with complacency about what, ideally, remains to be achieved, or at least aspired to in the evaluation of social work services. What are these important research challenges, and what responses are likely or feasible?

1 Capturing the content of social work

To start with the more difficult problems, research should, for example, attempt increasingly sophisticated accounts of individual needs and interventions, including the manner in which the latter are delivered, and of how both change over time. In short, the nature of much social work requires extremely detailed analysis if the whole of an encounter between a social worker and a client is to be captured; but since research findings should be generalizable, substantial numbers of similar cases have to be studied in this way. This is rarely, if ever, feasible. The depth of understanding of the case study and the potential strength of findings derived from research with large samples is a highly desirable but often unattainable combination.

Furthermore, any one social work approach or service, although bearing a single name, may well include several different modes of delivery. Thus care management will take many different forms; non-custodial supervision will include differing combinations of help, control and counselling; and domiciliary services may vary greatly from case to case, agency to agency and even from worker to worker. Ideally, therefore, any evaluative study of supposedly homogeneous interventions should capture and compare the different approaches which bear a single name before making any general claims about their efficacy. Indeed, some will argue that to do otherwise does violence to the complex interactions of need and intervention which should characterize social work.

2 Comparing the impact of changing intervention

Evaluative research should also be able to compare the impact of innovative services with each other and with established provision. Social work is an important instrument of social policy and as such is required to deliver services designed to fulfil some general objective, such as care management for people needing care in the community, non-custodial supervision for serious offenders or the prevention or deterioration of serious problems. Evaluative research ought to provide a commentary on the impact of these forms of social work intervention. This ideally requires a comparison with the coverage and outcomes of the former services. Such comparative data are rarely available, although the more comprehensive monitoring now being developed in many agencies will, theoretically at least, make historical comparisons feasible in the future.

3 Tracing the relationship between intervention and outcome

There is occasions and causes, why and wherefore in all things.
> Shakespeare, *Henry V*, Act V Scene i

A last and extremely important aspiration concerns the relationship between intervention and outcome. Most social work interventions consist of more than one component and may include, for example, any combination of different kinds of practical help, counselling, supportive visiting, oversight or control, the behavioural, psychotherapeutic or family therapies, all of which have their own varieties. Ideally, therefore, in the interests of economy and efficiency, studies of effectiveness should be able to identify (and perhaps to cost) the outcomes attributable to each component. What, for example, was the impact for an elderly widower of the different components of his 'package of care' – domiciliary services or bereavement counselling? Were both essential and interlinked? Could an equally good or (poor) outcome be achieved with one or the other? It is difficult enough, as Chapter 5 has shown, to capture all the more or less explicit and identifiable components of intervention. To disentangle their different or linked outcomes, taking account of the varied needs they address is, given the feasible scale of studies and the state of existing research methods at present, well nigh impossible.

Two of these research challenges, the detailed comparison of the content and effects of different modes of help, or components of that help, are both driven by the central conundrum of evaluative research: how is it possible to demonstrate a causal relationship between intervention and impact? Researchers should not quail if they are unable to use, as will usually be the case, the cross-institutional and experimental designs best able to tackle this problem. Disciplined comparisons of users' problems and state before and after intervention have their place, especially if studies can be replicated and their conclusions reviewed and synthesized. And while the consideration of causal relationships is by definition a central concern for effectiveness research, attempts to demonstrate them should not so dominate the agenda that this inhibits work which cannot meet this expectation but which has all the other contributions discussed earlier in this volume. Furthermore, the demonstration of causal relationships is not just a scientific issue when it concerns such everyday matters as the perceived impact of help on those in need. Here the comment and judgement of those who give and receive help, of those who have coped with problems and those who still endure them, have a place in considering whether it is plausible that certain events or conditions are the product of help received. There may not be consensus among such voices, and while this adds to the puzzles of evaluative researchers, they cannot ignore the authority of those who speak from personal experience about the impact of help they have received.

It is wiser to acknowledge these major problems in evaluative research than to encourage flights of fancy and to raise, prematurely, unrealizable hopes. It must also be recognized that to describe the existing state of the art is not to prescribe its future. A decade from now, as research experience accumulates and evaluative research evolves, these reservations about what can be achieved may appear unduly pessimistic or down right wrong. Distant dreams should also not deter more immediate aspirations. There are several areas of work in which progress is needed and can realistically be expected during the next few years.

Some immediate priorities

1 Users' reactions

First, as pressure mounts for measures of quality control and quality assurance in social work services, and with increasing interest in user choice, there will be calls for surveys of large samples of different types of recipient. Such studies have their place. They may, for example, be particularly suited to measuring reactions, at different points, to specific components of service provision, say the meals or leisure activities in a day centre. Here these surveys may be part of detailed monitoring to control or increase the quality of services. It can also be useful to study the opinions of people in residential care to some aspects of their home's provision, e.g. the degree of choice, privacy and security afforded as well as 'hotel features', food, heating, quality of furnishings, and so on. These enquiries can give some indication of gaps between stated policies and residents' experience and some measure of satisfaction with aspects of care.

The task of the evaluative researcher is to select those aspects of social work services that it is sensible to study through surveys which are relatively economic in the resources they require and those which require more detailed in-depth analysis, usually of small samples. These might be chosen because they have particularly complex needs or because they are receiving a combination of services, perhaps including some of the most contentious interventions, such as the supervision of behaviour associated with child abuse or offending. Surveys may also need to be supplemented by qualitative interviews to explore, for example, shades of opinion, views about issues respondents believe to be important which were not included in the survey, or any reservations about the usually high level of satisfaction revealed by studies of users' views. Such interviews are also important in exploring the important difference between relatively high satisfaction with the care provided and users' preferred style of life. For example, satisfaction with various aspects of care in old people's homes must not be taken, at face value, as indicating residents' satisfaction with this way of life. For some, it may be the preferred option; for others, a *faute de mieux*; and some residents' stated satisfaction may, on further enquiry, be offset by their sadness at their predicament, their feelings of desertion by relatives and their resentment at a lack of alternatives.

There has been no shortage in social work research of such qualitative studies; indeed, these may be regarded as one of its strengths. The interviews, transcription and analysis can, however, be time-consuming, and require considerable research skills. There may also be disputes about the extent to which the conclusions of qualitative research can be generalized. Indeed, the strength of such studies may well be their clear indication that in responding to some extensively complex and perhaps contentious problems, for example, juvenile delinquency or care of people with chronic mental illness, there is no single or majority view about best practice. In such cases, the conclusions of surveys which seek the inevitably simple responses they can produce are likely to be simplistic and misleading.

Not all evaluative research deals with such large and complicated questions. If users' views are to be important in practice, and not simply a fashionable rhetorical flourish, researchers need to become adept in selecting the topics appropriate for the various methods of enquiry, and combinations of methods, that are possible. They must also be firm and clear in their advice to policy makers, who will be increasingly hungry for user responses, about the strength, sense and validity of conclusions and findings likely to emanate from different types of study.

2 Quality of life

Second, studies of 'quality of life' need more analytical precision and comparison between the experiences of the general population and particular subgroups who may need a variety of social work services. For example, it appears that in general satisfaction with quality of life increases with age, while those experiencing more favourable living conditions are more likely to express dissatisfaction. Only recently, however, have more detailed explorations begun to be made of how these general principles vary across client groups and across different domains. How, for example, is 'quality of life' interpreted by elderly people who have the tragedies and misfortunes which are the often inescapable companions of advancing age: bereavement, disability, illness?

3 Making the most of small studies

Third, social work research needs to learn to move more easily between the analysis of the substantial databases which should accrue from the large-scale monitoring of user referral, requests, assessed needs and service delivery and the illumination which emerges from smaller more detailed studies. These proliferate in social work research and, on their own, each is likely to seem, for one reason or another, extremely limited and to bear little relationship to the larger studies, which may be primarily quantitative in nature or which include qualitative data as well.

Small studies may, however, be either particularly appropriate or, indeed, the only sensible option in certain situations. These include agencies' need to gain some swift, albeit impressionistic, understanding of the immediate impact of new legislation on certain user groups or on the operation of services. Innovative projects, or those using very unusual forms of intervention, may also best be examined by small studies, perhaps to list the feasibility of longer, comparative research. As discussed later, small studies of individual or team practice can encourage the critical evaluation of services, particularly when they become a regular feature of agencies' approach to their work. In such circumstances, small-scale research is also likely to be all that resources and especially time allow.

The value of small studies and their comparison with larger-scale research is enhanced by the systematic review and synthesis of findings in which general trends may be detected while allowances are made for differences in studies' focus and methods. In addition, the technique of meta-analysis, which focuses on how much difference something makes (the magnitude of the effect) and not on whether the difference in individual studies was statistically significant, may be particularly appropriate to social work research in which it is both inevitable and invaluable that small studies will proliferate. As yet, there has been little systematic use made of meta-analysis in studies of social work services, although the technique has been applied in the field of delinquency (see, e.g. Garrett, 1985; Andrews *et al.*, 1990) and is said to be promising in some studies of educational practice which have examined, for example, teacher style or classroom regime, and which may have some parallels in social work (Fitz-Gibbon, 1984). Unfortunately, the promise of meta-analysis often cannot be fulfilled because of the common failure of the reports of many small studies to report their samples, methods and findings in sufficient detail. Discipline and precision in such matters are thus as important in small studies as in large ones, issues which require attention as practitioners come to undertake more small-scale research and students continue to write research-based dissertations where time allows only small endeavours but where the academic context could encourage awareness of and, as far as possible, attention to the basic requirements of evaluative research.

The contribution of small, focused studies is considerable in encouraging practical interest in identifying the purposes of interventions, their form and impact. Chapter 1 has outlined the various pressures on social workers to think more clearly about the effectiveness of their endeavours and the Social Work Research Centre has found considerable enthusiasm among practitioners to learn some of the basic skills of evaluative research and to test them out in a context of small, highly focused studies of their own or their immediate colleagues' work. This has been done through an experimental programme which builds on the experience reported by Whittaker and Archer (1989) and Addison (1988) and which has been funded by the Joseph Rowntree Foundation. It involves practitioners spending six days over a nine-month period in lectures and workshops and individual sessions with members of the Centre. In addition, programme participants are expected to devote half a day a fortnight to their study, although some probably spend more. Studies have included a comparison of the expectations of elderly people about to enter residential care and a few weeks after their admission; an analysis of the congruence between family members' and family therapists' definition of problems at the beginning and end of therapy; carers' perceptions of a support group; potential adopters' assessments of an information and selection group; the reactions of parents of children with cancer to their initial contacts with the social work service of the oncology unit and the evaluation of respite care resources. The intention is that participants will produce a short report of their studies, methods and findings for the programme and their agencies and for other dissemination to be planned as appropriate. This experimental programme will be repeated and its outcomes, including the experience of the participants and the reports and other publications produced, carefully evaluated.

Such a modest programme demonstrates that small-scale evaluation studies are possible and productive. It also encourages practitioners to think critically about the relevance and feasibility of research and removes it from a distant and sometimes rather despised pedestal. It helps to place interest in effectiveness at the centre of agency practice, and it brings into a working alliance practitioners and researchers.

4 Linking social work, politics and social policy

The last and continuing priority for those who study the effectiveness of social work is to see this as inextricably linked with moral, social and political questions, central to social policy, on which there can be no general agreement. Much of the interest and worth of social work lies in its contribution to alleviating the enduring problems of the human condition, problems of poverty, ill-health, disability, struggling and disintegrating relationships. But since the responses to such troubles are often both contentious and ill-resourced, social work, by its association with them, can reap the whirlwind. Thus, when care management falls apart and old people deteriorate in residential care or their daughters collapse from overwork or anxiety, when children are killed by parents or removed from them, amid cries of protest, when supportive services fail to prevent deterioration or disaster, so will the storms break around the world of social work. Then all its audiences – the recipients of social work, practitioners, managers, politicians and ordinary citizens – can and should place their own value on what has happened. For these arguments to be fruitful, these voices must speak with authority which goes beyond anecdote, prejudice and individual experience. It is thus the responsibility of the researchers of social work to do their best to ensure that this debate can be grounded in knowledge about the suffering to be confronted, the means of so doing and the effects, for good and ill, of the designs of politicians and of the labours of practitioners.

ANNOTATED
BIBLIOGRAPHY

Addison, C. (1988). *Planning Investigative Projects: A Workbook for Social Services Practitioners*. National Institute for Social Work, London. A down to earth, practical and relatively brief guide, covering the development of a proposal (with useful worksheets) and some remarks on methods, with a stress on the qualitative.

Bailey, K.D. (1978). *Methods of Social Research*. Free Press, New York. An excellent introduction to the range of methods available to the social researcher. The pros and cons of different methods of data collection are discussed and clear illustrative examples presented.

Bowling, A. (1991). *Measuring Health: A Review of Quality of Life Measuring Scales*. Open University Press, Buckingham. Provides a comprehensive account of scales useful for both health and social care research.

Dawson, B.G., Klass, M.D., Guy, R.F. and Edgby, C.K. (1991). *Understanding Social Work Research*. Allyn and Bacon, Boston, Mass. This substantial textbook, written for American graduate and undergraduate social work students, explains and to some extent demonstrates research concepts and methods, including statistical procedures. It could be a useful reference book although, despite its title, the contents are not closely related to social work.

Everitt, A., Hardiker, P., Littlewood, J. and Mullender, A. (1992). *Applied Research for Better Practice*. Macmillan, London. Provides a useful approach for practitioners interested in researching their own work. The authors explore the possibilities of integrating research with practice.

Fisher, M. (ed.) (1983). *Speaking of Clients*. Joint Unit for Social Services Research, University of Sheffield. A useful collection of papers about studying the user perspective, which is both reflective and practice-oriented. Includes contributions by Eric Sainsbury, Tim Booth and Mike Fisher.

Goldberg, E.M. and Connelly, N. (1981). *Evaluative Research in Social Care*. Heinemann, London. Another collection of academic papers which report research and illustrate different methodological approaches, and one of the basic texts on evaluative research.

Kane, E. (1985). *Doing Your Own Research*. Marion Boyars, London. Another basic and user-friendly guide for the inexperienced researcher.

Knapp, M. (1984). *The Economics of Social Care*. Macmillan, London. Still the most comprehensive and comprehensible, if at times technical, introduction to cost-effectiveness and cost-benefit analysis in the field of social work.

Lishman, J. (ed.) (1983). *Research Highlights 8: Evaluation*. University of Aberdeen, Aberdeen (2nd edn, 1989, Jessica Kingsley, London). A collection of academic papers on different aspects of the theory and practice of evaluation aiming to represent different designs and methods (e.g. controlled experiments, illuminative evaluation, cost-effectiveness, etc.). Contains the important and influential paper by Smith and Cantley on pluralistic evaluation.

McDowell, I. and Newell, C. (1987). *Measuring Health: A Guide to Rating Scales and Questionnaires*. Oxford University Press, Oxford. Health in this volume is treated broadly with the scales reviewed dealing with functional, disability, psychological well-being, social health (via social support and social adjustment) and quality of life as well as physical illness. The range of scales considered is rather wider than those in Streiner and Norman (1989), which is half the length. Conceptual and practical issues are clearly discussed but the book is more suitable for those with some research experience than for complete novices.

Milne, D. (ed.) (1987). *Evaluating Mental Health Practice Methods and Applications*. Croom Helm, London. Aimed at mental health practitioners, a general introduction on principles of evaluation is followed by chapters contributed from a range of disciplines (including social workers) which provide an interesting overview and comparison of different strategies.

Patton, M.Q. (1980). *Qualitative Evaluation Methods*. Sage, London. An American book with features that some will find irritating, others attractive! A plea for qualitative evaluation methods, which many assume (wrongly, according to the author) do not carry conviction with policy makers; contains many examples, though few are drawn from social services.

Sainsbury, E. (1987). Client studies: Their contribution and limitations in influencing social work practice. *British Journal of Social Work*, **17**, 635–44. Sainsbury reflects on the methodological lessons to be learnt from client studies, seeks to clarify how they can be used, and suggests ways forward.

Sheldon, B. (1986). Social work effectiveness experiments: Review and implications. *British Journal of Social Work*, **16**, 223–42. A well-known review of evaluative research on social work which challenges the widely held view that social work emerges badly from studies of its effectiveness. Sheldon argues that when social work activities are clearly focused, problems clearly identified and modest and specified goals set with clients, then carefully controlled studies produce positive results.

Streiner, D.L. and Norman, G.R. (1989). *Health Measurement Scales: A Practical Guide to Their Development and Use*. Oxford University Press, Oxford. This is a useful critical review of a number of scales which can be used in social work research with some straightforward discussion of issues to consider in their selection. The hazards and possibilities of developing new scales are also explored thoroughly and practically.

Webb, E.J., Campbell, D.T., Schwartz, R.D. and Sechrest, L. (1966). *Unobtrusive Measures: Nonreactive Research in the Social Sciences*. Rand McNally, Chicago. From rummaging through dustbins to measuring the amount of wear on museum floors, Webb *et al.* present the case for the use of imaginative research methods to supplement more traditional techniques such as the interview and questionnaire.

Whittaker, D.S. and Archer, J.L. (1989). *Research by Social Workers: Capitalising on Experience*. CCETSW, London. Covers the same ground as Addison, but in much more detail – sometimes excessive in view of its target audience – but contains much that is useful. The book is very generous in the use of everyday examples, and covers a wide range of methods of data collection and analysis. Again, useful worksheets.

BIBLIOGRAPHY

Addison, C. (1988). *Planning Investigative Projects: A Workbook for Social Services Practitioners*. National Institute for Social Work, London.

Affleck, J.W. and McGuire, R.J. (1984). The measurement of psychiatric rehabilitation status: A review of the needs and a new scale. *British Journal of Psychiatry*, **145**, 517–25.

Andreason, N. (1984). *Scale for the Assessment of Negative Symptoms (SANS)*. Iowa, University of Iowa.

Andrews, D.A., Zinger, I., Hope, R.D., Bonta, J., Gendreau, P. and Cullen, F.T. (1990). Does correctional treatment work? A clinically relevant and psychologically informed meta-analysis. *Criminology*, **28**, 369–404.

Apte, R. (1968). *Halfway Houses: A New Dilemma in Institutional Care*. Occasional Papers on Social Administration, No. 27. London, Bell.

Audit Commission (1985). *Managing Social Services for the Elderly more Effectively*. HMSO, London.

Audit Commission (1986). *Making a Reality of Community Care*. HMSO, London.

Audit Commission (1989a). *Developing Community Care for Adults with a Mental Handicap*. HMSO, London.

Audit Commission (1989b). *The Probation Service: Promoting Value for Money*. HMSO, London.

Audit Inspectorate (1983a). *Social Services Care of Mentally Handicapped People*. HMSO, London.

Audit Inspectorate (1983b). *Social Services: Provision of Care to the Elderly*. HMSO, London.

Avebury, K. (1984). *Home Life: A Code of Practice for Residential Care*. Centre for Policy on Ageing, London.

Bailey, K.D. (1978). *Methods of Social Research*. Free Press, New York.

Bailey, S. (1987). *A Mental Health Centre: The User's View in its Evaluation*. Social Services Research, No. 3, pp. 25–38. Department of Social Administration, University of Birmingham.

Baldwin, S., Godfrey, C. and Propper, C. (eds) (1989). *Quality of Life: Perspectives and Policies*. Routledge, London.

Barclay, P.M. (1982). *Social Workers: Their Role and Tasks*. Bedford Square Press, London.

Barnes, M. and Miller, N. (1988). Performance measurement in the personal social services. *Research Policy and Planning (Special Issue)*, **6** (2).

Barnes, M., Bowl, R. and Fisher, M. (1990). *Sectioned: Social Services and the 1983 Mental Health Act*. Routledge, London.

Beecham, J., Knapp, M. and Fenyo, A. (1991). Costs, needs and outcomes: Community care for people with long-term mental health problems. *Schizophrenia Bulletin*, No. 3, August.

Beiser, M. (1974). Components and correlates of mental well-being. *Journal of Health and Social Behaviour*, **15**, 320–27.

Benjamin, S., Decalmer, P. and Haran, D. (1982). Community screening for mental illness: A validity study of the General Health Questionnaire. *British Journal of Psychiatry*, **140**, 174–80.

Berger, M. (1983). Towards maximising the utility of consumer satisfaction as an outcome. In M.J. Lambert, E.R. Christensen and S.S. DeJulio (eds), *The Assessment of Psychotherapy Outcome*. John Wiley, New York.

Berthoud, R. (1991). The Social Fund – Is it working? *Policy Studies*, **12** (11), 1–13.

Birchall, E. and Hallett, C. (1991). *Co-ordination and Child Protection: A Review of Literature*. HMSO, London.

Black, J., Bowl, R., Critcher, C., Grant, G. and Stockford, D. (1983). *Social Work in Context*. Tavistock, London.

Blagg, H. and Smith, D. (1989). *Crime, Penal Policy and Social Work*. Longman, London.

Bland, R., Bland, R.E., Cheetham, J., Lapsley, I. and Llewellyn, S. (forthcoming). *Efficiency Effectiveness and Quality of Care in Old People's Homes in Scotland*. Scottish Home and Health Department, Edinburgh.

Bland, R.E. and Bland, R. (1990). *Measuring Quality of Care in Old People's Homes*, Social Work Research Centre, University of Stirling.

Bland, R.E., Brooks, R., Cheetham, J., Fuller, R. and Lapsley, I. (1990). *Efficiency, Effectiveness and Quality of Care in Old People's Homes in Scotland: The Report of a Preliminary Study*. Social Work Research Centre and Institute of Public Sector Accounting Research, University of Stirling.

Booth, T. (1985). *Home Truths: Old People's Homes and the Outcome of Care*. Gower, Aldershot.

Booth, T. (1988). *Developing Policy Research*. Avebury, Aldershot.

Bottomley, A.K. and Pease, K. (1986). *Crime and Punishment: Interpreting the Data*. Open University Press, Buckingham.

Bottoms, A., Brown, P., McWilliams, B., McWilliams, W., Nellis, M. and Pratt, J. (1990). *Intermediate Treatment and Juvenile Justice: Key Findings and Implications from a National Survey of Intermediate Treatment Policy and Practice*. HMSO, London.

Bowl, R. and Fuller, R. (1982). *A Study of Research in Social Services and Social Work Departments*. Department of Social Administration, University of Birmingham.

Bradshaw, J. and Lawton, D. (1978). Tracing the causes of stress in families with handicapped children. *British Journal of Social Work*, **8**, 181–92.

Brown, L. (1989). *Perceptions of Prevention Held by Social Work Practitioners and Their Managers*. Social Work Research Centre, University of Stirling.

Brown, L. and Fuller, R. (1991a). *Joint Police/Social Work Investigation in Child Abuse: A Study of Central Region's Joint Initiative*. Social Work Research Centre, University of Stirling.

Brown, L. and Fuller, R. (1991b). Joint police and social work investigation in child abuse: an evaluation. *Children and Society*, **5**, 232–41.

Buckingham, K. and Ludbrook, A. (1989). *Costing Community Care – Some Problems and Proposals.* Discussion Paper, No. 6/89. Health Economics Research Unit, University of Aberdeen.

Bulmer, M. (1982). *The Uses of Social Research.* Allen and Unwin, London.

Bulmer, M. (ed.) (1987). *Social Science Research and Government.* Cambridge University Press, Cambridge.

Bulmer, M., with Bunting, K.G., Blume, S.S., Carley, M. and Weiss, C.H. (1986). *Social Science and Public Policy.* Allen and Unwin, London.

Burden, R.L. (1980). Measuring the effects of stress on the mothers of handicapped infants: Must depression always follow? *Child Care, Health and Development,* **6**, 111–25.

Campbell, A. (1976). Subjective measures of well-being. *American Psychologist,* **31**, 117–24.

Carnie, J. (1990). *Sentencers' Perceptions of Community Service by Offenders.* Central Research Unit, Scottish Office, Edinburgh.

Central Council for the Education and Training of Social Workers (1989). *Requirements and Regulations for the Diploma in Social Work.* Paper No. 30. CCETSW, London.

Challis, D. and Chesterman, J. (1985). A system for monitoring social work activity with the frail elderly. *British Journal of Social Work,* **15**, 115–32.

Challis, D. and Davies, B.P. (1986). *Case Management in Community Care.* Gower, London.

Challis, D., Knapp, M. and Davis, B. (1984). Cost effectiveness evaluation in social care. In J. Lishman (ed.), *Research Highlights No. 8: Evaluation.* University of Aberdeen, Aberdeen.

Challis, D., Darton, R., Johnson, L., Stone, M., Traske, K. and Wall, M. (1989). *Supporting Frail Elderly People at Home.* PSSRU, University of Kent.

Challis, D., Cheesum, R., Chesterman, J., Luckett, R. and Traske, K. (1990). *Case Management in Social and Health Care.* PSSRU, University of Kent.

Cheetham, J. (1989). Values in action. In S. Shardlow (ed.), *The Values of Change in Social Work.* Tavistock, London.

Cheetham, J. (1991). *The Effectiveness of Homemakers.* Social Work Research Centre, University of Stirling.

Cheetham, J. (1992). Conceptions of social work. In C. Crouch and A. Heath (eds), *Social Research and Social Reform: Essays in Honour of A.H. Halsey.* Oxford University Press, Oxford.

Cherlin, A. and Reeder, L. (1975). The dimensions of psychological well-being: A critical review. *Sociological Methods and Research,* **4**, 189–214.

Clarke, R.V.G. and Cornish, D.B. (1972). *The Controlled Trial in Institutional Research – Paradigm or Pitfall?* Home Office Research Study No. 15. HMSO, London.

Clear, T.R. and Hardyman, P.L. (1990). The new intensive supervision movement. *Crime and Delinquency,* **36**, 42–60.

Clifford, P., Leiper, R., Lavender, A. and Pilling, S. (1989). *Assuring Quality in Mental Health Services: The QUARTZ System.* Research and Development for Psychiatry, London.

Colton, M.J. (1988). *Dimensions of Substitute Child Care.* Avebury, Aldershot.

Cooper, B., Harwin, B.G., Depla, C. and Shepherd, M. (1975). Mental health care in the community: An evaluative study. *Psychological Medicine,* **5**, 372–80.

Cooper, J. (1978). *Patterns of Family Placement.* National Children's Bureau, London.

Cooper, P., Osborn, M., Gath, D. and Feggetter, G. (1982). Evaluation of a modified self-report measure of social adjustment. *British Journal of Psychiatry,* **141**, 68–75.

Corney, R. and Clare, A. (1983). The effectiveness of attached social workers in the management of depressed women in general practice. *British Journal of Social Work*, **13**, 57–74.

Cornish, D.B. and Clarke, R.V.G. (1987). Social science in government. In M. Bulmer (ed.), *Social Science Research and Government*. Cambridge University Press, Cambridge.

Coyle, D. (1988). *Prevention Clarified?* Queen's University, Belfast.

Darton, R. and Knapp, M. (1984). Factors associated with valuations in the costs of local authority old people's homes. *Ageing and Society*, **9**, 157–83.

Davies, B. and Knapp, M. (1981). *Old People's Homes and the Production of Welfare*. Routledge and Kegan Paul, London.

Davies, B. and Knapp, M. (1988). The production of welfare approach: Evidence and argument from the PSSRU. *British Journal of Social Work*, **18**, 1–73 (suppl.).

Dawson, B.G., Klass, M.D., Guy, R.F. and Edbgy, C.K. (1991). *Understanding Social Work Research*. Allyn and Bacon, Boston, Mass.

Denzin, N.K. (1970). *The Research Act*. Aldine, Chicago, Ill.

Department of Health/SSI (1989). *Homes are for Living In*. HMSO, London.

Dunlop, A. (1974). *The Approved School Experience*. Home Office Research Study No. 25. HMSO, London.

Endicott, J. and Spitzer, R.L. (1978). A diagnostic interview – The schedule for affective disorders and schizophrenia. *Archives of General Psychiatry*, **35**, 839–44.

England, H. (1986). *Social Work as Art*. Allen and Unwin, London.

Etzioni, A. (1968). *The Active Society*. Free Press, New York.

Evans, N., Kendall, I., Lovelock, R. and Powell, J. (1986). *Something to Look Forward To*. Report No. 15. Social Services Research and Intelligence Unit, Southampton.

Farrington, D.P. and West, D.J. (1981). The Cambridge study in delinquent development. In S.A. Mednick and A.E. Baert (eds), *Prospective Longitudinal Research*. Oxford University Press, Oxford.

Feragne, M., Longabaugh, R. and Stevenson, J.F. (1983). The Psychosocial Functioning Inventory. *Evaluation and the Health Professions*, **6**, 25–48.

Ferri, E.M. (1981). Evaluating combined nursery centres. In E.M. Goldberg and N. Connelly (eds), *Evaluative Research in Social Care*. Heinemann, London.

Fisher, M. (ed.) (1983). *Speaking of Clients*. Joint Unit for Social Services Research, University of Sheffield.

Fitz-Gibbon, G. (1984). Meta-analysis: An explication. *British Educational Research Journal*, **1**, 135–44.

Flanagan, J.C. (1982). Measurement of quality of life: Current state of the art. *Archives of Physical and Medical Rehabilitation*, **63**, 56–9.

Fogelman, K. (ed.) (1983). *Growing Up in Great Britain: Papers from the National Child Development Study*. Macmillan, London.

Folkard, M.S., Fowles, A.J., McWilliams, B.C., McWilliams, W., Smith, D.D., Smith, D.E. and Walmsley, G.R. (1974). *IMPACT (Intensive Matched Probation and After-Care Treatment) Vol. 1: The Design of the Probation Experiment and an Interim Evaluation*. Home Office Research Study No. 24. HMSO, London.

Folkard, M.S., Smith, D.E. and Smith, D.D. (1976). *IMPACT (Intensive Matched Probation and After-Care Treatment) Vol. 2: The Results of the Experiment*. Home Office Research Study No. 36. HMSO, London.

Freeman, C. and Tyrer, P. (eds) (1989). *Research Methods in Psychiatry*. Gaskell, London.

Fuller, R. (1985). *Issues in the Assessment of Children in Care*. National Children's Bureau, London.

Fuller, R. (1987a). *The Cross-Institutional Design: Paradigm or Pitfall?* Social Work Research Centre, University of Stirling.

Fuller, R. (1987b). *Researching Prevention.* Social Work Research Centre, University of Stirling.

Fuller, R. (1988). *The M.A.R.S. Project: A Study of Preventive Work.* Social Work Research Centre, University of Stirling.

Fuller, R. (1989). *The Prediction Method in the M.A.R.S Study: An Alternative to a Control Group?* Social Work Research Centre, University of Stirling.

Fuller, R. and Lovelock, R. (1987). Approaches to social work evaluation. *British Journal of Social Work,* **17** (6), 685–94.

Fuller, R. and Petch, A. (1989). *Organisation and Outcomes: Services to the Elderly (Report of the First Stage).* Social Work Research Centre, University of Stirling.

Fuller, R. and Petch, A. (1991). Does area team organisation make a difference? *British Journal of Social Work,* **21**, 471–89.

Garrett, C.J. (1985). Effects of residential treatment in adjudicated developments: A meta-analysis. *Journal of Research in Crime and Delinquency,* **22**, 287–308.

Gendreau, P. and Ross, R.R. (1979). Effective correctional treatment: Bibliotherapy for cynics. *Crime and Delinquency,* **25**, 463–89.

Gendreau, P. and Ross, R.R. (1987). Revivification of rehabilitation: Evidence for the 1980s. *Justice Quarterly,* **4**, 349–407.

Gibbons, J. (1981). An evaluation of the effectiveness of social work intervention using task-centred methods after deliberate self-poisoning. In E.M. Goldberg and N. Connelly (eds), *Evaluative Research in Social Care.* Heinemann, London.

Gilleard, C.J. (1984). *Living with Dementia: Community Care of the Elderly Mentally Infirm.* London, Croom Helm.

Glendinning, C. (1986). *A Single Door.* Allen and Unwin, London.

Goldberg, D.P. (1972). *The Detection of Psychiatric Illness by Questionnaire.* Oxford University Press, Oxford.

Goldberg, D.P. and Hillier, V.F. (1979). A scaled version of the General Health Questionnaire. *Psychological Medicine,* **9**, 139–45.

Goldberg, D.P., Cooper, B., Eastwood, M.R., Kedward, H.B. and Shepherd, M. (1970). A standardized psychiatric interview for use in community surveys. *British Journal of Preventive Social Medicine,* **24**, 18–23.

Goldberg, E.M. and Connelly, N. (eds) (1981). *Evaluative Research in Social Care.* Heinemann, London.

Goldberg, E.M. and Connelly, N. (1982). *The Effectiveness of Social Care for the Elderly.* Heinemann Educational, London.

Goldberg, E.M. and Fruin, D.J. (1976). Towards accountability in social work: A case review system for social workers. *British Journal of Social Work,* **6**, 3–22.

Goldberg, E.M. and Warburton, R.W. (1979). *Ends and Means in Social Work.* George Allen and Unwin, London.

Goldberg, E.M., Warburton, R.W., McGuinness, B. and Rowlands, J.H. (1977). Towards accountability in social work: One year's intake to an area office. *British Journal of Social Work,* **7**, 257–83.

Goldberg, E.M., Warburton, R.W., Lyons, L.J. and Willmott, R.R. (1978). Towards accountability in social work: long-term social work in an area office. *British Journal of Social Work,* **8**, 253–87.

Goldberg, E.M., Gibbons, J. and Sinclair, I. (1985). *Problems, Tasks and Outcomes: The Evaluation of Task-centred Casework in Three Settings.* George Allen and Unwin, London.

Gudex, C. (1986). *QALYS and Their Use in the Health Service.* Discussion Paper No. 20. Centre for Health Economics, University of York.

Gutek, B. (1978). Strategies for studying client satisfaction. *Journal of Social Issues*, **34**, 44–56.

HMSO (1989). *Caring for People: Community Care in the Next Decade and Beyond*. HMSO, London.

Hall, J.N. (1979). Assessment procedures used in studies on long-stay patients: A survey of papers published in the British Journal of Psychiatry. *British Journal of Psychiatry*, **135**, 330–35.

Hall, J.N. (1980). Ward rating scales for long-stay patients: A review. *Psychological Medicine*, **10**, 277–88.

Halsey, A.H. (1972). *Educational Priority*. HMSO, London.

Harris, M. (1988). *The Evaluation of Quality of Life in the Community*. Huddersfield Health Authority, Huddersfield.

Heclo, H. (1972). Policy analysis: A review article. *British Journal of Political Studies*, **2**, 83–108.

Hevey, D. (1984). *Linking Research and Practice: The Experience of a Research Liaison Officer*. ESRC, London.

Hewett, S. (1979). Somewhere to live: a pilot study of hostel care. In M.R. Olsen (ed.), *The Care of the Mentally Disordered: An Examination of some Alternatives to Hospital Care*. British Association of Social Workers, Birmingham.

Holman, R. (1988). *Putting Families First: Prevention and Child Care*. Macmillan Educational, London.

Holmes, N., Shah, A. and Wing, L. (1982). The Disability Assessment Schedule: A brief screening device for use with the mentally retarded. *Psychological Medicine*, **12**, 879–90.

Home Office (1988). *Report of the Work of the Prison Service 1978/88*. Cm. 516. HMSO, London.

Home Office (1989). *Probation Statistics, England and Wales 1982*. HMSO, London.

Home Office (1990). *Supervision and Punishment in the Community: A Framework for Action*. HMSO, London.

Hudson, B.L. and Macdonald, G.M. (1986). *Behavioural Social Work: An Introduction*. Macmillan, Basingstoke.

Hudson, H. and Dobson, B. (1991). *Evaluation of the Epic Project: Interim Report*. University of Stirling.

Humphrey, C. (1991). Calling on the experts: The Financial Management Initiative (FMI), private sector management consultants and the probation service. *The Howard Journal*, **30**, 1–18.

Hunt, S., McKenna, S.P., McEwen, J., Backett, E.M., Williams, J. and Papp, E. (1980). A quantitative approach to perceived health status: A validation survey. *Journal of Epidemiology and Community Health*, **34**, 281–6.

Hunt, S., McEwan, J. and McKenna, S.P. (1981). *The Nottingham Health Profile – User's Manual* available from Galen Research & Consultancy, Southern Hey, 137 Barlow Moor Road, West Didsbury, Manchester M20 8PW.

Huxley, P. (1986). *Quality Measurement in Mental Health Services: A Discussion Paper on Quality of Life Measurement*. Good Practices in Mental Health, London.

Ignatieff, M. (1984). *The Needs of Strangers*. Chatto and Windus, London.

Jenkins, S. (1987). The limited domain of effectiveness research. *British Journal of Social Work*, **17**, 575–94.

Jones, C.A. (1985). *A Second Chance for Families*. Child Welfare League of America, New York.

Kane, R.L. and Kane, R.L. (1981). *Assessing the Elderly: A Practical Guide to Measurement*. Lexington Books, Mass.

Kassebaum, G., Ward, D. and Wilner, D. (1976). *Prison Treatment and Parole Survival: An Empirical Assessment*. John Wiley, New York.

Kind, P. (1986). *Measuring Quality of Life: The State of the Art.* Centre for Health Economics, University of York.

King, R.D., Raynes, N.V. and Tizard, J. (1971). *Patterns of Residential Care.* Routledge and Kegan Paul, London.

Knapp, M. (1984). *The Economics of Social Care.* Macmillan, London.

Knapp, M. (1991). Cost. *Administration in Social Work,* **15**, 45–63.

Knapp, M. and Fenyo, A. (1988). Prison costs: Why the variation? *Home Office Research Bulletin,* **25**, 9–13.

Knapp, M. and Netten, A. (1991). *Reparation, Mediation and Prosecution: A Study of Comparative Costs.* Discussion Paper No. 710. PSSRU, University of Kent.

Knapp, M. and Robertson, E. (1986). Has intermediate treatment proved cost-effective? In A. Harrison and A. Gretton (eds), *Crime UK 1986.* Policy Journals, Newbury.

Knapp, M., Robertson, E. and McIvor, G. (1989). *Community Service Orders as Alternatives to Imprisonment: Evidence on Comparative Costs.* Discussion Paper No. 644. PSSRU, University of Kent.

Knapp, M., Beecham, J., Anderson, J., Dayson, D., Leff, J., Margolius, O., O'Driscoll, C. and Wills, W. (1990a). The TAPS Project 3: Predicting the community costs of closing psychiatric hospitals. *British Journal of Psychiatry,* **157**, 661–70.

Knapp, M., Cambridge, P., Thomason, C., Beecham, J., Allen, C. and Darton, R. (1990b). Care in the community: Lessons from a demonstration programme. *Care in the Community Newsletter,* No. 9.

Knapp, M., Cambridge, P., Thomason, C., Beecham, J., Allen, C. and Darton, R. (1991). *Care in the Community: Challenge and Demonstration.* Avebury, Aldershot.

Knapp, M., Robertson, E. and McIvor, G. (1992). The comparative costs of community service and custody in Scotland. *The Howard Journal,* **31**, 8–30.

Krawiecka, K., Goldberg, D. and Vaughan, M. (1977). A standardised psychiatric assessment scale for rating chronic psychotic patients. *Acta Scandinavica Psychiatrica,* **55**, 299–308.

Kurkowski, H. (1989). Adult mental handicap: Respite care and the older carer. Unpublished MSc Dissertation, University of Stirling.

Latessa, E.J. (1987). The effectiveness of intensive supervision with high risk probationers. In B.R. McCarthy (ed.), *Intermediate Punishment: Intensive Supervision, Home Confinement and Electronic Surveillance.* Criminal Justice Press, Monsey, N.Y.

Latessa, E.J. and Vito, G.F. (1988). The effects of intensive supervision on shock probationers. *Journal of Criminal Justice,* **16**, 319–30.

Lavender, A. (1987a). The measurement of the quality of care in psychiatric rehabilitation settings: Development of the Model Standards Questionnaires. *Behavioural Psychotherapy,* **15**, 201–214.

Lavender, A. (1987b). Improving the quality of care on psychiatric hospital rehabilitation wards – A controlled evaluation. *British Journal of Psychiatry,* **150**, 476–81.

Lawton, M.P. (1972). The dimensions of morale. In D.P. Kent (ed.), *Research Planning and Action for the Elderly.* Behavioural Publications, New York.

Lawton, M.P. (1975). Philadelphia Geriatric Center Morale Scale: A revision. *Journal of Gerontology,* **30**, 85–9.

Lehman, A.F. (1983a). The well-being of chronic mental patients: Assessing their quality of life. *Archives of General Psychiatry,* **40**, 369–73.

Lehman, A.F. (1983b). The effects of psychiatric symptoms on quality of life assessments among the chronically mentally ill. *Evaluation and Program Planning,* **6**, 143–51.

Lehman, A.F., Ward, N.C. and Linn, L.S. (1982). Chronic mental patients: The quality of life issue. *American Journal of Psychiatry,* **139**, 1271–5.

Le Touze, S. and Pahl, J. (1991). *Building New Lives? A Study of People Moving into a Community Care Scheme from Long Stay Hospitals.* Centre for Health Service Studies, University of Kent.

Levin, E.M., Sinclair, I. and Gorbach, P. (1985). The effectiveness of the home help services with confused old people and their families. *Research Policy and Planning,* **3** (2), 1–7.

Levine, S. (1987). The changing terrains in medical sociology: Emergent concern with quality of life. *Journal of Health and Social Behavior,* **28**, 1–16.

Lindblom, C. (1980). *The Policy-making Process.* Prentice Hall, Engelwood Cliffs, N.J.

Lipton, D., Martinson, R. and Wilks, J. (1975). *Effectiveness of Correctional Treatment: A Survey of Treatment Evaluation Studies.* Praeger, Springfield, Mass.

Lishman, J. (ed.) (1984). *Research Highlights 8: Evaluation.* University of Aberdeen Press, Aberdeen.

Logan, C.H. (1972). Evaluation research in crime and delinquency: a reappraisal. *Journal of Criminal Law, Criminology and Police Science,* **63**, 378–87.

Lyon, C. (1989). *Open Door – Closed Options: An Evaluation of the Open Door Accommodation Project.* Department of Housing Administration/Social Work Research Centre, University of Stirling.

Martinson, R. (1974). What works? Questions and answers about prison reform. *The Public Interest,* **23**, 22–54.

Mattinson, J. and Sinclair, I. (1979). *Mate and Stalemate.* Blackwell, London.

Mayer, J. and Timms, N. (1970). *The Client Speaks.* Routledge and Kegan Paul, London.

McCreadie, R.G. and Barron, E.T. (1984). The Nithsdale Schizophrenia Survey: IV. Social adjustment by self-report. *British Journal of Psychiatry,* **144**, 547–50.

McDowell, I. and Newell, C. (1987). *Measuring Health: A Guide to Rating Scales and Questionnaires.* Oxford University Press, Oxford.

McGlew, T., Robertson, A., Gilloran, A., McKee, R., McKinley, A. and Wight, D. (1991). *An Empirical Study of Job Satisfaction among Nurses and the Quality of Care Received by Patients in Psychogeriatric Wards in Scottish Hospitals.* Scottish Home and Health Department, Edinburgh.

McIvor, G. (1989). *An Evaluative Study of Community Service by Offenders in Scotland.* Social Work Research Centre, University of Stirling.

McIvor, G. (1990a). Community service and custody in Scotland. *The Howard Journal,* **29**, 101–113.

McIvor, G. (1990b). *Community Service Orders: Assessing the Benefit to the Community.* Social Work Research Centre, University of Stirling.

McIvor, G. (1990c). *Sanctions for Serious or Persistent Offenders: A Review of the Literature.* Social Work Research Centre, University of Stirling.

McIvor, G. (1991a). Community service work placements. *The Howard Journal,* **30**, 19–29.

McIvor, G. (1991b). Social work intervention in community service. *British Journal of Social Work,* **21**, 591–609.

McIvor, G. (1992a) *Reconviction Among Offenders Sentenced to Community Service.* Social Work Research Centre, University of Stirling.

McIvor, G. (1992b). *Sentenced to Serve: The Operation and Impact of Community Service by Offenders.* Avebury, Aldershot.

McIvor, G. (forthcoming). Community service by offenders: Agency experience and attitudes. *Research on Social Work Practice.*

McKeganey, N.P. and Bloor, M.J. (1981). On the retrieval of sociological descriptions: Respondent validation and the critical case of ethnomethodology. *International Journal of Sociology and Social Policy*, **1**, 58–69.

Miller, N. (1984). Under the Whitehall microscope. *Social Services Research*, **13**, 7–31.

Millham, S., Bullock, R., Hosie, K. and Haak, M. (1985). *Lost in Care: the Family Contact of Children in Care*. Gower, Aldershot.

Moos, R.H. (1974). *Evaluating Treatment Environments*. John Wiley, New York.

Neugarten, B.L., Havighurst, R.J. and Tobin, S.S. (1961). The measurement of life satisfaction. *Journal of Gerontology*, **16**, 134–43.

Nicol, A.R. (ed.) (1985). *Longitudinal Studies in Child Psychology and Psychiatry: Practical Lessons from Research Experience*. John Wiley, Chichester.

Nihira, K., Foster, R., Shelhass, M. and Leland, H. (1974). *AAMD Adaptive Behaviour Scale for Children and Adults*. American Association of Mental Deficiency, Washington, D.C.

O'Donnell, O., Maynard, A. and Wright, K. (1989). *The Economic Evaluation of Mental Health Care: A Review*. Discussion Paper No. 51. Centre for Health Economics, University of York.

Oliver, J. (1991). The social care directive: development of a quality of life profile for use in community services for the mentally ill. *Social Work and Social Services Review*, **3**, 5–45.

Palmer, T.B. (1973). Matching worker and client in corrections. *Social Work*, **13**, 95–103.

Parker, R.A., Ward, H., Jackson, S., Aldage, J. and Wedge, P. (eds) (1991). *Looking After Children: Assessing Outcomes in Child Care*. HMSO, London.

Pattie, A.H. and Gilleard, C.J. (1979). *Manual of the Clifton Assessment Procedures for the Elderly (CAPE)*. Hodder and Stoughton Educational, Sevenoaks.

Patton, M.Q. (1980). *Qualitative Evaluation Methods*. Sage, London.

Pease, K., Billingham, S. and Earnshaw, I. (1977). *Community Service Assessed in 1976*. Home Office Research Study No. 39. HMSO, London.

Petch, A. (1988). Answering back: Parental perspectives on the children's hearing system. *British Journal of Social Work*, **18**, 1–24.

Petch, A. (1990). *'Heaven Compared to a Hospital Ward': An Evaluation of Eleven Supported Accommodation Projects for those with Mental Health Problems*. Social Work Research Centre, University of Stirling.

Petch, A. (1992). *At Home in the Community*. Avebury, Aldershot.

Petersilia, J. and Turner, S. (1990). Comparing intensive and regular supervision for high risk probationers: Early results from an experiment in California. *Crime and Delinquency*, **36**, 87–111.

Platt, S. (1981). Social adjustment as a criterion of treatment success: Just what are we measuring? *Psychiatry*, **44**, 95–112.

Platt, S., Weyman, A., Hirsche, S. and Hewett, S. (1980). The Social Behaviour Assessment Schedule (SBAS): Rationale, contents, scoring and reliability of a new interview schedule. *Social Psychiatry*, **15**, 43–55.

Polanyi, M. (1958). *Personal Knowledge: Towards a Post-critical Philosophy*. Routledge and Kegan Paul, London.

Quay, H.C. (1977). The three faces of evaluation: What can be expected to work? *Criminal Justice and Behaviour*, **4**, 341–54.

Quine, L. and Charnley, H. (1987). *Evaluating the Malaise Inventory as a Measure of Stress in Carers*. Discussion Paper No. 551. PSSRU, University of Kent.

Quinton, D., Rutter, M. and Rowlands, O. (1976). An evaluation of an interview assessment of marriage. *Psychological Medicine*, **6**, 577–86.

Raynor, P. (1984). Evaluation with one eye closed: The empiricist agenda in social work research. *British Journal of Social Work*, **14**, 635–8.

Raynor, P. (1988). *Probation as an Alternative to Custody*. Avebury, Aldershot.

Rees, S.J. (1978). *Social Work Face to Face*. Edward Arnold, London.

Rees, S. and Wallace, A. (1982). *Verdicts on Social Work*. Edward Arnold, London.

Reid, W.J. and Hanrahan, P. (1981). The effectiveness of social work: Recent evidence. In E.M. Goldberg and N. Connelly (eds), *Evaluative Research in Social Care*. Heinemann, London.

Renshaw, J. (1985). *Care in the Community: Measuring Outcomes for Mentally Ill People*. Discussion Paper No. 310/2. PSSRU, University of Kent.

Richardson, A., Jackson, C. and Sykes, W. (1990). *Taking Research Seriously*. HMSO, London.

Roberts, C.H. (1989). *Hereford and Worcester Probation Service Young Offender Project: First Evaluation Report*. Department of Social and Administrative Studies, University of Oxford.

Robertson, A. and Gandy, J. (1983). Policy, practice and research: An overview. In J. Gandy, A. Robertson and S. Sinclair (eds), *Improving Social Intervention*. Croom Helm, London.

Robertson, E. and Knapp, M. (1987). Promoting intermediate treatment: A problem of excess demand or excess supply? *British Journal of Social Work*, **17**, 131–47.

Robertson, E., Knapp, M., Crank, D. and Wood, C. (1986). *The Comparative Costs of Intermediate Treatment and its Alternatives in Tameside*. Discussion Paper No. 374/3. PSSRU, University of Kent.

Rothschild Report (1971). *A Framework for Government Research and Development*. Cmnd. 4184. HMSO, London.

Rowe, J. (1985). *Social Work Decisions in Child Care*. HMSO, London.

Rowe, J. and Lambert, L. (1974). *Children Who Wait: A Study of Children Needing Substitute Families*. Association of British Adoption Agencies, London.

Rowe, J., Hundleby, M. and Garnett, L. (1989). *Child Care Placements: Patterns and Outcomes*. British Agencies for Adoption and Fostering, London.

Rushton, A. (1990). Community-based versus hospital-based care for acutely mentally ill people. *British Journal of Social Work*, **20**, 373–83.

Rutter, M. (1967). A children's behaviour questionnaire for completion by teachers: Preliminary findings. *Journal of Child Psychology and Psychiatry*, **8**, 1–11.

Rutter, M., Tizard, J. and Whitmore, I.C. (1970). *Education, Health and Behaviour*. Longman, London.

Rutter, M., Quinton, D. and Liddle, C. (1983). Parenting in two generations: Looking backwards and looking forwards. In N. Madge (ed.), *Families at Risk*. Heinemann, London.

Sainsbury, E. (1975). *Social Work with Families*. Routledge and Kegan Paul, London.

Sainsbury, E. (1987). Client studies: Their contribution and limitations in influencing social work practice. *British Journal of Social Work*, **17**, 635–44.

Sainsbury, E., Nixon, S. and Phillips, D. (1982). *Social Work in Focus: Clients' and Social Workers' Perceptions of Long Term Social Work*. Routledge and Kegan Paul, London.

Salend, S.J. (1984). Therapy outcome research: Threats to treatment integrity. *Behaviour Modification*, **8**, 211–22.

Saran, R. (1973). *Policy Making in Secondary Education: A Case Study*. Open University Press, Buckingham.

Scheirer, M.A. and Rezmovic, E.L. (1983). Measuring the degree of program implementation: A methodological review. *Evaluation Review*, **7**, 599–633.

Sechrest, L., White, S.O. and Brown, E.D. (1979). *The Rehabilitation of Criminal Offenders: Problems and Prospects*. National Academy of Sciences, Washington, D.C.

Sechrest, L., Perrin, E. and Bunker, J. (eds) (1990). *Research Methodology: Strengthening Causal Interpretations of Nonexperimental Data*. US Department of Health and Human Services, Washington, D.C.

Segal, S.P. and Moyles, E.Q. (1979). Management style and institutional dependency in sheltered care. *Social Psychiatry*, **14**, 159–65.

Sheldon, B. (1983). The use of single case experimental designs in the evaluation of social work. *British Journal of Social Work*, **13**, 477–500.

Sheldon, B. (1984a). 'Evaluation with one eye closed: The empiricist agenda in social work research' – a reply to Peter Raynor. *British Journal of Social Work*, **14**, 6.

Sheldon, B. (1984b). Group-controlled experiments in the evaluation of social work services. In J. Lishman (ed.), *Research Highlights No. 8: Evaluation*. Jessica Kingsley, London.

Sheldon, B. (1986). Social work effectiveness experiments: Review and implications. *British Journal of Social Work*, **16**, 223–42.

Shipman, M. (1981). *The Limitations of Social Research*. Longman, London.

Simic, P., Gilfillan, S. and O'Donnell, O. (1992). *A Study of the Rehabilitation and Discharge of Long Term Psychiatric Patients from the Royal Edinburgh Hospital*. Scottish Office, Edinburgh.

Sinclair, I. (1971). *Hostels for Probationers*. Home Office Research Study No. 6. HMSO, London.

Sinclair, I. (1990). Research and caring for people: An example of the influence of social scientists on government reports? *SRA News*, Social Research Association.

Sinclair, I. and Clarke, R.V.G. (1981). Cross-institutional designs. In E.M. Goldberg and N. Connelly (eds), *Evaluative Research in Social Care*. Heinemann, London.

Sinclair, I. and Walker, D. (1985). Task-centred casework in two intake teams. In E.M. Goldberg, J. Gibbons and I. Sinclair (eds), *Problems, Tasks and Outcomes: The Evaluation of Task-centred Casework in Three Settings*. George Allen and Unwin, London.

Smith, D. (1987). The limits of positivism in social work research. *British Journal of Social Work*, **17**, 401–416.

Smith, G. and Cantley, C. (1984). Pluralistic evaluation. In J. Lishman (ed.), *Research Highlights 8: Evaluation*. Jessica Kingsley, London.

Smith, G. and Cantley, C. (1985). *Assessing Health Care*. Open University Press, Buckingham.

Smith, G. and Smith, T. (1992). From social research to educational policy. In C. Crouch and A. Heath (eds), *Social Research and Social Reform: Essays in Honour of A.H. Halsey*. Oxford University Press, Oxford.

Smith, R. (1991a). *A Study of Mental Health Officer Work in Scotland*. SWRC, SSRG, BASW, ADSW, Social Work Research Centre, University of Stirling.

Smith, R. (1991b). Users' views: A study of mental health services in Grampian Region. Unpublished MSc Dissertation, University of Stirling.

Social Security Research Consortium (SSRC) (1991). *Cash Limited Limited Cash: The Impact of the Social Fund on Social Services and Voluntary Agencies and Their Uses*. Association of Metropolitan Authorities, London.

Social Services Research Group (Scotland) and Social Work Research Centre (1989). *Monitoring the Impact of the Social Fund on Social Work Departments: The National Report*. SSRG/SWRC, University of Stirling.

Spitzer, R.L., Endicott, J., Fleiss, J.L. and Cohen, J. (1970). The Psychiatric Status Schedule: A technique for evaluating psychopathology and impairment in role functioning, *Archives of General Psychiatry*, **23**, 41–55.

Stanley, B. and Gibson, A. (1985). The prevalence of chronic psychiatric morbidity: A community sample. *British Journal of Psychiatry*, **146**, 373–6.

Stewart, G. and Stewart, J. (1991). *Relieving Poverty*. Association of Metropolitan Authorities, London.

Streiner, D.L. and Norman, G.R. (1989). *Health Measurement Scales: A Practical Guide to Their Development and Use*. Oxford University Press, Oxford.

Suchman, E.A. (1967). *Evaluative Research*. Russell Sage Foundation, New York.

Surtees, P.G. and Tansella, M. (1990). The interval General Health Questionnaire and its relationship with psychiatric disorder in community and general practice samples. *British Journal of Psychiatry*, **157**, 686–93.

Sylva, K.D., Painter, M. and Roy, C. (1980). *Childwatching at Playgroup and Nursery School*. Grant MacIntyre, London.

Team for the Assessment of Psychiatric Services (1990). *Better Out Than In?* Report from the 5th Annual Conference of the Team for Assessment for Psychiatric Services.

Thomas, N. (1984). Evaluative research and the personal social services. In J. Lishman (ed.), *Research Highlights 8: Evaluation*. Jessica Kingsley, London.

Thomas, P. (1985). *The Aims and Outcomes of Social Policy Research*. Croom Helm, London.

Thyer, B.A. (1989). First principles of practice research. *British Journal of Social Work*, **19**, 309–323.

Thyer, B.A. (1992). Single systems designs. In R.M. Grinnell (ed.), *Social Work Research and Evaluation*, 4th edn. Peacock, Ithaca., N.Y.

Tizard, B. (1977). *Adoption: A Second Chance*. Open Books, London.

Tizard, J., Sinclair, I. and Clarke, R.V.G. (eds) (1975). *Varieties of Residential Experience*. Routledge and Kegan Paul, London.

Tonry, M. (1990). Stated and latent features of ISP. *Crime and Delinquency*, **36**, 174–91.

Truax, C.B., Wargo, D.G. and Silber, L.D. (1966). Effects of group psychotherapy with high accurate empathy and nonpossessive warmth upon female institutionalised delinquents. *Journal of Abnormal Psychology*, **71**, 267–74.

United States General Accounting Office (1990). *Intermediate Sanctions: Their Impacts on Prison Crowding, Costs, and Recidivism are Still Unclear*. Report to the Chairman, Select Committee on Narcotics Abuse and Control, House of Representatives, Washington, D.C.

Vass, A.A. (1984). *Sentenced to Labour: Close Encounters with a Prison Substitute*. Venus Academia, St Ives.

Wallace, A. and Rees, S. (1984). The priority of client evaluations. In J. Lishman (ed.), *Research Highlights No. 8: Evaluation*. Jessica Kingsley, London.

Ware, J.E. (1978). Effects of acquiescent response set on patient satisfaction ratings. *Medical Care*, **16**, 327–36.

Warner, S. (1992). *Making Amends: Justice for Victims and Offenders*. Avebury, Aldershot.

Webb, E.J., Campbell, D.T., Schwartz, R.D. and Sechrest, L. (1966). *Unobtrusive Measures: Nonreactive Research in the Social Sciences*. Rand McNally, Chicago.

Weissman, M.M. (1975). The assessment of social adjustment. *Archives of General Psychiatry*, **32**, 357–65.

Weissman, M.M., Prusoff, B.A., Thompson, W.D., Harding, P.S. and Myers, J.K. (1978). Social adjustment by self-report in a community sample and in psychiatric outpatients. *Journal of Nervous and Mental Disease*, **166**, 317–26.

West, D.J. and Farrington, D.P. (1973). *Who Becomes Delinquent?* Heinemann Educational, London.

West, D.J. and Farrington, D.P. (1977). *The Delinquent Way of Life*. Heinemann Educational, London.

Whittaker, D.S. and Archer, J.L. (1989). *Research by Social Workers: Capitalising on Experience*. CCETSW, London.

Wilkin, D. and Thompson, C. (1989). *Users' Guide to Dependency Measures for Elderly People*. Joint Unit for Social Services Research, University of Sheffield.

Williams, A. (1985). Economics of coronary artery by-pass grafting. *British Medical Journal*, **291**, 326–9 (CHE Reprint 1).

Wing, J.K. (ed.) (1982). *Long-term community care: Experience in a London borough. Psychological Medicine Monograph* (suppl. 2).

Wing, J.K., Nixon, J.M., Mann, S.A. and Leff, J.P. (1977). Reliability of the PSE (ninth edition) use in a population study. *Psychological Medicine, 7*, 505–516.

Wykes, T. (1982). A hostel-ward for 'new' long-stay patients: An evaluative study of a ward in a house. In J.K. Wing (ed.), Long-term community care: Experience in a London borough. *Psychological Medicine Monograph* (suppl. 2).

Wykes, T., Sturt, E. and Creer, C. (1982). Practices of day and residential units in relation to the social behaviour of attenders. In J.K. Wing (ed.), Long-term community care: Experience in a London borough. *Psychological Medicine Monograph* (suppl. 2).

Yin, R.K. (1989). *Case Study Research*. Sage, London.

Zautra, A. and Goodhart, D. (1979). Quality of life indicators: A review of the literature. *Community Mental Health Review, 4*, 2–10.

INDEX

Index compiled by Ann Barham